THE COMPLETE BOOK OF
DOG TRAINING AND CARE
is the kind of book that thinks of
EVERYTHING—for example:

"CHANGES IN BEHAVIOR
in the aging dog

"The old dog can be very jealous and possessive. After all, he's been the center of your
pet world for years. He'll resent children and
other animals, particularly when you show
them affection. Keep up the old dog's morale
by letting him know that he is still important. . . ."

*If you have a dog, or are planning to acquire
one, this will be the most valuable book in
your library.*

The Complete Book of
Dog Training
and Care
J. J. McCoy

A BERKLEY MEDALLION BOOK
published by
BERKLEY PUBLISHING CORPORATION

For BASIA and CORDELIA

Coward, McCann, & Geoghegan, Inc.
200 Madison Avenue
New York, New York 10016

Library of Congress Catalog Card Number: 70–118061

SBN 0-425-04311-8

BERKLEY MEDALLION BOOKS *are published by*
Berkley Publishing Corporation
200 Madison Avenue
New York, N.Y. 10016

BERKLEY MEDALLION BOOKS ® TM 757,375

Printed in the United States of America

Berkley Medallion Edition, July, 1974

FOURTH PRINTING

CONTENTS

Part Four
RESPONSIBLE DOG OWNERSHIP

Part Six
REPRODUCTION

Part Seven
OLD AGE

Foreword

Nobody really knows the exact number of dogs kept in American homes. Various estimates or censuses have given the number as 26, 30, and even 40 million dogs. The true figure probably lies between 25 and 30 million.

Actually, the number of dogs in America doesn't matter, except as a vital statistic. What does matter, however, is that our dogs are given proper care and that they are managed in such a manner as to make them pleasures and assets to the family and community, rather than nuisances and pests.

And this brings us up to the purpose of this book. *The Complete Book of Dog Training and Care* is intended as a handy guide for the dog owner and prospective dog owner. It is, I hope, a manual that will prove helpful in the everyday care of your dog. I have tried to make this book as complete as possible, without turning out a technical or tedious volume.

In writing this manual, I have drawn heavily from my more than twenty-five years of experience with dogs in various situations—from my years as manager of the famous Bide-A-Wee Home for Animals, where I personally handled hundreds of dogs; from my years as assistant to the director at the Gaines Dog Research Center, where I came into contact with dogs, veterinarians, breeders, and professional and amateur "dog people"; from my experiences as a syndicated pet columnist and my many years as a dog owner; and from my current experience as a pet consultant to several municipalities and humane societies.

Although this book contains detailed material on the causes, symptoms, and treatment of dog diseases and injuries, such information is not presented with the view toward encouraging home veterinary treatment. Veterinary medicine is a complicated and technical science; the diagnosis and treatment of dog diseases and injuries are and should be the province of the veterinarian.

However, I firmly believe that an informed dog owner—one who is familiar with dog diseases and injuries—will be in a position to render a service to his faithful pet. A general knowledge of dog diseases and injuries will help the dog owner understand what has happened to his pet or why the veterinarian does certain things or requests certain aftercare. Furthermore, the informed dog owner will be able to give intelligent follow-up care when the veterinarian so directs.

A final word: Reading this book will not make you an expert on dogs. It can make you an expert on *your* dog. And that, after all, should be your main interest.

Fort Washington, Pennsylvania   J. J. McCoy

THE COMPLETE BOOK OF
DOG TRAINING AND CARE

Part One

UNDERSTANDING THE DOG

1. Instincts and Behavior

The dog is a remarkable animal. Consider this unusual trait: he is the only animal that gives his friendship and loyalty for nothing more than a word of praise or a scratch behind the ears. He is unique among all other animals in this respect.

Man and dog have been friends for more than 10,000 years. It has been a lasting friendship, starting out as a collaboration for mutual benefit. The dog volunteered his services as a hunting companion, and was tossed a bone or chunk of meat for his help. Next, he took to sitting outside the caves, waiting for any cast-off bones or meat. While he waited, he chased away any predatory animals that skulked nearby.

Our hardy ancestor, the caveman, was quick to see the advantage in having the dog stay around the caves. The dog was not only a big help in hunting and guarding the caves, but he also acted as a scavenger and kept the cave grounds clean. All in all, it was a satisfactory arrangement for both dog and man.

Gradually, as man and dog learned they had nothing to fear from each other, their relationship became more intimate. The dog graduated from being just a watchdog and hunting aide to the more exalted position of trusted friend. He moved into the caves, sharing the food and hearth of the cave family. And when he moved closer to man, an emotional bond was formed. The dog was no longer a mere animal servant or chattel, but a member of the family.

Our dogs today are not much different from those of the Ice Age. Despite the variation among the breeds, modern dogs are still basically predatory animals, geared to run and hunt. They have the same fundamental instincts and behavior as the prehistoric and wild dogs. Our modern dog is, after all, nothing more than a tame wolf.

But by his long association with man, the domestic dog has often been forced to adapt to an abnormal environment. He does this willingly, even though it may make great demands on him. However, by his willingness to live with man and serve him, the dog has put himself in a position of dependency. He no longer has complete freedom and must look to man for the physical necessities and his emotional well-being.

If we are to have a pleasant relationship with our dogs (and uphold our part of the friendship pact), we must see to it that these physical and emotional needs of the dog are fulfilled. And to meet these needs, we must understand our dogs—their instincts, behavior and whatever else makes them "tick."

THE WORLD FROM THE DOG'S STANDPOINT

Let's try to form an image of the world as your dog views it. Since some of our senses are not as highly developed as those of the dog, we'll have to be satisfied with an approximation.

Smell

First of all, your dog lives in a world of smells. His nose is an intricate organ, telling him many things about people, animals and objects. He can detect hundreds of odors that are missed by us. No matter where those odors are—in the air, on the ground, on objects, hands or clothing—the dog easily picks them out and sorts them. He has a vast range of smells—all unconsciously classified and available for quick identification.

The Bloodhound, for example, has such a keen sense of smell that he can select one scent from among hundreds in the same area. And he can do this even though the one scent he is searching for is several days old or mixed with many others. Scientists studying the olfactory sense have learned that dogs can detect the difference between natural and artificial musk. Even to a human being with an unusual sense of smell, natural and artificial musk have identical odors.

Your dog's nose, therefore, is his guide to the identification of people, objects and other animals. Regardless of how many times your dog sees people or animals, he will

not accept them until he puts his nose to work. Then—
and only then—will he be satisfied.

But for the dog to bring his sense of smell into play, he
must be within range. If he is too far away or the wind is
blowing away from him, he will be unable to identify a
person or animal. There is a classical experiment for this.
Put on an old coat and hat. Pull the hat down over your
ears and turn up the coat collar. Now get downwind from
the dog, so that he cannot pick up your scent. Crawl toward him or approach him in an apelike walk. Watch his
reaction. He'll either bark and run off, or stand still. If
he stands still, he'll growl and the hairs on the back of
his neck will rise. The chances are he'll assume an attack
position: body rigid, tail lowered and teeth bared. Don't
push this experiment too far. When you see that he
doesn't recognize you, straighten up, take off the hat and
coat, and call out to him. Then let him approach and
sniff you.

Vary the experiment and approach the dog upwind
with the same costume and stance, and you'll get a different reaction. Once he whiffs your scent, he'll bound
toward you with tail-wags and yelps of recognition. No
doubt, if he could talk, he'd say, "Come on, take off the
disguise. I know you!"

Sight

Most dogs have poor eyesight. There are exceptions,
notably the sight hunters or gaze hounds. These gaze
hounds, such as the Saluki, Afghan and Greyhound, are
lean, speedy dogs that hunt with their eyes fixed on the
quarry. They have good vision and are farsighted. But the
majority of dogs are nearsighted. The Bloodhound, keen-
nosed though he may be, is one of the most myopic of all
dogs.

Despite his nearsightedness, your dog will react to
motion. In fact, he has a high degree of sensitivity to
motion. And this is a main reason why many dogs recoil
from a hand that is suddenly thrust at them. The dog's
ability to see motion can be likened to a similar reaction
in human beings. We can notice motion that is outside
the direct line of vision. We may be looking straight
ahead and at the same time notice something moving to

the right or left and slightly behind us. We refer to this as seeing something move "out of the corner of our eye."

While your dog may not be able to identify a person or animal by sight, he can tell in which direction they are moving. That is, he can tell a clockwise or counterclockwise movement. He also has the ability to see at night and a facility known as eyeshine or *tapetum lucidum*. Eyeshine can be seen at night when your headlights or flashlight are focused on the dog's eyes. It is caused by the light bouncing off a layer of cells at the back of the dog's eyes. The facility of eyeshine is also present in some other animals, such as the cat and raccoon. Human beings do not have eyeshine.

When it comes to color vision, your dog has a low score. His color range is limited to black and white, possibly gray. Interestingly enough, dogs do make choices between colors. Or so it seems. They do not select green over red, or blue over yellow. But if given a choice of three colored toys—one bright red, one dull green and one black—your dog will probably pick the red one. He'll make this choice because of the difference in brilliance among the three toys. In short, he'll pick the red toy because it is *bright* red. But in the final analysis, your dog's color vision is very weak, and it can become confused when the shape or position of an object is changed or altered.

To sum up, your dog's eyesight is poor and he has an undeveloped color-vision range. Nature, to compensate for these two weaknesses, has given him a highly developed sense of smell and sound. And in these two senses, your dog has no peer.

Sound

Dogs have exceptionally keen hearing and can pick up sounds too faint for human ears. They can also detect sounds of a higher pitch. The silent dog whistle is designed on the principle of your dog being able to hear the high-pitched sounds. Blow on one of these silent whistles and *you* hear nothing, except maybe some expelled air. But if the dog is nearby and he's well trained, he'll dash over to you in short order.

Dogs are very responsive to the human voice. By changing your inflections and tones, you can get a variety of reactions from your dog. An encouraging word will set off a barrage of joyful barks or a series of frenzied tail-wags. Speak harshly to him, and he'll become depressed, perhaps slinking away or cringing before you. You may have noticed how some dogs back away from a loud or harsh-voiced person. Some dogs may even run off and hide if a voice "hits" them the wrong way.

Your voice and how you use it are the most important factors in communicating with your dog. Remember, it will be the tone, inflection and shading in your voice that will provoke a response, not the words. But more about this in the chapter on training your dog.

Taste

Your dog's sense of taste is closely related to his sense of smell. What he will not accept with his nose, he'll rarely, if ever, eat. Some dogs have acquired unusual tastes and will eat foods that border on the exotic. But the majority of dogs have plain tastes and will stick to standard foods.

Touch

What we're referring to here, of course, is the dog's degree of sensitivity to *being* touched.

Dogs react in various ways when touched by the human hand. Most dogs don't mind being petted. In fact, they will almost beam with pleasure while you scratch behind their ears or massage their stomachs. Many of us have met the old house dog that, after he's sniffed and checked you out as a friend, thrusts his rear end at you to be scratched.

But there are dogs that violently object to being touched. This touchy-type dog will quickly let you know that he doesn't want to be petted. He may cringe, pull back, run off or snap at anyone who tries to pet him. This is especially true when you suddenly thrust your hand at his head.

Unfortunately, people get bitten because they either ignore a dog's objection to being touched or are unaware of it. Many people assume that *all* dogs like to be petted and just can't resist stopping to pat every dog they meet.

Considering what we've just learned about the dog's poor eyesight, need to identify everything with his nose, and a possible objection to being touched—we can understand why some dogs snap at people.

A dog's objection to being touched may be an inherited or acquired trait. Genetics, environment and state of health all have a bearing on the dog's degree of sensitivity to being touched. But regardless of the cause, you and others will have to respect the dog's dislike of being petted.

Protective instinct

Most dogs have an innate sense of protection for the people with whom they live. This protective sense is stronger in some dogs than others. But once your dog gets accustomed to the house and occupants, he will assume a guardianship over the household. He will bark a warning, possibly launch an attack when danger threatens his charges. Now, he may not be able to do this with the dash and skill of Rin-Tin-Tin or Lassie, but his concern is genuine. He will, if necessary, risk bodily harm or death to protect you.

Your dog will also show an instinct to guard property. This is a deep-rooted instinct that is dominant in the wild, as well as domestic, dogs. Wolves and coyotes carefully stake out property lines and defend them against all aggressors, canine and otherwise. They do this by urinating on trees, rocks and bushes around the perimeter of their domain. The domestic male dog's habit of lifting his leg and urinating against trees, poles and fireplugs is a remnant of this powerful instinct. But your dog doesn't have to "stake a property claim." Your home is well defined—fences, shrubbery and so forth—and the dog gets to know the boundaries. And once he is familiar with the property, he will defend it. (Even though this "defense" consists of barking shrilly from the safety of the porch or house!)

Individual dogs with a strong protective instinct and a tendency toward overaggressiveness, are trained as guard dogs. But there is a big difference between the average watchdog and guard dog. The guard dog is taught to be hostile to everyone except his master, and is always a potential hazard. Such a dog is not for the average person.

Intelligence

Finally, we come to the matter of intelligence in the dog. Much has been written about how smart or dumb dogs are when faced with various psychological tests. Unquestionably, the dog doesn't measure up to man or the great apes in intelligence. He does rank high above most of the other animals below the primates.

Some dogs are more intelligent than others. Similarly, certain breeds have a higher intelligence quotient. The German Shepherd Dog and Collie, for example, are two breeds with high I.Qs. For practical purposes, your dog's I.Q. should be based on two factors: 1) his *readiness to learn* and 2) the degree to which he *remembers and uses what he learns*. There's no point in hoping for a dog whose intelligence matches that of a highly inventive chimpanzee.

BEHAVIOR

Your dog's general behavior depends on various factors, some subject to your control, others beyond it. Inheritance, experience and environment—all play a vital role in your dog's behavior.

Aggressiveness

Individual dogs are more aggressive than others. So are certain breeds. The Doberman Pinscher, for instance, is an aggressive dog, and it is his aggressiveness that makes him an outstanding police dog. Breed fanciers object to the statement that temperament (shyness, aggressiveness, snappiness, etc.) is related to specific breeds. Nevertheless, it is related. We have only to remember that the various breeds and groups of dogs were developed with definite purposes in mind. And among these purposes was a need for aggressive or snappy dogs. Furthermore, scientific experiments have shown that behavior, i.e., aggressiveness, shyness, sociability, etc., vary among individual dogs and breeds.

Overaggressiveness in dogs may be caused by environment, as well as inheritance. If you keep your dog in close confinement or chained in the yard all of the time, he's going to build up excess energy. Since he's chained up, he's got no way to let off steam. As a result, his excess energy turns into aggression. Chaining a dog and annoying him was a method used in the army to make a dog overly aggressive.

The lack of sexual gratification also contributes to overaggression in dogs. Dogs are polygamous, with a strong sexual drive. Both the male and female have this drive, although the female displays it only during her semiannual heat periods. The male is sexually alert all year round. When unable to expend this sexual energy, male dogs are apt to become overly aggressive. (For a fuller discussion on abnormal behavior and examples, see Chapter 9.)

Shyness

Shyness may also be inherited or acquired. Certain breeds, such as the Bloodhound and Shetland Sheepdog, tend toward shyness. But individual dogs of any breed can acquire shyness out of fear and anxiety, prevalent during the critical weeks of early puppyhood. Dr. J. P. Scott, former Director of the Animal Behavior Laboratory, Roscoe B. Jackson Memorial Laboratory, Mt. Desert Island, Maine, conducted special experiments on the inherited and acquired behavior of dogs. Dr. Scott and his co-workers found that when 7- to 12-week puppies were raised in isolation, without human contact, they grew up like wild animals. These dogs were suspicious, fearful of people, even showing marked aggression and shyness. When kept in isolation for three or four months, it was almost impossible to rehabilitate the puppies.

SOCIALIZATION AND THE LEARNING PROCESS IN YOUNG PUPPIES

Not too long ago, a puppy under 6 months of age was not supposed to have any set of behavior pattern. He was more or less expected to learn a few rules (such as using his newspapers or going outside) and gradually develop his sociability, reaching his peak when about a year old. He was not of school age. A young pup's life was spent in playing, eating and just physically growing up.

The story is different today. Dr. Scott and his group found that the learning and socialization process begins very early in the pup's life. Young puppies are ready to learn and adapt to their environment when they are from 19 to 20 days old. One of the major conclusions of Dr. Scott's experiments was that there are five critical stages in a puppy's life. And all of these stages occur before a pup is 4 months old.

THE FIVE CRITICAL STAGES IN A PUPPY'S LIFE

Stage one: The first stage is from birth to about 13 days. At birth, the puppy is practically helpless. He's blind, deaf, toothless and is restricted in motion (he can crawl or slither on his stomach, with his paws making swimming motions). He experiences very little in the way of learning. He's strictly a creature of reflexes. His total behavior pattern is built around reflexes dealing with food, elimination and bodily contact with his mother and litter mates. When deprived of food or bodily contact, the pup will object by whimpering or whining. During this first stage, he lives in a half-world, aware only of his physical needs.

Stage two: This stage extends from the 13th day to the 19th, according to Dr. Scott. It begins on the 13th day when the puppy opens his eyes (13 days is an average; some pups open their eyes earlier, some later). For the next 7 days, the puppy moves very quickly through sensory, motor and psychological changes. At the end of the 7 days, the pup can see, hear and walk. His milk teeth appear and he can eat solid food. He can also form conditioned reflexes and adapt to a variety of situations. But he still shows no signs of any permanent learning ability.

Stage three: The third stage begins on the 19th or 20th day after birth and continues until the puppy is 7 to 10 weeks old. It is a crucial stage in the puppy's development, one that sets the pattern for future behavior. And it is the stage when socialization begins and the pup forms a relationship with human beings and other animals.

The third stage is ushered in by the pup's startled reaction to sounds. In stages one and two, the young puppies ignore sounds. But the puppy in stage three will really jump if you make a loud noise. He will also show an investigative curiosity about people and animals, and will tussle and scrap playfully with his litter mates. During this stage, the puppy's nervous system is still immature.

Neglect or faulty handling of the puppy during this third stage can result in serious damage to the behavior pattern. We've already learned what complete isolation can do to young puppies in this age group. Dr. Scott's group studied another effect of environment on the young puppy. Three-week-old pups were raised in individual cages, away from people and other dogs. They had no contact with the physical or social world beyond their cages. After three to four months in the cages, the puppies were taken out. They all seemed more or less physically sound, but they were woefully lacking in experience! These ivory-tower puppies couldn't adapt to the competitive life with other puppies their age, nor could they comprehend the world outside their cages.

In general, what happens to a pup during the third stage of his life will determine his future behavior.

Stage four: Stage four begins when the puppy is from 7 to 10 weeks of age. This is the usual age at which puppies are weaned from their mothers. The pup is not completely independent, but he now has some increased motor skills and his nervous system is similar to that of an adult dog. The 7- to 10-week age group is ideal for raising a puppy. It is the best age at which to establish a sound relationship between dogs and people. If the puppy has had a happy third stage, he's eager to form an attachment. And what's more, he's ready to learn.

Stage five: The fifth and final critical stage starts at about 12 weeks of age and lasts until the pup is 4 months old. Now the puppy starts to assert himself. He'll be bold, perky; testing you in all kinds of situations. It is time to teach him discipline.

An understanding of your dog's instincts and behavior is a must for intelligent dog ownership. It's true that dogs just grew up in the "old days." But don't compare the "old days" with today. Know your dog and know him well. He's an extraordinary animal!

Part Two

A DOG IN THE HOME

2. Selecting Your Dog

The right dog can be a source of fun and companionship for many years. But the wrong dog may well turn out to be a nuisance and cause of family dissension. So, give some serious thought to the matter of picking your dog. Avoid a spur-of-the-moment choice. And don't dash out to buy a certain breed just because it's in fashion or you've been impressed by a dog in a television show. Remember, with reasonable care your dog will be a part of your life for ten to twelve years. That's a long time to live with a mistake.

PUREBRED, CROSSBREED OR MONGREL

To paraphrase Gertrude Stein: "A dog is a dog is a dog." No one breed or mixture is better than another. It all depends on *why* you want a dog and what kind of a dog your particular situation will maintain. There's only one species of dog, *Canis familiaris*, with 116 breeds registered in the American Kennel Club. As to the crossbreeds and mongrels, their numbers and combinations are best left to the mathematicians. You may be sure, though, the crossbreeds and mongrels far outnumber the purebreds.

The purebreds, crossbreeds and mongrels are much alike in their general behavior and instincts. Any one of them will offer friendship, loyalty and companionship. And with reasonable care, a dog from any of these groups will turn into a fine pet.

Purebred dogs

A purebred dog is one whose parents and ancestors are of a single breed. It is a dog with a traceable pedigree. In America, purebred dogs are registered with the American Kennel Club. Foreign purebred dogs are registered in the official kennel club of the specific country. The American Kennel Club now registers 116 breeds, divided into six groups.

THE SIX GROUPS OF DOGS

The Sporting Dogs (24 breeds)

The Sporting Dogs are hunters, specifically bird dogs. They hunt, point and retrieve, depending on the breed. Rangy, rugged, with a love of the outdoors, the bird dogs have great stamina in the field. The retrievers are expert swimmers and will leap into icy water to retrieve a duck.

In size, the Sporting Dogs range from 14 inches for the Cocker Spaniel to 28 inches for the Pointer. Weights go from 26 pounds for the Cocker to 75 pounds for the Golden and Labrador Retrievers. The popular breeds among the Sporting Dogs are the American Cocker Spaniel, Springer Spaniel, Brittany Spaniel, Pointer, English Setter, Irish Setter, Labrador Retriever, and the Weimaraner. Two dogs in this group were developed in America: the Chesapeake Bay Retriever and the American Water Spaniel.

While basically hunting dogs, the Sporting group make good pets. But they are not for the apartment house or hotel suite. An exception here is the Cocker Spaniel. But the rest of the Sporting Dogs are very energetic, requiring plenty of exercise, not just a walk to the curb or down the street.

The Hound Dogs (19 breeds)

The dogs in this group are also hunters, but specialize in animals rather than birds. They are subdivided into *sight hunters* (or gaze hounds) and *scent hunters*. Afghans, Salukis and Greyhounds are examples of the sight hunters. These sight hunters are tall, rangy and speedy dogs that chase their quarry by sight. Bloodhounds and Beagles are examples of the scent hunters. They are stocky dogs with pendulous ears and keen noses. The scent hunters trail their quarry with noses to the ground, while their long ears flap and stir up the spoor.

Hound dogs have good dispositions, lots of stamina and make good pets. They range in size from the Dachshund at 5 to 9 inches to the big Irish Wolfhound standing at 34 inches. In weight, the hounds vary from 5 to 20 pounds for the Dachshund to 105 to 140 for the Irish

Wolfhound. The Dachshund is bred with three coat varieties: short-haired or smooth, wire-haired and long-haired. There is also a miniature Dachshund bred for work in small burrows. The Dachshund was developed primarily to hunt the badger.

Among the popular breeds in the hound group are the Beagle (two sizes: 13 and 15 inches), Basset, Dachshund (three varieties), Norwegian Elkhound, Bloodhound, Greyhound and Afghan. The hound dogs need space and a chance to hunt. City life is a bore for most of them. The smaller hounds, such as the Dachshund and Beagle, manage to get along in the city.

The Working Dogs (28 breeds)

The Working Dog group contains some of the most useful dogs in the world. Sled dogs, guide dogs for the blind, cattle and sheep dogs, police and war dogs, rescue dogs—all of them render faithful service. We've all read or heard stories about the heroic exploits of these wonderful dogs.

Intelligent, strong, with just enough aggressiveness to make them good watchdogs, the Working Dogs are very popular as house pets. The Cardigan and Pembroke Welsh Corgis are the smallest, standing 12 inches, while the Great Dane is the giant of the group at 34 inches. Weights range from 15 to 22 pounds for the Cardigan Welsh Corgi to 170 pounds for the Saint Bernard.

All of the 28 breeds in the Working Dog group are found in the United States. The most popular breeds are the German Shepherd Dog, Collie (rough), Doberman Pinscher, Boxer, Great Dane, Saint Bernard, Old English Sheepdog, Shetland Sheepdog (or Sheltie), and the Siberian Husky. These are big dogs and they need plenty of exercise. You'll find them in the cities, often showing the strain of their confined life. They do better in the suburbs and country.

The Terrier Dogs (20 breeds)

The Terriers are small to medium-sized dogs with plenty of pep and courage. They are also hunters, bred to track down and root out rodents and other burrowing animals. Terriers are very alert and make excellent watchdogs.

The smallest of the Terriers is the Dandie Dinmont at 8 to 11 inches, and the tallest is the Airedale at 23 inches. Heavyweights are the Airedale and Staffordshire Terrier at 50 pounds; the lightweight is the Norwich Terrier at 11 pounds.

Terriers make good house pets and manage to adapt well to city life. The favorite breeds are the Scottish, Welsh, Kerry Blue, Irish, Airedale, Bedlington, Smooth and Wirehaired Fox, Cairn, Skye, Bull, Miniature and Manchester Terriers. The Bull Terrier was developed in the United States.

The Toy Dogs (16 breeds)

The Toys are the world's midget dogs. Tiny, alert, with very keen hearing, these little dogs have the courage and audacity of dogs ten times their size. Some of them tend toward nervousness, but respond to affection.

Toy Dogs are all under 12 inches. The smallest are the Chihuahua and Pekingese at 5 inches; among the tallest are the Miniature Pinscher and the Italian Greyhound at 10 to 12 inches. The Toys are all lightweights, with the Chihuahua weighing 4 pounds and the Pug averaging 15 pounds.

These little dogs make ideal house dogs. Their alertness and keen hearing, plus their small size, qualify them as apartment house or hotel pets and watchdogs. Since they are small and on the delicate side, they can't stand rough handling. Especially the kind of play and fondling to be expected from young children.

The most popular of the Toys are the Chihuahua, Maltese, Pug, Italian Greyhound, Miniature Pinscher, Pekingese, Pomeranian, Toy Poodle, Manchester Terrier, and Yorkshire Terrier.

The Non-Sporting Dogs (9 breeds)

The Non-Sporting Dogs are the miscellaneous purebred breeds, the odd fellows. Just why this is so, is not clear. Some of the so-called Non-Sporting Dogs have excellent qualifications as hunters and workers. The Dalmatian, for example, is a working dog of ancient lineage. He was used as a draft, war and shepherd dog. He also has hunting prowess and will catch rats and other vermin.

Since this is a catch-all group, there is a wide variation among the 9 breeds. Consequently, no generalization as to characteristics can be made. The Bulldog weighs 40 to 50 pounds and is the heaviest. At the other end of the weight scale is the Miniature Poodle at 12 pounds. The shortest dog in this group is the Schipperke at 12 inches and the tallest is the Dalmatian at 21 inches. One dog in this group, the Boston Terrier, was developed in the United States. The breed is a result of crossing an English Bulldog and a white English Terrier. Most popular among the Non-Sporting Dogs are the Boston Terrier, Bulldog, Chow Chow, Dalmatian, French Bulldog, Poodle (Miniature and Standard) and the Keeshond.

Breeds not registered with the A.K.C.

Some breeds, while popular, are not registered with the American Kennel Club. The Club recognizes them (*ipso factor*, they exist and can't be ignored!), but doesn't open its registry to them. However, these breeds are thriving and have many fanciers, so they do not appear to be held back by their exclusion from the Club.

Three of these breeds are American-bred hunting dogs, scent hounds. These are the Bluetick, Redbone and Plott hounds. They are all of Foxhound blood crossed with Bloodhound or other hound stock. Highly prized in the South and Southwest, these three hounds are used to hunt coon.

Included in this group is one of the best shepherd dogs in the world, the Border Collie. Developed on the Scottish border, the Border Collie is used to guard and herd sheep, cattle, pigs and poultry. Border Cattle breeders have their own registry. Others in the group are the Drathaar, a German dog; the Spitz and American Toy Fox Terrier.

THE ADVANTAGES OF A PUREBRED DOG

There are some decided disadvantages in owning a purebred dog. First of all, the purebred breeders have spent a lot of time, money and effort in developing their breeds.

You, as the buyer, profit by all of these. Most of the purebred kennel operators have high standards in the selection
of breeding stock, sanitation, dog care and business transactions. They are not "fly-by-night" enterprises.

Another important advantage in buying a purebred
dog is that you can be sure what the dog will look like
when mature. This is not so with the crossbreed or mongrel. Finally, a purebred dog can be entered in dog shows
or field trails. All of these advantages justify the higher
price you will pay for a purebred dog.

Once you've decided on a purebred dog and a specific
breed, your next step is to shop around. And now it is
time for a warning or *caveat*, as the lawyers say. Many
pet shops offer purebred dogs at bargain prices. And in
most instances, you will get registration papers. But that
is not where the *caveat* comes in; it's the *quality* of these
bargain purebreds that you must consider.

Very few pet shop operators are dog breeders; they
get their dogs from kennels, middlemen and private owners. Most of the stock in the pet shops are runts, poor
dog show prospects and possibly in ill health. Furthermore, pet shop dogs don't always get the best care or attention. They are usually kept in individual cages, and
you will recall from Chapter 1, what can happen to
puppies raised in cages or isolation. Puppies in the pet
shops don't get much handling, other than when fed or
the cage is cleaned. The pet shop proprietor has too many
other charges to look after, from tropical fish to monkeys.
But the kennel operator specializes in dogs and gives them
his full attention.

Locating a kennel

Try to find a kennel for the breed of your choice that
is nearby. Look in the classified ads in your local newspaper or the yellow pages of the telephone book. A handy
directory, *Where to Buy, Board or Train a Dog*, is available from the Gaines Dog Research Center, White Plains,
New York. Three magazines that cater to the dog world
also list kennels. These are *Popular Dogs*, 2008 Ranstead
Street, Philadelphia 3, Pennsylvania; *Dog World*, Chi-
cago, Illinois; and *All-Pets Magazine*, Fond du Lac, Wis-
consin. *Dog World* is available at some newsstands. The

American Kennel Club will also help you to locate a kennel near your home.

There are some dog "trade" magazines, such as *Mountain Music*, the *American Foxhound* and the *American Coonhound*. These magazines have listings for coonhounds and other dogs. You can also order a dog by mail through one of these magazine ads. But this is not for the tyro. You can get yourself into quite a predicament, what with being disappointed in the dog, writing a lot of letters, paying shipping costs and feeling sour about the whole deal. Buy your dog from a kennel within commuting distance.

CROSSBREEDS AND MONGRELS

You may have decided that you just want a dog, nothing fancy—animal or price. If so, you have a wide range of choice from among the many combinations of crossbreeds and mongrels. They have little monetary value, but they'll give every bit as much loyalty and companionship as the purebreds. Don't think that because crossbreeds and mongrels are purchased cheaply or obtained gratis, they are not highly prized by their owners. Of the 26 million dogs in the United States, more than two-thirds are crossbreeds and mongrels. And, along with the purebreds, these "cheap" dogs are the best-fed and best-cared-for dogs in the world.

The crossbreed dog is the result of cross-mating two different purebred dogs. Thus, the puppies born from a mating between a German Shepherd dog and a Boxer are crossbreeds. The mongrel is a mixture of many breeds. You'll have an idea of how complex the background of a mongrel can be when you consider the following possible lineage: a purebred Collie bitch is accidentally mated with a purebred Doberman Pinscher. She has six crossbred puppies, four of them females. These four females are given away, raised to sexual maturity and mated to mongrels. The female puppies from this mating, when mature, are bred to mongrels, and so on.

There are some disadvantages in getting a crossbreed or mongrel dog. To be sure, the crossbreed will grow up to look somewhat like his sire or dam. But not the mongrel; what he will look like is anybody's guess. Neither the crossbreed nor the mongrel can be entered in dog shows or field trials. So take this fact into consideration if you want to take part in the competitive areas of the dog world.

You will not experience much difficulty in finding a crossbreed or mongrel. And often they are yours for the asking. Consult the classified ads in your newspaper, visit a humane society, or reputable pet shop, and check with any neighbors who have puppies they cannot keep.

MALE VS. FEMALE

The choice between a male or female should be based on facts, not prejudice. There are pros and cons for both sexes. The usual objection to the female is her estrus cycle or heat periods. She has a discharge during her periods, wants to go out and roam, and attracts a horde of canine Romeos. Add to this the excellent chance of unwanted puppies and you have the case against the female.

It's really not a very strong case. Let's consider some of the pros for the female. You'll find she is cleaner around the house, with better control of her bladder than the male. This is an important factor if you live in an apartment. You will recall that the male dog has an instinct for lifting his leg and urinating against trees, poles and fireplugs. He won't hesitate to use table and chair legs, doorjambs or floor lamps as substitutes.

The female has a strong maternal and protective instinct. She will guard children (especially if raised with them) as closely as she will guard her puppies. Some dog trainers consider the female to be more tractable, more willing to learn and with a longer attention span than the male.

A female dog in the home with children can be a valuable aid in educating the children to the "facts of life." What better way is there to show the children the miracle of reproduction than to let them see how puppies are born? And the bridge between animal and human reproduction is more easily spanned when the children can see for themselves.

Owning a female can be less of a problem than you think. Granted, you'll have to watch her when she comes into heat twice a year. But this is not an impossible task. Once you've learned to recognize the onset of heat, you can take some precautions to see she is not bred. (See Chapter 19 under THE FEMALE) If you think this is too much bother but still want a female, you can have her spayed.

The male presents no major problems in care or handling. He makes just as good a pet as the female. There are a few situations involving the male dog that will require special handling, such as mounting. These are covered in Chapter 9.

LARGE AND SMALL DOGS

Choosing between a large and small dog should be more than a matter of personal preference. More to the point: it's a matter of *space, time* and *cost.* The large dog needs plenty of *space;* medium-sized and small dogs can get along with less. A large dog will suffer, mentally and phsyically, from being penned up all day; therefore you will have to take *time* to exercise him. The smaller dog can get enough exercise running around the yard or house. To complete the space-time-cost trilogy; large dogs *cost* more to feed. The Saint Bernard, for instance, will eat over 5 pounds of food a day.

LONG-HAIRED AND SHORT-HAIRED DOGS

The type of coat is an important factor in the selection of a dog. Unless you send the dog to a canine beauty salon, you'll have to spend time grooming a long-haired dog. There's also the problem of shedding hair. All dogs shed hair, usually twice a year. (The Bedlington Terrier breeders claim their breed doesn't shed.) Shedding takes place in the spring and fall; more often if the dog is kept indoors or fed a faulty diet.

Short-haired and smooth-haired dogs require no trimming, and a vigorous brushing will keep them looking their best. Long, thick-coated dogs, such as the Collies, Saint Bernards and Samoyeds, need more frequent brushings and possibly combing out of burs and other foreign matter. The fancy-trim dogs—Poodle and Bedlington Terrier—need to be trimmed and groomed according to their breed standards. You'll have to learn how to do this special trimming and plucking, or else pay a professional dog groomer for the job. Trimming instructions can be secured from the specific breed clubs. Wire-haired dogs need to be trimmed and plucked about twice a year. If neglected, their coats become soft, fuzzy and matted. Needless to say, if you don't want to be bothered with trimming and elaborate grooming, your choice is narrowed down to the short-haired or smooth-haired varieties.

PUPPY OR OLDER DOG

There should be no question about this. Get a puppy in the 7- to 10-week-old group. There's certainly more work involved in raising a puppy, but when he grows up, he'll be the product of *your* care and training. And this care and training starts with the day you bring him home. It may be possible to teach an old dog new tricks, but you're going to have a lot of headaches doing it.

TRAINED GUARD DOGS

What about getting a mature trained guard dog to protect your family and home? Our answer is for you to think twice about it and then to get a trained guard dog if you must, but only if you are aware of the responsibilities and dangers that go with the keeping of such a dog.

The steadily rising crime rates in our cities and suburbs have prompted many frightened and concerned citizens to go out and purchase a large dog for protection. Some people have brought home an especially trained guard dog, such as a German Shepherd, Doberman Pinscher, Great Dane, or Mastiff. Certainly every citizen has the right to protect his life, that of his family, or his property from muggers, sex offenders, thieves, and other criminals who infest our urban and suburban areas. A well-trained guard or attack dog can deter criminals from carrying out their crimes. However, the trained guard dog, particularly the attack dog, poses a danger to people other than criminals; the owner or keeper of such a dog must be constantly on the alert to protect innocent people from injury, possibly death.

Look at it this way: A trained guard or attack dog is a potentially lethal weapon. The animal may be compared to a loaded, cocked gun; it can wound or kill at the slightest provocation or misuse. The trained guard dog will generally attack any person the animal thinks threatens the property or lives of the people with whom it lives—or if it thinks its own life is in jeopardy.

Most reputable guard dog dealers and trainers will not sell an attack dog to people wanting the animal for home protection. They are well aware of the dangers and consequences contingent on such a sale. In addition to the physical and emotional damage which an attack dog is capable of inflicting, the owner or keeper faces all kinds of legal entanglements, from lawsuits arising out of dog bites to eviction of the "vicious" dog by petition and court order.

Then what recourse is left to the person who needs a dog to protect his home and family? Our advice is to get a young dog, preferably one that is three to four months old, of a breed that has strong protective instincts, such as a German Shepherd, Boxer, etc. Forget about a highly trained attack dog. Raise the dog yourself; in another three or four months the animal will be almost mature and of an impressive size. Furthermore, the dog will be the product of your training and—what is most important —it will (assuming the dog is normal) have become a member of the family, with attachments to people and property.

Even untrained dogs are useful as guardians; they will at least bark a warning, alerting you to danger. Many ordinary housedogs have prevented crimes. Remember that even the highly trained attack dog can be eliminated by a knowledgeable criminal, particularly one who is armed or who carries Mace and other dog deterrents. Therefore, the presence of a highly trained attack dog does not guarantee 100 percent protection. But the chances are that a would-be housebreaker or mugger will move on if he sees a large, aggressive-looking dog around, regardless of the dog's training or lack of it.

SOME POINTERS ON PICKING
THE INDIVIDUAL DOG

Avoid basing your selection of the puppy solely on his looks or appealing expression. Pick a dog that you like, but make sure he meets all of the requirements. Examine him carefully for a happy, perky and alert nature. He should be plump, but not potbellied. Stay away from the potbellied or shy puppy; it may mean trouble.

Here are some further suggestions:

Examine the puppy's eyes for any redness or discharge. A thick discharge from the eyes or nose may be a symptom of distemper or other serious illness.

The nose should be moist. A hot, dry nose is not necessarily an indication the pup is ill. Overheated rooms will cause a dog's nose to become cracked and dry. But beware of a discharge from the nose.

Examine the skin and hair. A healthy puppy's hair should be soft and glossy. The skin should be free from sores, rashes and parasites.

Hold the puppy up and examine his rectal area. Look for signs of diarrhea (damp or dried feces clinging to the rear end or legs). Diarrhea may mean internal parasites or intestinal disorder.

Look the puppy over for fleas, lice and ticks. (See Chapter 15.)

Be on the alert for any deformities in the feet or legs, especially enlarged bone joints that may indicate rickets.

Check the puppy's teeth. At three to four months of age, the pup still has his baby or temporary teeth. The permanent teeth usually appear after four months. Discolored or stained teeth may mean the puppy has been exposed to a virus disease.

Find out about the puppy's inoculations: what kind and when. Also inquire as to whether the pup was wormed and for what kind of worms.

Arrange to buy the puppy on a trial basis, say for two or three weeks. He may possibly be incubating a disease when you purchase him.

Be sure to obtain the necessary registration papers and signature of the breeder, if you buy a purebred dog.

Finally, inquire as to what the puppy has been eating, so that you can continue this diet for a week or so.

The decision to get a dog is a big step and one that may involve the entire family. Since children quickly fall in love with any puppy, it's wise to hold a family conference to decide what kind of puppy is best. And this conference should be held *before* going to the kennel, pet shop or humane shelter. This way, you will avoid having disappointed children and puppies.

3. The New Puppy

Raising a puppy is a comparatively simple project, providing you make liberal use of patience and common sense. The young puppy cannot be expected to act like a grown dog; he needs direction and supervision. But the pup will quickly grow up and the period of close daily supervision becomes correspondingly shorter as the puppy matures. Naturally, raising a young puppy will cause some changes in your life and home. Whether these changes are pleasant or unpleasant depends largely on you and the regime you set for the puppy.

SETTING THE STAGE FOR THE NEW PUPPY

If there's anything that will get the family and puppy off to a bad start, it's bringing the pup home without any preparation. Resist the temptation to surprise the family with a new puppy. No doubt your family will quickly recover from the excitement stirred up by the sudden appearance of a captivating pup, but what about the puppy? It can be a trying time for him.

Ever since he was first aware of his surroundings, the puppy has lived with his mother and litter mates. He's eaten, slept and played in a familiar environment. Now he's taken away from all this and his security is shattered. This is a time when the puppy needs a friend and he'll need plenty of affection and consideration. But this doesn't include hounding or mauling him to the point of collapse. Nor does he want to be isolated; he just wants time to become accustomed to the change and a chance to get his "sea legs." You can help a lot by seeing to his comforts.

Sleeping arrangements

Decide whether the pup is going to sleep indoors or outdoors. Make this decision *before* you bring him home. The type and location of his bed are important. His bed

42

or doghouse should be his own, a place where he can curl up and nap, away from the clatter of family life. And once he takes over bed or doghouse, respect his right to privacy. A regular baby playpen makes an ideal bed or place in which to confine the very young puppy. It has the added advantage of controlling a puppy until he is housebroken or when you want him out from under your feet. Cover the bottom of the playpen with several layers of newspaper.

Indoors

The puppy's bed can be an ordinary cardboard box with a mattress of cedar shavings, shredded newspaper or a washable blanket. Or it can be one of the more elaborate commercial beds. If you use a cardboard box, cut down about one-half of one side, so the pup can climb in and out. Whatever the type of bed you buy or make, it should be so constructed that it is easily cleaned.

Place the pup's bed in a room, away from cracks under the door or drafty windows. Dogs can stand the cold, but not drafts. Any room will do, just so long as it is not the cellar. Cellars are usually damp, dank, lonely places. It would be more considerate to let the dog sleep outdoors than to banish him to the cellar. Keep the bed away from radiators and other heaters; too much heat will make him uncomfortable and dry his nose.

Once you've located the bed, avoid shifting it around after the pup has taken over. Moving the bed from spot to spot and room to room will only serve to confuse the puppy. He may well give it up altogether and find himself another nook.

Outdoors

If you provide the puppy with a dry and snug doghouse, he will manage very well outdoors all year round. Most dogs do, except the toy and miniature breeds. Nature will help the dog that lives outdoors by giving him a heavier coat.

Have the doghouse set up before the puppy arrives. If you don't have it ready, you'll find yourself coping with two sleeping arrangements: one, his sleeping in the house until you can get a doghouse; and two, again when you put him outdoors. And once he gets accustomed to sleeping in the house, he'll not want to go outdoors. Eliminate this double work by having the doghouse on hand.

You can either buy a doghouse or make one. The Gaines Dog Research Center, White Plains, New York, will send you without charge a blueprint for building a doghouse from a wooden barrel. This barrel doghouse is sturdy and weatherproof. When painted and set up in a sheltered spot, the barrel will make a good all-weather house for your dog. Your local library will also have information on how to build a doghouse. Or, if you are creative, you can design your own.

Whether you buy or make the doghouse, it should meet certain specifications. The house should have four walls, a tight roof, a solid floor, a draft-free door, be at least twice as large as the dog (when mature), and be easily cleaned. A hinged roof will facilitate cleaning.

The dog's bed must be built off the floor. A wooden platform raised three or four inches from the floor will make a good bed. Nail a three-by-one-inch furring strip around the perimeter of the platform to hold the bedding material. Fasten a wooden ramp from the floor to the bed for the small puppy; later, when he is larger, he can jump up into his bed. Finally, add about two inches of bedding—cedar shavings, straw, or shredded newspaper—and the doghouse is ready for occupancy. (Sawdust is unsatisfactory for bedding since it will cling to the dog's coat. So will the others, for that matter, but they are much easier to brush off.)

Locate the doghouse where it will be protected from the hot summer sun and the winter winds. If a southern exposure is not practical, you can reduce wind-draft by erecting a canvas or burlap shield around the doghouse area. In summer, an awning will provide shade if no trees are nearby.

Equipment and accessories

A lot of running around and using makeshift equipment can be avoided if you have the necessary equipment and accessories before you bring the puppy home. Your pup's "layette" should include a feeding dish, water pan, brush, comb, collar, leash, and some indestructible toys.

Stainless-steel or aluminum food and water pans are best. Enamelware splits and cracks. The food dish should not be too large, otherwise the pup will step into it. Later on, you can get him a larger pan. If you are getting a long-eared dog, you would be wise to buy one of the special food dishes for these breeds. The pans have a wide base and taper to a smaller opening at the top; they resemble hollow cones with the upper part or point cut off. These pans allow the dog to get his face and mouth inside, but keep his ears hanging outside. Thus, food stays off the ears and saves washing or combing. A piece of foam or sponge rubber placed under the food and water pans will help keep the floor clean and dry.

Car-sickness

The pup may get car-sick on the way home or soil himself with excretion. When this happens, the brush and comb will come in handy. Use a long-bristled brush for long-haired dogs; a short-bristled one for the short- or smooth-haired varieties. One of the commercial "dry" cleaners would be helpful in cleaning the puppy. These come in pressurized cans or plastic bottles. Simply spray the soiled spots, wipe with a damp cloth, then dry with a rough towel and brush.

Toys

A few toys will help the puppy to forget his fears on finding himself in a strange environment. Don't go overboard on the toys; one or two safe ones are all he needs. You'll find all kinds of toys in the pet shops and department stores, from squeaky gadgets to brilliantly painted rubber balls. Pass them by, as most of them are impractical and potentially dangerous.

Young puppies have needle-sharp teeth and a craving to gnaw and chew. Select toys that cannot be splintered, torn apart or swallowed. The safest toys are those made out of tough leather, processed natural bone, or hard rubber. Stay away from painted toys, sponge rubber and plastics.

Food supply

Since young puppies have delicate digestive systems that can be easily upset, feed the pup the same diet he received at the kennel or pet shop. Bring a supply home with you. Or else feed the diet recommended for young puppy feeding in this chapter.

BRINGING THE PUPPY HOME

The trip from the kennel or pet shop to his new home can be an ordeal for the young puppy. Make it as easy on him as you can. Take along a container to carry him. This can be a cardboard box, basket or commercial dog carrier. If you use a box, punch holes in the sides for ventilation. Baskets that are not too tightly woven have breathing space between the reeds. The commercial dog carriers are well supplied with vent holes.

Remember, the pup may get sick, so cover the bottom of the container with shredded newspaper. If you are driving, place the container well back on the seat or on the floor to prevent it from toppling over, should you have to apply the brakes fast or go around a sharp curve. Most dogs are uneasy when riding in cars; imagine, then, what it is like closed up in a box. Yet the container is the best way to bring home the puppy.

When the puppy meets the family

The puppy's first day in a new home is a crucial time in his life. He's got to adjust to a new world of strange people, smells and sounds. Whether he adapts well after a reasonable time or turns into a nervous wreck depends on how he is handled the first few days.

If there are young children in the home, there's going to be shrieks of delight when the pup arrives. Everyone will want to pick him up and hold him. This will be his most hectic moment, and you've got to rescue him. Explain to the children (and any persistent adults) that the puppy is frightened, that he needs time to get acquainted with the house and people. Stress the fact that the pup is not a toy, but a living creature that must be treated with care. He can easily be injured by squeezing, mauling or falling to the floor. And he can be made ill by too much excitement.

You can allow everyone to hold the puppy just once. But show them the proper way to lift and hold him.

Place your right or left hand under the pup's chest, with the forefinger between his front legs. Put the other hand under his rear end for support. Now the puppy can be lifted and held with safety.

After the introductions are over, it's time to show the puppy to his sleeping quarters. He's just gone through quite a trial, and he'll welcome the opportunity to regain his equilibrium. Place him in his bed, playpen or doghouse and then let him alone. You can stop by now and then to reassure him that the bottom has not dropped out of his world. Give him a pat on the head and some words of praise. Most likely he'll huddle in a corner, shivering or shaking, but with your help, he'll recoup his confidence.

It is best not to feed the puppy the first hour or two. He may have a "nervous stomach" after the car ride and meeting the family. You can offer him a little warm milk or water. If he refuses it, take it away and wait until later. You can be sure that when he sees things aren't so bad after all, he'll be hungry and will let you know it.

FIRST-NIGHT LONELINESS

His first night in a strange surrounding will be a big hurdle for the puppy. If he was confused and bewildered during the day, he's going to be lonely and depressed at night. Where once he nestled close to his mother or curled up against his litter mates, he now has to sleep alone. He will not take this drastic change without a loud protest, so be ready for some whimpering or howling. But make a resolution to be firm about his sleeping in *his* bed, not *yours*.

Learning to sleep alone is an important lesson the young puppy must learn. It is one that will have a future bearing on his behavior in the house. Sleeping or staying alone without barking or howling is a *must* for city dogs. (See Chapter 7) So, start teaching the pup this important lesson the first night.

Be sympathetic, but be firm. Place him in his bed, give him a pat and a few words, and then go away. When he complains, you'll have to resist the impulse to pick him up. If he persists in whimpering or howling, go back to him and tell him "No!" Don't bring him into your bedroom, unless you want him there for the rest of his life. You can help him to console himself by placing a hot-water bottle in his bed. He'll nestle up to this and may go to sleep. Or you can put a loud ticking clock alongside his bed. The ticking of the clock is often a comforting sound and will help overcome the pup's self-imposed insomnia. A few more "sleep-inducers" are a dish of warm milk just before bedtime and one of his new toys. You may have a sleepless night yourself, but once you and the puppy get through it, you should have an easier time next night.

THE PUPPY'S SECOND DAY AND THEREAFTER

The situation should appear somewhat brighter for the pup the next morning. Unless he is ill, he'll be wide-awake, hungry and ready for the day's events. Don't expect him to be completely over his feeling of strangeness; he's still going to walk with care and more or less nose his way for another few days. But he will be very glad to see you.

Feeding the puppy

You will recall that one of the pointers we gave you on selecting your puppy was to inquire about what he has been eating at the kennel or pet shop. This suggestion was made with a definite purpose. Young puppies are radically affected by sudden changes in their diet. More intestinal upsets are encountered in young puppies than during any other stage. The pup's digestive system is very sensitive and he simply cannot stand any sudden changes, poorly mixed foods or overfeeding. Commit any of these errors and you will end up with the pup having gas, diarrhea; possibly vomiting.

More than likely, your pup was fed a high-quality dog meal at the kennel or pet shop. Continue with this diet for at least a week. Set regular feeding hours, spacing them about four hours apart. If he's under 7 weeks, feed him five times a day; if 7 to 10 weeks, he should have four meals a day.

The puppy meal can be mixed with milk or gravy. At least one of the puppy's meals should include milk. The mix should have the consistency of gruel; not too lumpy, pasty or watery. One or two tablespoons of chopped meat and a teaspoon of animal fat (lard, bacon grease, melted suet, etc.) may be added to one of the rations.

If you've been unable to get the same brand or type of dog meal fed the pup at the kennel or pet shop, you can feed him baby cereal and milk. This is a safe, bland diet. After a few days, you can introduce a good-quality dog meal and meat ration. When you do add a meal, do so by adding a small amount each day, and reducing the baby cereal by the same amount. Spread this process out over a week; it will pay off. Add a teaspoon of animal fat once a day.

How much should you feed the pup at each meal? This is a question without a ready answer. You can find all kinds of feeding charts, diagrams and menus. At best, they can only generalize. Dogs differ in their requirements and appetites. And because of these differences, *you* are going to be the judge of what and how much your dog will eat.

Until you are familiar with your dog's needs and appetite, here are some emergency feeding guides:

First, feed the puppy all the food he'll clean up at one feeding. And here's where a little common sense is needed. Don't mix a half-pound of meal with a pint of milk for a young pup. Granted, you'll have to experiment with the amount for one or two feedings. After that, you will be able to gauge the amounts without too much difficulty. Start with ¼ to ½ cup of meal per feeding. If the pup doesn't eat what you've set down, remove it and reduce the amount at the next feeding. If he cleans it up and seems to want "seconds," increase the amount next time. Allow about 20 minutes for the meal. Some pups may gobble their food, others may dawdle.

If your pup skips a meal or two, it doesn't necessarily mean he is ill. He may not be hungry. But if he should go a whole day without eating, then you can assume that something is wrong and consult a veterinarian.

Here are some more feeding tips: Feed all food at room temperature (70° to 72°F.), never right off a hot stove or out of the refrigerator. Allow the pup to eat without interruption. Keep the children away from the pup or permit them to watch (if they must) from a distance.

The feeding instructions given here are intended as an emergency measure, until you can learn more about the pup's feeding habits. A fuller discussion on puppy feeding and dog nutrition will be found in Chapter 4.

Housebreaking

Housebreaking seems to be the one chore that new or prospective dog owners dread. Actually, it isn't as difficult or time-consuming as you may think. By following some simple rules and exercising patience, you will have the pup housebroken in a short time.

Dogs are naturally clean animals. They dislike soiling their beds or living area, and will make every effort to urinate and defecate elsewhere. Keep this in mind if you decide to paper-train the puppy and *he* decides not to use any newspapers spread near his bed.

Housebreaking can be divided into two techniques: paper-training and training to go outdoors. You can either housebreak the puppy in two steps, first to paper and then outdoors; or you can start him outdoors right away.

The majority of puppies take to paper-training with little trouble, often retaining this habit long after they have been going outdoors. For the apartment house or hotel suite dog, paper-training is a must. This is especially true when the city owner is away from home most of the day. (See Chapter 7)

Step number one in paper-training the puppy is to restrict his living or play area. Allowing him to run all through the house is an invitation to trouble. If his newspapers are placed several rooms away or far down the hall, the pup is not going to make it every time. And if he's having a good time with the children or his toys, he will not take time out to race into another room. He'll use the first handy spot.

Spread several thicknesses of newspaper over the floor

in the designated toilet area. This area can be a room or part of a room, gradually reduced in space when the pup becomes paper-trained. Immediately after the pup has eaten or you see signs that he has to go, pick him up and place him on the newspaper. Keep him there until he has a bowel movement or urinates.

Young puppies usually have a bowel movement after each meal (sometimes in between) and will urinate upon waking from a nap. Your pup will show definite signs when he has to go: he'll whimper, sniff around for a spot, turn around in circles or squat. Get to know the signals and act on them. Praise him lavishly when he does use the newspapers.

Expect mistakes. A young puppy is similar to a very young child; he doesn't have much control over his bladder or bowel movements. But once he understands that you expect him to use the papers, he'll try to make it there. But there will be times when he misses. And nine times out of ten, these near-misses will be on a rug or carpet!

When a pup makes a mistake, handle it intelligently. Yelling at him or rubbing his nose in his mistake is the wrong tactic. It will get you nowhere. No dog or animal likes having his nose rubbed in his own offal (even though dogs enjoy rolling in other odorous matter), and it will mean nothing to him, except that he's being subjected to an insult. When you catch him doing his business away from the newspapers, go to him, scold him with a stern "No!," maybe tap him on the rear end with a rolled-up newspaper and place him on his newspapers. He'll soon get the point.

Next, take care of the mistake. If it's a bowel movement, pick it up in newspapers and discard it. If he wets on a rug or carpet, apply a blotter of newspapers to the spot right away. When you have the excess urine soaked up, scrub the spot lightly with a soft-bristled brush or a cloth. And now, since the spot will entice the pup again, clean it with one of the various commercial preparations put out for this purpose.

When the puppy does use the newspapers, roll up two thicknesses and discard them. Leave one or two down.

They will have a faint odor that will act as a lure for the puppy the next time he has to go. When the pup goes to the paper every time, you can reduce the area.

After you have the puppy paper-trained, you may want to train him to go outdoors. If you live in a congested city, it's safer to wait until the pup has had all his inoculations before taking him outdoors. Teaching him to go outdoors is, in a sense, a retraining process. Once he gets used to the newspapers indoors, he will not take to going outside without balking. This is easy to understand; the pup will be moving from the security of the house to the uncertainty of the outdoors. For the city pup, this is a big step and he has to contend with people, traffic and countless noises.

A simple way to help the puppy get used to going outdoors is by bringing out some of his newspapers. Spread these on the ground or in the street near the curb and place him on the paper. Keep reducing the newspapers each time you take him out. Don't be surprised if the pup waits until he's back in the house before having a bowel movement. If he does hold it until he's in the house, scold him and take him outside. Keep reassuring him and keep him outside for awhile, even though he's already gone in the house. He'll gradually get used to going outdoors.

Occasionally, however, a puppy is so badly frightened by the street noises that he refuses to go, no matter how much you scold him. In this case, you'll have to resort to mechanical means of inducing him to go. Buy some baby suppositories, insert one in the dog's rectum and take him outside. Reassure him. The suppository will force him to have a bowel movement. Repeat this routine until the puppy goes of his own accord. And he will, once he sees that nothing is going to harm him.

If you live in the suburbs or country or have a backyard, you can train the puppy to go outdoors right from the start. Follow the outline for paper-training: immediately after each meal and nap, take or put the puppy outdoors. Be regular about this and keep on the alert for the telltale signs that the pup has to go. If he holds it and messes in the house, scold him and put him outside again.

As the puppy learns to control his bladder and bowel movements, he'll let you know when he wants to go out. Take him up on this right away. Don't postpone the outing. If you do, you're violating your own training rules. As the pup grows older, you can take him out for regular walks. Keep him out long enough to go and follow the same route, if possible. When he goes over his old trail, he'll find spots that will remind him what he's supposed to do.

Bathing

What about bathing the young puppy? Don't, unless it's *absolutely* necessary and certain optimum conditions prevail. We'll discuss these "optimum conditions" shortly. Bathing the young pup can be risky; he can be chilled and his resistance to disease lowered. Bathing also removes the essential hair oils and too many baths may cause skin irritations.

When your pup gets so soiled that brushing won't remove the dirt, use a commercial "dry" bath preparation. Wipe him with a damp cloth and then rub vigorously with a rough towel. You'll be surprised how clean you can get him with one of these treatments.

Returning to the "optimum conditions," if you must bathe the puppy, wait until he is at least four or five months old. The older the dog, the less risk. If winter, pick a sunny day and have the house a little warmer than usual. Take the pup outside for a romp, because after his bath he will have to stay indoors for three or four hours. There's less risk in summer, of course, bathe the dog, towel him dry and let the sunshine do the rest. But in summer or winter, make sure that you dry his chest and undercoat, not just the surface hair. For bathing equipment and technique, see Chapter 5.

Fleas, lice and ticks

Your puppy may be harboring fleas, lice or ticks. Of the three, he's more likely to have fleas and ticks. Lice are not as common, although they do infest dogs. If your puppy is a playground for any of these parasites, dust him with a non-toxic insecticide. Detailed information on these parasites and their control will be found in Chapter 15.

Worms

Even though you were told at the kennel or pet shop that your puppy was wormed, you would be wise to make a check for these parasites. But don't make the mistake of just worming the puppy without positive evidence that he has worms. More puppies have been made ill or killed by faulty worming techniques than by the worms themselves. Worm medicines or vermicides are powerful poisons and an overdose can kill, particularly if the puppy is suffering from a disease or is malnutritious.

Dogs may become reinfected with worms from time to time, depending on various factors, such as sanitation, for example. Your best procedure in checking for worms is to take a specimen of the puppy's bowel movement to the veterinarian. The veterinarian will place the specimen (or part of it) in a centrifuge, whirl it around, put a sample on a slide and examine it under a microscope. From this microscopic examination, he can tell if your puppy has worms, and if so, what kind. He will then prescribe the correct vermicide and proper dosage. The money you spend on this fecal examination is money well spent. A neglected infestation of worms can cause considerable harm in a young puppy. (See Chapter 14)

Inoculations

Your puppy may or may not have had all his distemper inoculations when you brought him home. If you have secured the pup's inoculation history from the kennel or pet shop, you will know where he stands. If not, you should assume he's had no shots and take him to the veterinarian, who will advise you on the proper immunization program for your puppy. The pup will also need to be inoculated for hepatitis and leptospirosis (usually given in combination with distemper inoculations). After the pup is six months old, he can be given a rabies inoculation.

There are several schools of thought on distemper immunization. These are discussed in the chapter on Distemper. But regardless of the school of thought to which your veterinarian belongs, don't delay getting the puppy inoculated. His life may depend on it. (For specific inoculations, see Chapter 12)

The veterinarian

The best friend your puppy will have, besides yourself, is the veterinarian. Therefore, you should select a veterinarian with the same care as you would your own physician. While it's not *you* who will be treated, you want a veterinarian in whom you have confidence. The dog, of course, has no choice.

Start looking around for a veterinarian *before* the pup is ill or injured. If you wait until an emergency occurs, you will have to rush the pup to the first veterinarian that will see him. Inquire among your dog-owning friends and neighbors as to which veterinarians they would recommend. Evaluate these opinions with care; many a good man has had his reputation maligned by people with an ax to grind. Granted, the veterinarian who suits your friends will not necessarily suit you. But you will get an idea of which veterinarians in your neighborhood are highly regarded and those who are not.

What to expect of the veterinarian

First, don't worry about degrees, accredited colleges and licenses. All veterinarians (with very few exceptions) have a degree from one of the 19 accredited colleges of veterinary medicine, and all are licensed to practice.

Your main concern is the veterinarian's competence with animals. Does he have an understanding and a knack for handling dogs? Fancy equipment is no substitute for a good "bedside" manner with pets. But a thorough understanding of dogs and a quiet approach to their physical and emotional problems is what you are looking for in a veterinarian.

Size the veterinarian up as a person. After all, you've got to work with him on your puppy's health problems. Don't rule the man out just because he doesn't want to spend an hour chatting with you or philosophizing about world conditions. If he is a good veterinarian, he'll be a very busy man. His time must be budgeted, if he's to give his patients (including your dog) the care and attention they need. You can expect him to devote a reasonable amount of time for discussion and questions.

Again, don't be overly impressed with a brand-new hospital and clinic. Older equipment, while not giving off the sparkle of new, may be just as serviceable. When you visit the veterinarian, pay more attention to the sanitation, handling of the animals and hospital personnel. Soiled cages, strong odors, filthy dogs and rough handlers —these should be enough to tell you that *this* particular veterinarian is not for your dog.

The collar and leash

Your puppy's collar and leash are important parts of his equipment; they are tools used to teach and restrain him. The pup will have to get accustomed to wearing a collar. Buy a lightweight, inexpensive collar, for he will soon outgrow it. Put the collar on just before feeding him; he'll probably be concentrating on his meal and will not object too strenuously to the collar. It should fit comfortably, not too tight or loose. If it is too tight, he'll gasp or choke when you try to lead him with a leash. A loose collar can be pawed or scratched over his head.

The puppy may want to sniff and examine the collar before you put it on him. Let him, but don't permit him to chew it. He may object to the collar in various ways: biting or pawing at it, rolling on the floor, running away and hiding, etc. He'll soon get over it, particularly if you have his food ready.

Once the pup is accustomed to the collar, you can introduce the leash. Here again, let him smell and examine the leash. After he's satisfied the leash isn't going to bite him, snap it onto the collar and let him drag it around for awhile. Make sure the leash doesn't get snagged on something or the pup become entangled in it. Buy a flat, pliable leather leash; chain leashes get kinks in them, are hard on the hands and not as effective in training as the leather leash.

When you first try to walk the puppy on the leash, he'll probably balk. After you snap on the leash, move a few steps away from the puppy, holding onto the end of the leash. Call to him, slapping your knee with one hand and giving a gentle tug on the leash with the other. Don't drag him, keep coaxing him over to you. He'll soon get the hang of the leash and will be keen for a walk whenever he sees you get out the leash. Later on, you can teach the pup to heel and other basic obedience training by means of the leash. (See Chapter 6)

Pre-schooling for the puppy

Actually, the puppy's pre-schooling started the day you brought him home. He had to learn to sleep alone, use the newspapers, go outside, and various other lessons. But he has to learn more. He has to learn the difference between good and bad conduct, advanced obedience training, and a host of rules of dog etiquette. All of this will take time and patience on your part. As for the puppy, he's eager to please, just so long as you let him know what you want.

The meaning of "No!"

The only way to teach the puppy the meaning of "No!" is to make liberal use of the word whenever he gets into mischief or disobeys. Until the puppy has grown up and become more reserved, the word "no" will be the most-used word in your dog-training lexicon.

Yanking on the leash, climbing on people or furniture, continually barking, growling, nipping or getting hold of something he shouldn't have—these are all situations requiring a stern "No!" For example, if the pup takes off with your shoe or hat, go to him, take the object away from him and tell him "No!" Be stern and shake your finger at him. Repeat "No!" several times, then give him one of his toys. Praise him well if he starts playing with the toy. Learning the meaning of the word "no" will often be difficult for the pup, but it will be one of the most useful lessons in his life.

Growling and nipping

Your puppy should never be allowed to growl at or nip you or anyone else. "Nip" these tendencies in the bud! Unfortunately, some people get a kick out of watching a puppy grab hold of a trouser cuff or hand, nipping and growling while he "shakes" it. The pup may look "cute" while he's pretending to be fierce, but he's being allowed to indulge in a habit that will put him in the canine delinquency class later on. If you neglect to correct the puppy when he does this or are foolish enough to encourage it, you may find yourself with a chronic biter.

Some puppies become resentful nippers, growling and nipping when they don't get their own way. Children do the same when they kick and scream at their parents. Stop the puppy's growling and nipping the *first time he does it*. Tap him sharply across the nose and tell him "No!" in a loud, stern voice. If he tries again, repeat the disciplinary action. After a few "tests" the pup will go off and take out his aggression on his toys.

You will find that your puppy will be happier and better adjusted when taught discipline and kept within certain behavior boundaries. There is no room today for permissive rearing of dogs; crowded cities, mushrooming suburbs—these spell trouble for the untrained dog. Train your puppy well and he will be a pleasure, not a nuisance. But in your training—whether pre-school or advanced obedience—make liberal use of the three "P's" of dog training: patience, persistence and praise.

4. The ABC's of Dog Nutrition

Query a dozen dog breeders as to what they feed their dogs and you'll more than likely get a dozen different answers. You'll find the subject of dog feeding very similar to politics; it will start an argument most any time. How and what you feed your dog are for you to decide. But while the dog experts don't agree on the how and what of dog feeding, they *do* agree on the basic nutritive requirements of the dog.

A working knowledge of the dog's nutritive requirements and how to provide them is essential to intelligent dog care. Your dog's health and longevity will depend a great deal on your ability to feed him properly. There's an old saying: "The eye of the feeder fattens the cattle." Of course, you are not especially interested in fattening your dog. But you can apply to your dog-feeding program the basic principle of this old saw: *Feed your animal well and observe the daily results.*

THE ESSENTIAL NUTRIENTS

Your dog needs the same basic nutrients that you do. He requires daily amounts of protein, fat, carbohydrates, vitamins and minerals. Where the dog differs from human beings is in the *amount* and *form* in which these essential nutrients should be supplied.

Proteins

Proteins are often referred to as body-building blocks and are necessary for growth and repair. They are biological compounds made up from various combinations of amino acids. Approximately 20 amino acids—capable of forming many combinations—intermix to form the different proteins. The known protein requirements of the dog are 18 to 20 percent of the daily ration.

Regardless of the form in which they are taken into the dog's body, proteins are broken down into their component amino acids. Assimilation takes place and the amino acids are distributed and used for growth, body repair, heat and energy. If these amino acids are to be properly utilized by the dog, certain amounts of fatty acids, carbohydrates, vitamins and minerals must also be present.

Fats

The importance of fat in the dog's diet has been revealed in many dog nutrition experiments. Fat is a source of energy and heat. It is composed of essential fatty acids. Three of these fatty acids—*linoleic, linolenic* and *arachidonic*—are necessary in your dog's daily diet. *Linoleic* acid is found in vegetable and animal fats, such as corn oil, linseed oil, pure lard, bacon grease, beef suet, etc. *Linolenic* acid is found only in oils. *Arachidonic* acid is present to a limited degree in animal fats.

Fatty acids have other functions besides providing heat and energy. The presence or absence of adequate amounts of these three fatty acids in the dog's diet has a marked effect on his skin condition, nervous system and resistance to disease. Young puppies will show a definite reaction to the absence or insufficient quantities of the three essential fatty acids.

When young puppies are fed one percent or less fat in their daily diet, they develop dry, coarse hair and the skin becomes flaky or scaly. If this fat-deficient diet is continued, the pups have a peeling skin and falling hair. As the fat-deficiency progresses, the paws swell, followed by a reddening of the skin. When kept on a low-fat diet, puppies become highly excitable, shaky and timid. They are also more susceptible to infections than pups on a high-fat diet.

Although linolenic and arachidonic acids are necessary, the accent should be on *linoleic* acid. Of the three, *linoleic* is the most essential. And since it is readily available in pure lard, bacon grease, pork, beef and lamb fat, there is no reason why your puppy should suffer from a deficiency. Cod-liver oil, while a source of vitamins, will not provide any of the three essential fatty acids. It contains highly unsaturated fatty acids which have no preventive or curative effect on the fat-deficiency syndrome.

Carbohydrates

Carbohydrates are also a source of energy. They are present in green plants or vegetables as sugars and starches. In the commercial dog foods, carbohydrates are supplied in the form of fiber or bulk. Old wives' tales to the contrary, dogs can digest limited amounts of starch, preferably cooked.

Minerals

Minerals are needed to promote the proper growth of your dog. Calcium and phosphorus aid in the formation of sound teeth and bones, as well as blood. Iron, copper and cobalt are involved in the makeup of red blood cells. Iodine prevents goiter. There are other minerals, traces of which are needed to maintain good health.

Vitamins

Vitamins are food constituents necessary for the normal nutrition of the dog. All of the vitamins—A, the B-complex, D and E—are utilized by the dog. Vitamin C is synthesized within the dog's body, so it is not necessary to supply it. A deficiency of vitamins can result in rickets, poor skin and hair, lack of appetite and nervous disorders.

FEEDING YOUR DOG

Before discussing the various prepared dog foods and wholesome meats and leftovers, it is appropriate to mention some pitfalls in dog feeding.

Your dog-feeding program involves more than just shoveling the essential nutrients into the dog by way of high-powered dog foods. Again, your dog must be treated as in individual. And in feeding him properly, you will have to take into account his age, breed, size, kind of hair, activity and climate.

Too many dog owners think in terms of human nutritional requirements or their own tastes when it comes to feeding their dogs. Your food requirements or likes and dislikes have nothing to do with your dog's diet. Forget them. On the other hand, don't overbalance the other way and cater to your dog's taste buds. His ration should be palatable, but not exotic.

What about adding supplements, such as vitamins and minerals, to the daily diet? If you feed your dog a balanced diet, there is no need for supplements. There are some exceptions to this: orphaned newborn puppies, pregnant and lactating bitches, and when your veterinarian prescribes supplements—these are conditions under which vitamin and mineral supplements should be added to the diet. Nature intended for the dog to get his essential nutrients from natural foods. So, unless there is some metabolic dysfunction, there is no need for you to load the diet with vitamin and mineral supplements. Puppies fed on one of these "high-powered" diets can develop nutritional disturbances just as well as the pup getting a diet low in vitamins and minerals.

THE VARIOUS DOG FOODS

Your dog will maintain normal growth when fed a commercial dog food or a combination of commercial dog food and meat or wholesome leftovers. However, if you read the pamphlets put out by the dog food companies, you will be told that there is nothing like prepared dog foods for your dog. There are some high-quality commercial dog foods, fortified to provide your dog with all the essential nutrients. Most of these dog foods are palatable and dogs like them. But the manufacturers, in recommending their products via large-scale advertising, overlook the basic principle of dog feeding; to wit, the dog is an individual and must be fed according to his needs.

Considerable research and manufacturing know-how have gone into the production of dry and canned dog foods. They are an economical and easy-to-use source of essential nutrients. When used as a part of the dog's ration, in combination with approved meats and leftovers, the prepared dog foods help to produce healthy dogs. You can approximate the natural diet of the dog by feeding him a ration composed of 25% meat and 75% dry meal or kibble biscuit with added fat.

There are any number of high-quality dry and canned

dog foods on the market. (Some 3,000 manufacturers make one or more brands of dry and canned dog foods.) It must be remembered that dry dog foods deteriorate with storage, especially in their fat and vitamin content. Nutritional tests have shown that animals fed on old or stale dry foods have a tendency to develop rough coats, baldness and general unthriftiness. If you are feeding just one dog, don't overstock on dry dog food. Buy the smaller packages or boxes.

Prepared dog foods

There are many types of dog food sold today. Here are some of the more common types:

Canned dog foods are a mixture of meat or meat by-products (or both) and cereals (corn, oats, soybeans, wheat, barley, etc.), vitamins, minerals and fat. They are generally high in moisture, about 72% (moisture is in the meat products and is also added), and low in solids, about 28%. Canned dog foods are low in fat (but not as low as the fat content of dry foods). You can feed the food directly from the can, with added fat, or mix it with gravy and leftovers, preferably beef, cooked pork or lamb.

Dog biscuits are a mixture of unbleached wheat flour and other cereals, dehydrated meat by-products, vitamins, minerals, fats, and water or skim milk. Dog biscuits are baked. They are low in moisture (about 10%) and high in solids (90%). The fat content is low.

Biscuits are available in three sizes: whole biscuits, "bits," and "kibbles." Bits are biscuit meal baked in small cubes. Kibbles are broken biscuits available in assorted sizes. Bits and kibbles make a good ration when mixed with meat, gravy or leftovers. When fed as a basic ration, add fat. Whole biscuits can be fed as tidbits or snacks.

Dog meal is available in various forms, including *"old-fashioned meal,"* containing cereals and meat by-products (usually what is known as tankage or blood meal); *homogenized meal,* composed of cereals, meat products, vitamins, minerals, and fat (these ingredients are blended, cooked, and dehydrated); and the newer cereal-based foods that are kept soft or semisoft by certain additives (*e.g.,* the so-called dogburgers, etc.). In general, the dry or semidry dog foods are low in moisture, high in solids, and low in fat. The vitamin content of the dog meals is subject to deterioration.

Meats, vegetables and wholesome leftovers

While your dog is basically a carnivorous animal, feeding him solely on meat is neither economical nor nutritionally sound. Meat is expensive today and a balanced diet consisting of meat alone is not feasible.

Then how do the wild dogs manage to get a balanced diet? Simply by eating various parts of their victims. When the wild coyote or wolf kills a rabbit or bird, he eats the muscle meat for proteins; the heart, lungs and other organs for vitamins; the contents of the stomach and intestines for carbohydrates (present as vegetable matter eaten by the bird or animal) and bones for minerals. Despite his selective eating, however, the wild dog is not as well fed as the domestic dog. The wild dog eats only when he is able to bring down game; his existence is one of either a feast or a famine.

Beef, lamb and pork livers, kidneys, hearts and muscle meat are all excellent sources of proteins and vitamins. The glandular organs of cattle, sheep and swine, such as brains, tripe, spleen, are also nutritious. Pork should be cooked because of the danger of trichinosis, an infestation of worms in the muscles and intestines. Fish and chicken are also good meats. Fish should be *boned* and *cooked*, especially trout and salmon. (For symptoms and treatment of salmon or fish poisoning, see Chapter 14, under FLUKES.)

Vegetables, especially the green and yellow varieties, may be fed for bulk and vitamin value. Vegetables are more easily digested by the dog when cooked. Avoid feeding cabbage, lima beans, peas or other legumes.

Stewed, dry or raw fruits (peaches, apples, pears, prunes or apricots) may be added to the ration or fed alone. Not all dogs will eat fruit. Citrus fruits are not necessary, and are rarely relished by the dog.

Eggs

There's no doubt about eggs being a nutritious food for human beings. But they are not necessary in the dog's diet. In fact, eggs can be a source of digestive trouble.

Dogs don't easily digest raw eggs, especially the egg whites. Raw egg white contains a substance that interferes with the work of *trypsin*, an enzme present in the pancreas. Egg whites also contain a substance called *avidin*, which hinders *biotin*, a vitamin.

Raw or cooked eggs may cause flatulence in some dogs. Boxers, Boston Terriers and Bulldogs seem to have more flatulence than other breeds. The condition is aggravated by feeding eggs. As for eggs being "good for the dog's coat," there's no truth to this belief. Your best coat and hair conditioner is fat of animal origin.

Bones

The subject of feeding dogs bones is another argument-provoker. Some dog experts say bones have no nutritional value, others claim bones wear down a dog's teeth and may pierce his stomach and intestines. We say it all depends on what kind of bones you give your dog.

A dog needs a bone now and then simply for his well-being. Watch a dog gnaw on a big knucklebone; he's got an ecstatic look as he worries the bone, rolling it this way and that. It's a pacifier, a soothing source of pleasure and, incidentally, tasty marrow.

Admittedly, some bones may cause damage to the teeth, mouth, stomach or intestines. Steak, chop, fish and fowl bones have sharp ends, are splintery and can pierce the mucous membrane or viscera. Don't deny your dog a bone, but use common sense. Toss the steak, chop, fish and fowl bones into the garbage pail, and keep the shinbones or knucklebones for the dog. Take the bone away from him when he's got it gnawed down to the point where it may cause damage. Refrain from giving very young puppies or old dogs large bones, because of possible wear or breakage of their teeth.

Water

Hardly anyone thinks of water as anything but a thirst-quencher. Actually, water has another use. It helps to transport the proteins and other nutrients throughout the dog's body. Also, the dog's body weight is made up of 70% water, and he must drink water every day to maintain this percentage.

Provide the dog with water every day and several times a day if the weather is hot. Crockery-ware retains the coolness of the water much longer than metal or ceramic pans. Place the water pan where the dog can easily find it. If he lives outdoors, put his pan in a cool, shady place. It is advisable to withhold water for a short period after vigorously exercising the dog. Also, young puppies will often drink too much water. This can cause diarrhea or soft bowel movement.

Feeding regime

It's important to set regular feeding hours and stay with them. As mentioned before, puppies under three months of age can be fed four or five times a day, with each feeding about four hours apart. You'll have to work this out according to your situation, but whatever system you set, avoid changing it.

Puppies three to six months old need three meals a day—morning, noon and evening. When the dog is six months old, you can eliminate the noon feeding. Once-a-day feeding is best for the dog over one year. You can, if you wish, take the amount that you would feed him once a day and divide it into two parts, feeding one in the morning and the other at night. Special feeding instructions for the overweight and aged dog will be found in Chapter 20.

Self or dry feeding

The self or dry feeding system consists of keeping dry dog food in a pan where your dog can go to it when he's hungry. It is a system that works well for poultry and livestock. The chief advantage of the dry feeding is that you can fix a supply of food for the dog if you plan on being absent from home all day. If you are out for two or three of the pup's meals, he can get his own from the pan without having to eat sour or congealed meal that would result if you left a large portion of mixed meal. The dry system has some disadvantages, though. Young pups are apt to gorge themselves the first time and there is no way to include the proper amount of fat. Also, dry feeding increases his need for water, so you will have to allow for it.

Some "old wives' tales" about dog feeding

Dog care, like child care, has its "old wives' tales," especially when it comes to feeding dogs. But modern dog feeding is based on scientific experiments and not on superstitions or rumors. You, as an intelligent dog owner, will prefer the modern way.

Garlic and worms: Legend has it that garlic is a prevention and cure for worms. That's all this is—a legend, and a tall one at that. So far, there is no evidence that garlic has any vermicidal value. It *might* be objectionable to worms, but until there is more conclusive proof, you'll find the worm medicines effective in ridding your dog of worms.

Raw meat: Raw meat does not make a dog vicious. More dogs are made vicious by a poor environment than by feeding them raw meat. Your dog will enjoy an occasional chunk of raw meat. Don't feed him raw pork. Beef is good and it will not change his disposition when fed raw.

Milk and worms: Does milk cause worms in dogs? No, worms are not caused by milk or any other food. They are hatched from eggs. There is a remote possibility that worm eggs may accidentally get into milk or other food. If this should happen, the eggs could be transmitted to the dog. But, as we've just stated, the chance of this is very remote. The usual carriers of worms and worm eggs are insects, soil, offal and other unsanitary matter.

TABLE MANNERS

We've advised you elsewhere to allow the puppy to eat without interruption. He should be taught to let you and the family alone when you eat. Don't encourage him to beg at the table. If you do, he will forever pester you and any guests. Keep him away from the table. He can, of course, have an occasional tidbit, but not from the family table.

5. Grooming and General Care

A regular grooming will keep your dog clean, free from parasites and improve his general appearance. The grooming period will also enable you to keep a check on the condition of the dog's skin, coat, ears, eyes and teeth.

It's best to set a definite time for the grooming period. It doesn't have to be every day, but can be two or three times a week; certainly not less than once a week. Young puppies will need to be cleaned more often than older dogs, but as the pup matures, he can go on a semiweekly grooming routine.

Your pup may need to have his face cleaned daily, until he learns how to eat without sticking his face into his food. Use a damp cloth and wipe off the pup's mouth, muzzle and throat. If he has food on his ears, wash them too. Otherwise, the hair will become matted.

CARE OF THE HAIR

Brushing

Brushing and combing the dog should be made into a pleasant ritual. Select a place to do the grooming—a chair, table or bench will be satisfactory. Lift the dog onto the chair or table, talking to him, reassuring him that all is well. Let him know that he's in for a treat, not an ordeal. Let him sniff each tool; the comb, brush, nail clippers and scissors. It's very important that he learn to associate these tools with a pleasant experience. Handle the situation with tact and care, and the pup will look forward to it. Botch the job and *you* will be looking for the pup the next time you bring out the grooming tools.

When brushing the puppy, stroke the brush with and against the lie of the hair. This will help to loosen dead hair and stimulate the skin. Use a brush with the correct bristle length; short for medium- and short-haired dogs, long bristles for long-haired dogs. If you do any combing, use a fine comb for the short-haired dog and a comb with widely spaced teeth for the long-haired, medium-haired and wirehaired dogs. You can bring out the gloss in your dog's coat by polishing with a flannel cloth or one of the commercial grooming gloves. These grooming gloves are available in pet shops or pet supply stores.

Shedding

Under natural conditions, the dog sheds twice a year, in spring and fall. In spring shedding, the dog loses his heavy undercoat, and in fall he sheds dry, dead hair to make way for the winter coat. Dogs kept indoors all year may shed over a longer period of time. Overheated rooms, lack of exercise, illness and unbalanced diet—all of these will increase the amount of hair shed and the period over which it is shed. Too many baths can also contribute to excessive shedding.

You can help hurry the process during the periods of natural shedding by vigorous brushing and massaging of the skin. If the dog is allowed outside, he will help with the job by rolling in the grass or brush. Do a good job of brushing and massaging, and there will be very little hair dropped in the house.

Matted hair

If you have a short- or smooth-haired dog, you will not have to worry about matted hair. But medium- and long-haired dogs do get tangled or matted hair from burs, paint, tar, chewing gum or other sticky or prickly objects. Dried food will also contribute to matted hair, and this is common in puppies and very old dogs. Matted hair is not only unsightly, but it can pinch and iritate the dog.

If the hair is not too snarled, try combing out the mats. Do this gently. Hold the matted hair or tuft in one hand and gently comb it. If it is too tightly matted, you will have to cut it off. Use blunt-end scissors. Puppies are very quick and wriggly, so be careful not to jab your pup with the scissors. There's very little danger with blunt-end scissors. Gently pull the mat away from the dog's body, then carefully cut the hair between the skin and the mat or tuft. Avoid pulling or yanking the tuft; it hurts. Tar, paint, and other sticky or gummy matter can be softened with acetone (nail-polish remover) and then combed out.

Trimming

Just how much trimming your dog needs depends, of course, on his breed. The very short-haired breeds require no trimming, except an occasional shortening of the whiskers and eyebrows. Dogs with long, fine hair, such as Cocker Spaniels, Setters and Afghans, need to have the dead hair removed from time to time. The process of removing this dead hair is called stripping, and a special tool called a stripper or dog dresser is used. You can get one of these gadgets in most pet supply stores. Or you can obtain one called the "duplex dog dresser" from the Durham-Enders Razor Company, Mystic, Connecticut. This company also publishes charts for all breeds requiring trimming, except the Poodle. These charts are easy to follow and have the trimming process outlined in numbered steps.

Trimming and stripping are necessary to shape or balance the dog's coat. And this finishing must be done according to the breed standards. This is where the charts mentioned above will come in handy. If you don't want to tackle this job yourself, you can take the dog to a professional who specializes in your breed.

Terriers accumulate dead hair in their coats and will require trimming. They, too, must be trimmed according to specifications. Long-haired breeds don't need trimming, but they do require plenty of brushing. You may, if you wish, trim the hair on and between the toes of your long-haired dog. Also trim the hair or feathering below the hocks on the hind legs. But check the breed standards before you start to do any snipping or trimming.

Poodles are in a class all by themselves when it comes to "beauty" treatments. There are various Poodle trims and styles, all requiring some experience if the dog is to look neat. Let a professional show you how to do the job. Watch how it is done and then, if you want, you can take care of any subsequent clips. Don't expect perfection on your first few attempts; it takes time and skill to turn out a perfectly groomed and trimmed Poodle. That's why the job costs so much. But if you spoil the first clip, you can let the hair grow back again.

Summer or crew haircuts

Never clip a dog's hair close to the skin in summer. His hair acts as an insulator against heat and protects him against insects. When you give him a crewcut, you're exposing him to sunburn, the bites of flies and other insect pests. Also, the short hairs will prick and itch him every time he moves. You will not be doing him a favor by shaving him close, no matter how hot he looks. He'd rather be hot than put up with the misery that accompanies a crewcut.

TOENAILS

Overgrown or ingrown toenails can be very troublesome. The nails of young puppies grow rapidly, particularly if the puppy doesn't get outdoors where he can wear down the nails by digging. Consequently, you can expect sharp nails, capable of putting holes in your stockings, trousers and skin. If neglected, the nails can become quite curved, snagging on clothes, rugs and other objects. Also, a pup can dislodge a nail when he tries to yank them out of a rug or cloth. Long nails make a dog slip-prone and interfere with his traction on smooth or glazed floors.

Approach the first nail-clipping session with caution. A young puppy may put up a fight and it will be safest to have someone restrain the dog while you do the nail trimming. Work quietly and easily, reassuring the pup as you work. Use blunt-end scissors or your own toenail clippers. Just snip off the transparent end of the nails; if you cut too much, you may cut into the "quick." The quick is sensitive and likely to bleed. If you should happen to cut into the quick and bleeding occurs, take a piece of gauze, clean cloth or tissue and press against the bleeding part. Keep the pup quiet and off his feet for a few minutes, until the blood has had time to clot. After clipping the nails, you can smooth the rough edges with an emery board.

Older dogs that live indoors most of their lives need to have their nails trimmed every two weeks or so. You can easily judge when the nails need trimming. Either the nails make a clatter when the dog walks on the floor or they touch the floor when he is standing up straight. If your dog has noisy nails or they are too long, a nail-trimming session is in order. Use regular human toenail clippers for small dogs. Larger breeds need special nail clippers available in most pet shops or pet supply stores.

Clip the older dog's nails carefully and watch out for the quick. Some dogs have dark nails and the quick is not readily seen. In this case, it is better to take off small bits, enough to stop any clattering or dragging on the floor. After clipping, file off any rough edges or snags. A routine nail clipping will cause the quicks to recede and they will remain short, just so long as you trim the nails about every two weeks.

Dewclaws or dog thumbs

On the inside of your puppy's legs, just above the paws, you will find some extra claws. These are the dewclaws. They are vestigial claws, once having served as thumbs during the early evolution of the dog. In young puppies, the dewclaws are attached rather loosely to the leg with cartilage. Later on, they become more firmly fastened to the leg bone. They are useless and should be removed.

Removing the dewclaws is a job for the veterinarian and should be done while the puppy is still young. The operation is a comparatively simple one. Two breeds, the Great Pyrenees and Briard, feature the dewclaws as a desirable breed characteristic. If you own one of these breeds and wish to show the dog, you will have to leave the dewclaws on.

If you have an older dog with dewclaws, clip the dew-claw nails when you trim the other nails. Dewclaw nails also have quicks, so watch out for them. Occasionally, dewclaw nails grow backward and into the surrounding skin. When they do this, they become a source of pain and infection. Overgrown dewclaw nails may have to be surgically removed.

BATHING

You have already been cautioned about bathing the young pup. Avoid too many baths when he is grown up.

There are still the same risks involved for the older puppy or dog. Bathing should be resorted to only when you cannot clean the dog by other means. But give those "other means" a fair trial before you decide to bathe the dog.

The most practical place to bathe the dog is in the bathtub. There are several good reasons for this choice: the bathtub is usually large enough for any dog, it is easily flushed and cleaned, and the bathroom floor is tiled, thus allowing for a quick mopping when water is splashed out of the tub (as it will be!). Place a rubber mat on the bottom of the tub so that the dog will not slip or fall. The dog doesn't care for the bath to begin with, and if he slips and gets upended, it will only make him more eager to jump out.

Use *warm* water, not hot. Test it with your elbow; if it's too hot for you, it's too hot for the dog. Put in enough water to reach the dog's stomach. Next, gradually wet the dog all over, either by cupping it on him with your hands or pouring with a pot. Protect his eyes with Vaseline or eye ointment. Soap will sting his eyes and, unlike you, he can't reach for a towel. Castile or Dial soap are mild and will not harm the dog's skin or coat. Coconut-oil shampoos are also satisfactory. Work up a foamy lather all over his body, avoiding his eyes and mouth, then rinse with clean warm water. Make sure that no suds stay on him; dried suds can cause itching and possibly dandruff later on.

After you've rinsed the soap off him, lift the dog out of the tub onto some newspapers. Unless you want to be mopping the floor and bathroom fixtures, quickly envelop him in a large towel. Give him a brisk rubbing with the towel, paying attention to his chest and undercoat. If it is winter, keep him indoors for at least three or four hours. In summer, he can go outside, providing it is a clear and sunny day.

Fleas, lice and ticks

Full instructions on the control of these pests are given in Chapter 15. However, you can use the dog's bath to get rid of fleas, lice and ticks. A commercial "dip" added to the bath will control these parasites. Follow directions explicitly. Most of the commercial "dips" are standardized and contain lindane, chlordane, rotenone or pyrethrum, all of which are non-toxic when used as directed.

EARS

Your dog's ears should be an important checkpoint during the grooming period, or more often if the dog is running loose. Long-eared dogs have more trouble with their ears than the short-eared varieties. Look for dirt, cuts, scratches, swellings, parasites or discharge. (See Chapter 13 for symptoms of serious ear troubles)

Most of the time, you will find that your dog's ears just need to be cleaned. With care, you can do the job. Remember, dogs are very sensitive about having their ears touched. Until your dog gets used to having his ears cleaned, it's best to have someone restrain him. Lift the dog onto a table or bench and have him sit. While it is best not to make a large production out of the ear-cleaning project, it is wise to take some precautions. Put an emergency muzzle on the dog. (See illustrations 1 to 4) Next, have your assistant stand opposite you at the table or bench. Instruct him to put one hand under the dog's jaw and around his neck. The other hand is to be placed on the dog's rear end, forcing him to stay in a sitting position. (See illustration 5) Now you can begin to clean the dog's ears.

Place a few drops of light mineral or sesame oil on a cotton swab. Carefully wipe off any dirt or foreign matter from the ridges and crevices in the ear. Clean only as far down as you can see without stretching the ear tissue. Avoid poking or jabbing the cotton swab. When the swabs become soiled, change them. If you come across dried blood, scabs or a thick discharge, clean the ear, apply mineral or sesame oil and watch the ear for a day or two. If the condition persists, consult your veterinarian. (See Chapter 13)

EYES

When all is well, your puppy's eyes will be clear and bright, free from discharge and inflammation. But his eyes are vulnerable and he can easily get something in his eye that will cause him to weep or have reddened eyes. Minor colds will also affect the eyes, as will the more serious diseases.

If the dog has something in his eye, you can remove it by rolling the corner of a clean handkerchief, and after lifting up the eyelid, flicking out the object. You'll need to have someone restrain the dog while you do this. When you have the object out, bathe the eye with a boric-acid solution. Do not apply boric-acid powder to the eye or surrounding areas. Boric-acid powder contains boron, which is an internal poison. Puppies and older dogs can become seriously ill or possibly fatally poisoned if they ingest boric acid. Boric acid has been used to help alleviate the tear stains common on white-haired breeds, such as the Maltese and Sealyham. However, cases of death following the ingestion of boric-acid powder have been reported. In solution, boric acid is relatively safe.

After bathing the eyes, you can apply an eye ointment such as mercuric oxide or butyne sulfate. These usually come in small tubes. Squeeze a small amount of the ointment into the corner of the eye, pull down the lid and then let the dog blink. When he blinks, he will distribute the ointment around the eye.

At this point it is apropos to state a general rule for treating your dog. It is one that should be followed throughout his life. When you are in doubt as to the severity of a condition or injury—or when what at first appears to be a minor condition or injury · persists for more than a few days—seek professional advice. (See Chapter 13).

TEETH

Under normal conditions, your dog's teeth should not need much attention until he is a year old. However, it will not be amiss to glance at his teeth whenever you groom him. You might turn up a potentially troublesome condition.

The puppy is born without any teeth and begins to cut his first teeth when he is about three to four weeks of age.

When he is 6 or 7 weeks old, he will have a full set of temporary or milk teeth. When they are all in, the pup will have 32 temporary or milk teeth. These temporary teeth are satisfactory for the pup at this stage of his life. He can chew and gnaw objects that are not too hard, but he lacks the tooth strength and jaw power of the older dog. His milk teeth can be broken if subjected to a strain. So resist the temptation to lift him up by letting him grab hold of the leash or a stick. He'll enjoy this roughhousing, but he may end up with a broken tooth.

About the fourth or fifth month, the pup's gums will become swollen and inflamed. His milk teeth loosen and fall out of their own accord, and the second or permanent teeth appear. Now, your puppy may not whine or howl while he is cutting his second teeth, but you can be sure that the process bothers him. He may have a sore mouth, go off his feed, vomit and take on a woeful expression. His swollen gums make him want to chew and gnaw things, and he may forget his training and grab your shoe or other forbidden objects. Give him a shinbone or knucklebone to gnaw on; this will satisfy his craving to gnaw and will also help massage his gums.

Occasionally, a milk tooth fails to yield the right of way to an upsurging permanent tooth. The result is that the new tooth may be shunted aside. When this occurs, the milk tooth should be extracted to allow for the normal growth of the permanent tooth. This is best done by the veterinarian, who has all the tools for the job.

Tartar begins to form on the dog's teeth after a year. The molars are mostly affected. Feeding him hard biscuits or an occasional knucklebone or shinbone will help keep tartar from forming on the teeth. Heavy deposits of tartar cause mouth odors and will have to be scraped off by a veterinarian.

EAR CROPPING AND TAIL DOCKING

You may have purchased a puppy of a breed that requires ear cropping and tail docking as show standards. Boxers, Doberman Pinschers, and Great Danes are among the breeds requiring cropping or docking or both. Docking and cropping are relatively minor operations performed under anesthesia, usually when the pup is 6 to 8 weeks old.

Most kennel operators specializing in the breeds requiring cropping or docking usually have the work done before selling the pups. There are some, however, who consider cropping and docking the new owner's responsibility. If you get a pup that needs cropping and docking, and you decide to have the work done, don't delay; the earlier the better. Ear cropping and tail docking are against the law in some states, so be sure to check the legality of these operations in your state.

GENERAL HEALTH

The chances are your puppy will have some off-days, times when he will not feel good. When he does, you should be able to recognize these off-days and be prepared to help him.

A normal, healthy puppy is amiable and happy. He's responsive and eager to please you. He'll run, play and romp at the drop of the proverbial hat. His eyes are clear, bright, and free from inflammation, and his nose clean and moist. (A dry hot nose, however, does not mean he is ill.) The pup will "talk" to you with barks or yelps or transmit his exuberance in sign language with expressive tail-wags. He'll eat his food with pleasure, often bolting it down with gusto, and drink moderate amounts of water. His bowel movements will be regular and well formed (most of the prepared dog meals will contribute to large, bulky bowel movements); he'll have a bowel movement at least three times a day and perhaps more, depending on the number of feedings and type of food. In short, the healthy puppy is a bundle of energy and mischief.

But when he has an off-day, there is a drastic change. He gets a woeful expression. He'll lack pep, become listless, sluggish, and lose his usual eagerness for fun and adventure. He may refuse to eat, or just pick at his food. His need for water may be increased, and he'll have an unusual thirst, drinking more than his customary amount.

He may have frequent bowel movements, possibly watery or bloody with a foul odor. Or he may be constipated. He may also vomit or gag.

Your puppy's eyes are a very good indicator of his general health. When ill, his eyes may be inflamed, weeping or discharging a thick matter. His nose may be plugged with a thick discharge or just "run." Finally, a check of his temperature may show that it is above or below the normal rang of 101° to 102° Fahrenheit.

EXAMINING THE PUPPY

When the puppy is not feeling well, he will not be his old cooperative self. Talk to him and reassure him. If he is snappy put on an emergency muzzle. His snappiness and irritability should not be taken personally or mean that you've got a dog that "bites the hand that feeds him." The pup may have an injury or tenderness in a spot and when you accidentally touch him there, he does what is natural for him—yelps or snaps.

First, walk the puppy slowly to see if he is lame. Next, place him carefully on a table or bench and examine him all over. Look for cuts, wounds, injuries, lumps, parasites or signs of disease. Keep reassuring him and work quietly and gently.

TAKING THE DOG'S TEMPERATURE

The dog's normal temperature range is 101° to 102° F. It may go above or below this range, depending on what is wrong with him. Use an ordinary human rectal thermometer. Dip the bulb end in Vaseline or light mineral oil (baby oil will do), and gently insert it into the pup's rectum about one or two inches. (See illustration 6) Hold the thermometer there for at least three minutes. Remove it, clean it on some absorbent cotton and take the reading.

The grooming and general checkup period will contribute considerably to the health and well-being of your puppy. It should not be one of those hurry-up-and-get-it-over-with-quickly affairs; but a careful and thorough cleaning and examination. You will be much better off setting a semi- or twice-weekly grooming period than in starting out with the resolve to do it daily and then not getting around to it. Remember, the old adage—"An ounce of prevention is worth a pound of cure"—still holds true.

Part Three

MANNERS AND OBEDIENCE

6. Basic Training for Dog and Owner

Up until now, your puppy's training has consisted of a series of corrections when he erred. You've been pointing out his mistakes after he's committed them. When he jumps on the furniture, you push him off and tell him "No!" If he misses his newspapers and stains your rug, you reprimand him with a stern "No!" and rush him, belatedly, over to the newspapers. He's lived and grown in a world of "do's" and "don'ts" and it's all been very bewildering for the young pup. But the time has come when the pup needs to be taught simple commands that will permit you to *guide* his actions. These simple commands are what we will call the pup's formal training.

Basically, the formal training is a command and response program; you issue the commands with the proper voice inflections, gestures and demonstrations, the pup learns to respond and perform the commands. He repeats and repeats the action of the command until he learns to associate the command with the proper action. It is the old "trial-and-error" routine. Eventually, the pup learns the commands well enough to make them part of his regular behavior pattern.

How well he learns his lessons depends a great deal on what and how you teach him. Make no mistake about it, teaching your dog the basic obedience commands calls for plenty of perseverance and patience. But you have a very important factor working in your favor. You are the pup's idol and he'll do everything he can to please you. He wants your approval and upon this factor you will base your formal training program. The pup will not spare himself in his efforts to win your good graces. But you will have to help him by making it clear just what you want him to do. You cannot expect the pup to make good marks in his schooling unless he knows what you want and has the ability to do it.

DOG-AND-TEACHER RELATIONSHIP

The pup will pick up his cue from your behavior. Approach the lessons in a playful manner and the dog will respond in a similar manner. Both you and the dog should enter into the lessons with a serious intention. You are not out to make the lessons a grueling marathon of learning, but neither are you supposed to make a big game of them. The pup is in school to learn some important lessons that will have a bearing on his future in your home and community. Show him that you will not tolerate any fooling and he'll fall into line.

You will find that the pup will definitely respond to your attitude during the training and thereafter. He will be affected by your pleasure or displeasure, *as shown in your voice.* You will recall from the chapter on instincts and behavior, that dogs are very responsive to the human voice. Your voice, then, will be the most valuable training tool. Learn to use it correctly.

There's no need to acquire the harsh or snappy voice of a drill sergeant. You will have to speak loudly and clearly, with enough firmness in your voice to show the pup you mean business. A lackadaisical or indifferent tone will simply not work. If you do use this approach, you'll soon find your pupil gazing off into the distance, his mind far away from the job at hand.

YOUR STUDENT

The young pup is very much like a young child: he would much rather play than go to school. You will have to get and keep his attention. And you will have to win his confidence. These are important reasons why there must be no distractions during the training lessons. Furthermore, since the pup has a relatively short attention span, the lessons should be kept to a minimum; fifteen minutes twice a day will be adequate.

The pup needs security. He's going to make mistakes and become confused during the training. He must be made to feel that his failure to execute a command with precision the first few trials will not affect his relationship with you. He'll have to work for your approval, but let him know he's not going to be banished if he fails to get 100% on his first test. Give him boundaries. When he knows that a certain response on his part will evoke a specific action from you, his security will be bolstered. But his response to a command must always yield the same action from you. Switching your praise technique or manner of reprimand will undermine his security, as well as confuse him.

Some dogs learn more readily than others. Very often their ability to learn is affected by behavior. Shyness, aggresiveness, stubbornness—these traits will be factors in the pup's progress. If your pup falls into one of the following categories, you'll have to adjust your teaching methods:

The aggressive pup

The aggressive or bold puppy is sure of himself. He'll enter the lessons with a "show me" attitude and will be constantly testing you. He needs to be reined in and kept under control, but not cowed. Bold as he is, he'll want to please you. And as long as he does, he can be trained.

The shy pup

The shy pup is more of a problem. He hangs back, cowers and shivers, especially when you reprimand him. He requires careful handling. Keep reassuring him, building up his confidence and security. It's best to ease up on the disciplining of the shy pup. Be very patient with him, give your commands in a clear voice, and be lavish with the praise. The shy pup needs all the confidence you can give him.

The stubborn pup

This fellow simply refuses to cooperate. He balks, sits down when he's supposed to heel and vice versa. You'll have to be firm with him. Make him work. Find some way to arouse his interest and curiosity, but don't give in to his stubbornness.

The backward pup

Don't confuse the backward pup with the stubborn pup. The backward pup doesn't seem to know what he's expected to do. He gets all mixed up and confused. This is the time when the three "P's" of training need to be applied in force; they are patience, perseverance and praise. Use them liberally, working all the time to build up the backward pup's confidence, give him more time to learn his lessons, not by lengthening the daily lessons, but by extending the semester. Where the average pup can learn to execute all the basic commands in three weeks, the backward pup will need four to five weeks. But stay with him, he'll catch on.

THE CLASSROOM

If you are an average city dweller, classroom space is at a premium. Apartments are small, the streets and sidewalks are crowded with people and distractions, and the empty lots have NO TRESPASSING and NO DOGS ALLOWED signs. Then where can you work with the dog if these conditions prevail? There are several places in the average apartment house that can be used as classrooms. One of these is the hallway. While not ideal, it can be used as an emergency measure until the pup has enough grasp of the lessons to be taken outdoors. Another area is the basement, providing it does not have too many distractions, such as tenants using community washing machines. An excellent place to school the dog is on the roof. The rooftops of most apartment houses and hotels are the least utilized areas in the buildings. There is plenty of room, usually a wall or parapet, and enough solitude to conduct lessons without distractions. You should, of course, secure the landlord's permission to use the hall, basement or roof for your dog's training.

Once your pup has learned the rudiments of the basic commands, it is imperative that you take him outside the classroom. Otherwise, he'll be a star performer in familiar surroundings and a dunce elsewhere. Since the dog will probably be accompanying you on walks in the city or trips out of town, he should be accustomed to obeying commands under all kinds of conditions. Introduce him to as many as you can and do it early in his training.

The suburban dog owner has less of a problem when it comes to classroom space. Backyards, fields, even patios, will serve as classrooms. Again it must be stressed that the areas selected must be free of distractions. And upon mastering the ABC's of training, the pup should be taken into town, schoolyards, playgrounds and the highway for orientation in these areas.

Out in the open country, classroom space is yours for the taking. But, here again, the pup will have to be taken into unfamiliar areas and put through his lessons. Unless you do take him, the country dog will be like his bucolic master in a big city: he won't know how to behave.

WHO'S TO DO THE TRAINING?

If you are to be the sole trainer of the puppy, the problem is simplified. Set regular daily training periods and follow them faithfully. However, if several members of the family are to help train the pup, there should be a clear understanding about what to teach and how to go about it. Above all, there has to be a standard training technique. Every member of the family in on the training must use the same commands, voice control and gestures. Sudden changes in the training technique are just as harmful to the pup as sudden changes in his diet. They will only confuse him and set him back in his lessons.

In the average home, it's Mother who ends up with most of the work of raising a dog. She feeds him, paper-trains him and conducts his pre-school training. All of this is usually done while Father is at work and the children are at school. Most of the time, the pup's pre-school training is done during and between Mother's household chores. The formal lessons require concentration on the part of dog and teacher. They shouldn't be hurried or skimmed through because the cake is burning in the oven or the clothes have to be hung up. It is better to let Father and the children (if old enough) take over the formal training of the pup. But Mother should conduct some lessons herself.

TRAINING EQUIPMENT

A slipchain collar and a long leather leash are all the equipment you will need. The slipchain collar should have links that are smooth and close-forged. It should be a wide collar. A narrow chain will dig into the pup's neck when you exert pressure on the end ring.

The leash should be made of strong, flat leather, about ¾ inches wide. It should have a small, strong, lightweight snap. As for the length, get a leash that is one foot longer than your height.

Slipchain collars come disassembled. To form the collar, take the chain in both hands, the right hand on one ring, the left hand on the other ring. (The chain has two rings, one on either end.) Lift the right ring higher than the left, flip the bottom ring (left) over to a horizontal position, then bring your right hand down. As you bring it down, the chain will form a loop which you will pass through the lower ring. You will now have a slip noose.

When you are ready to put the slipchain collar on the dog, face him and drop the chain over his head. If you do this correctly, the free end of the chain (with a ring) will be hanging to your left and the dog's right side. This is very important; the dog will be walking and heeling on your left side, and the chain has to exert the proper leverage to control him. After you have the slipchain on the dog, snap on the leash and you are ready.

GIVING COMMANDS

Limit your commands to the fewest words possible. Make them clear, loud and to the point. Long sentences intended to cajole the pup into doing what you want are meaningless to him. He responds to your voice tone and inflections, not your grammar and syntax. If you want the pup to sit, for example, give the command "Sit!" Refrain from the imploring-type command: "Come on, nice doggie, sit down." In making him come to you, simply order him to "Come!" Or you can substitute his name for the word "come." That is, you can if his name doesn't have too many syllables. Short, one-syllable names, such as Jack, Duke or Buck, are more practical. This is one reason why purebred dogs with long-winded registry names are given short kennel or "call" names.

PRAISE AND REPRIMAND

Your most effective training persuaders are praise and reprimands. Don't be stingy with the praise; when your dog performs correctly, let him know it. Your praise signifies to him that he has your approval. Furthermore, praise should not be forthcoming only when the pup gets a lesson down pat. It should also follow a reprimand. By reprimanding the pup when he errs and then following with some praise, you will be getting across two important points: 1) if the pup doesn't do what you command, you will be displeased and 2) even though you've reprimanded him, you are still his friend. You need have no fear that praise after a reprimand will lessen the impact of the reprimand. It will not. It has the effect of impressing him and at the same time wiping the slate clean. You can look at it this way: the pup makes a mistake and you correct him. Now he knows that he has done wrong. He'll try to do better next time. Then you praise him and he knows that everything is all right. Now, he'll do his darndest to get it right next time!

You will have to be judicial in your reprimands. Make the "punishment fit the crime." And to make an honest judgment, you should not only consider the fault but also the pup's age, aptitude, and the difficulty of the assignment.

The form of the reprimand, whether it is to be a scolding or a physical demonstration, depends on the circumstances. For example, if the pup doesn't get the idea of sitting down, you should show him how by pushing his haunches down. This is, in effect, a reprimand, and your voice and attitude during the demonstration should convey your displeasure. On the other hand, if the pup balks at a lesson, you reprimand him with your voice. But regardless of the form, the reprimand should be administered *immediately* after the error or omission. It must be an on-the-spot correction. Calling the pup aside fifteen minutes later and telling him he made a mistake is a sheer waste of time.

Ignoring his friendly overtures when he bolts a lesson or keeps making errors is another form of reprimand. Instead of getting a pat on the head or a playful tussle, he gets the "deep freeze" treatment. But when you do ignore him, don't walk away in a huff. Bring him back into line and start the lesson over again.

The leash can also be used to reprimand the dog. In heeling, for instance, the pup may try to rush ahead or lag behind. A sharp yank on the leash followed by the command "Heel!" will let him know he's done wrong. When he does get back at your heels, praise him.

Threatening or striking a dog during traning is a controversial subject. Some trainers use physical force, resorting to threatening gestures or striking the dog when he balks or errs. Others scorn the use of physical force and stoutly maintain it is not necessary. Doubtless there will come a time when the pup really gets you irked and you feel like giving him a good swat. When the pup is stubborn or incorrigibly lax, a slap with the end of the leash may help put his mind to the task.

There will be those who will object to this statement, saying that it is cruelty to animals to strike a dog. When administered as an instructive rebuff, the slap or swat is not cruelty. It is a *natural punishment*. Let us see how domestic and wild animals teach their offspring. When a bear cub doesn't head for a tree when his mother gives the danger signal, or if he stops to sniff at a rattlesnake, the mother bear gives him a cuff on the head. The cub gets the point and scampers up a tree. If a pup misbehaves or tries to eat his mother's food, she nips him. This helps him to learn not to misbehave or steal his mother's food. A mother cat will whack her wayward kitten with her paw, letting the kitten know he has erred. These examples go on and on, in the animal as well as the bird world. These physical reminders to obey are absolutely necessary. Nine times out of ten, the bird or animal may find that his life depends on instant obedience. He must learn the lesson well, even if it has to be cuffed into him. And none of the bird or animal youngsters ever seems any the worse for the experience.

But *you* will have to learn the difference between slapping to teach and striking out of danger. The animal or bird parents do not cuff, bite or peck out of anger. Likewise, your slap or cuff should not be used as an outlet for rage or frustration. Whipping the dog while in a fury, beyond the point of reason, is cruelty. When you get to that stage, stop the lesson and cool off. Or, better still, dismiss the class and wait for next time.

YOUR CLASSROOM DEPORTMENT

Each lesson should be approached with a businesslike attitude. Both you and the dog are there for work. You have a definite schedule and objective. Conduct the lessons in a professional manner, using slow, deliberate movements. Avoid fast, jerky motions; the chances are the pup will misinterpret them.

How you use your body and arms during the lessons will have an important bearing on your ability to communicate with the dog. He's going to watch your body and your hand movements, as well as listen for your voice. Avoid miscues. Always synchronize hand signals with the proper voice command. Do this by giving the voice command and then following it with the hand signal.

THE BASIC COMMANDS

Sit!

Teach the pup to sit as his first lesson. There are several good reasons why you should start with this command. First, sitting comes naturally to dogs since they often sit to rest. Two, teaching the pup to sit is relatively easy, a lesson that he will learn very quickly. Three, you will find the sit position an excellent base or jump-off spot from which to launch the other commands. When the pup is sitting, he is quiet and under control. The sit position is akin to the five basic foot positions of the ballet dancer. From the five positions, the ballet dancer can execute any number of steps or combinations, from an entrechat to a capriole.

The sit position has practical applications, it is not just a trick. When walking the pup, you will find the sit useful at intersections, when meeting a friend, and in various other situations where you want the dog to be quiet and under control.

Start the lesson with the pup on the leash. You can place him on your left side; later he'll be walking or heeling from that position. Hold the leash in your right hand, give the command "Sit!" and lift up on the leash. This will raise the pup's head. With your left hand, push down on his rear end. Repeat these movements until the pup sits down without your having to lean on him. Then unsnap the leash and give the command. If he balks or sits down only halfway, put him back on the leash and start over. He'll soon learn that when he doesn't obey, he'll be restrained with the leash. Praise him well when he gets the lesson right.

Next, introduce him to the appropriate hand signal. Move a pace or two in front of the dog, give the command "Sit!" and hold up your forefinger in an admonishing gesture. Let him see it. Keep repeating the lesson, using both the command and the hand signal. While the hand signal has its best use when working at a distance, such as in the field, there are many situations in which you will find it useful. One of these is when there is too much noise for your dog to hear your voice.

Stay!

Teaching the pup to stay after he's learned to sit at your command is a natural step. The combination of sit-stay is one that will help keep your dog out of trouble or possibly save his life. See that he learns it.

Even though the pup can now sit without being restrained on the leash, snap on the leash while you are teaching him to stay. This will be a more difficult lesson, for the pup will want to move or race after you. Hold the leash short in your left hand, give him the command or signal to sit, then follow with the command "Stay!" Show him the hand signal: palm of the right hand raised toward him. Keep repeating the command "Stay!" and at the same time emphasize the command by pushing your palm at the dog.

After the pup is staying (even though you are still very close to him), you can advance the lesson. Back away a few steps, give the command and hand signal, and hold him in position with the leash. Remember, the farther away you move, the more eager the pup will be to go to you. Hold him in place with the leash, repeating the command and hand signal. Give him some praise.

Once you have him staying a few feet from you, the next move is to increase the distance between you and the pup. Move backward to the end of the leash. Give him the command to stay and reinforce it with the hand signal. If he breaks out of the sitting position and dashes over to you, reprimand him, give him a pat on the head, and take him back and start over again.

Gradually increase the distance between you and the dog. In a few weeks, you will be able to leave him and go out of sight. This will be the supreme test; if he sits and stays when you are out of his sight, he rates plenty of praise!

Come!

Most of the time the pup will come when you call him. Notice we said *most* of the time. That is not enough. You want him to come *every* time you call him, not when he feels like it or expects something. You cannot consider your dog properly trained unless he instantly obeys your command to come. There must be no hesitation on his part; come means come.

In addition to wanting to please you, the pup also wants to come to you. In fact, it's all he can do to restrain himself from dashing over to you. Fine. This makes a good place to start. Later, you will want him to come from any position and place.

Before starting the "come" lesson, give the pup a warm-up. Run him through the sit-stay a few times to get him into the spirit of the lessons. Next, give him the command or hand signal to sit, follow it with stay, then move off about twenty feet. Now, give the sharp, clear command "Come!" (or use his name), at the same time slapping your knees as you bend over.

If the pup dawdles or bolts away for a romp, *go to him*, issue a reprimand and give him the sit-stay commands. Move back from him and repeat the command "Come!" If he still insists on giving you the "you-chase-me" treatment, go to him, chastise him, and make him sit-stay again. This time fasten a twenty-foot rope to his collar. Walk to the end of the rope, turn around and give the command "Come!" As you give the command, tug on the rope. If he digs in, haul him toward you and keep repeating the command. He'll come to you when you pull him, albeit very unwillingly. But when he gets hauled over to you three or four times, he'll prefer to come without the rope. Try him. If he goes astray, put him back on the rope.

Some trainers use a hand signal for "Come!" This hand signal has its uses, mostly in the field. But even in the field it is limited, especially when you are out of sight of the dog. For general use, the voice command is best or you can use a "silent" whistle.

Heel!

There is nothing more exasperating to watch (or get in the way of) than an untrained dog on a leash moving along a crowded sidewalk. He crisscrosses in front of the dog-walker, trips people, and lunges his way through traffic. He's a pest and a peril.

Once you've taught your pup to heel, walking with him will be a pleasure. When he's mastered the lesson, the pup will walk close to your left side, his head on a line from your left foot. And whenever you stop, the pup should automatically drop into a sitting position without a command.

Heeling is taught on the leash. Start from the sit-stay position, but first give the pup a warm-up by running him through the three commands he's already learned.

When the pup is warmed up and ready to go, put him into the sit-stay position on your left side. Hold the leash in your right hand, letting the leash loop toward the ground. Your left hand should grasp the leash halfway between the dog and your right hand, giving you a corrective hold when needed. You are now ready to start.

Give the command to "Heel!"—followed by the dog's name; e.g., "Heel, Buck!" As you give the command, step briskly forward with your left foot. You can expect one of several maneuvers from the pup: he will dash forward, remain sitting or lag behind. Each one of these requires instantaneous correction. If he dashes forward, feed out the leash and, when he gets to the end of it, stop him with a hard yank. Walk up to him, make him sit-stay, pat him on the head and start over again. If he remains sitting, step backward to him and repeat the command to heel, urging him forward with the leash. If he lags behind, don't drag him; wait for him to come up to you, then make him sit-stay and start again. Praise him each time after the reprimand, whether it's a voice or leash correction.

After the pup is heeling well on the leash, you can teach him to come to a sitting position when you stop. The pup already knows how to sit on your command. When he is heeling, walk him a short distance, then stop and give the command or signal to sit. Keep repeating this walk-and-sit routine and eliminate the voice command. Repeat the walk-and-sit, using the hand signal, until the pup has it down pat. Then do away with the hand signal. In a short time, the pup will automatically sit down when you stop.

TURNING

You'll have to teach the pup to turn right or left while heeling. Otherwise, he'll be walking straight when you want to turn and you will trip over him.

Right and left turns

You can easily teach the pup to make forty-five- or ninety-degree turns to the right or left. Teach him while he is on the leash. To make a ninety-degree turn to the right, first alert the dog by *shortening* your steps. When you think he is alerted, and when your left foot is forward, pivot on your right foot and proceed in the new direction.

If the dog fails to turn right, stop and start again. This time, hold the leash in your right hand, using up about half of the length. As you turn right, pull the leash and dog around with you in a semicircle and step off in the new direction. Ease up on the leash pressure when you're on the new course, give the command "Heel!" and give the dog some praise.

The left turn is made in a similar manner, except that you have an extra persuader. Alert the dog for the turn by shortening your steps. Then, while your right foot is forward, pivot on your left foot. As you turn, bring your right knee up and across your left leg and bump the dog's right shoulder, pushing him around to the left. If you have a small dog, you can't use your knee to nudge him to the left. Use the side of your right foot. When the pup gets the nudge, he'll turn out of your way. The right and left turns have the same steps as the right- or left-flank movement in military drill.

The forty-five-degree turn right or left is made in a similar fashion as the ninety-degree turns. Simply shorten your steps, pivot on the right or left foot (depending on which way you want to turn) and make half-turns. Keep practicing all turns until the pup automatically swings right or left when he sees you shorten your steps.

HEELING WITHOUT THE LEASH

Make no attempt to heel the dog off the leash until he is letter-perfect on the leash. If he still makes errors walking on the leash, whether heeling or turning, eliminate them before proceeding to off-the-leash training.

The first step in the off-leash training is to suggest to the dog that he is not being restrained, except when he makes a mistake. You do this by exerting no hold or strain on the leash (although you should be ready to make a quick correction). Give the dog a warm-up of the lessons he knows, then order him into the sit-stay position. Attach the leash to the slipchain and stick the end of the leash into your pocket or drape it over your shoulder. This will take the pressure off the leash. In a sense, this is similar to the dual controls of a trainer airplane. The novice holds onto one control stick, the instructor has the other. But the instructor has a light grasp on the controls, allowing the novice to fly the plane. He's ready to take over at the first error or sign of danger. So it is with you and the pup; he's really walking unrestrained, but you are ready to take over when necessary.

With the leash dangling from your pocket or shoulder, give the command to heel and step out briskly. At the first sign of hesitation or mistake, immediately correct the dog. Either give him a jerk with the leash or reach down, hook your finger into the ring of his slipchain and yank it. Praise him and start over.

When the dog is responding well to this dual-control lesson, you are ready to put him on his own. Make him sit-stay and unsnap the leash. Give the command to heel and step forward. Put him through his paces: walking, running, turning and stopping in the correct position. Correct any error or omission, either by hooking your finger in the slipchain ring or stopping him and giving him a voice reprimand. If he runs ahead of you (now that he's discovered he's off the leash), call him back and begin over again. If you want to reprimand him, go to him, tell him "No!" and repeat the lesson. Be lavish with the praise.

TEACHING THE PUPPY ETIQUETTE

Now that your pup has learned the basic commands, he will be a better citizen. He is not, by any means, a trick dog, nor is he browbeaten. He's a dog under control.

You may, if you wish, go on with the dog to more advanced training that will lead to competitive obedience trials or proper etiquette in the show ring. Among these are advanced maneuvers such as figure-eights and circles while heeling; tracking, fetching and other advanced work. What he knows now, though, makes him an obedient dog.

However, by way of finishing school, you can teach him some simple etiquette. He can be taught to stand and not to jump on people or chase cars.

Standing

Teaching the dog to stand is usually done for the purpose of examination in the show ring. But you may find it useful when you and the dog meet someone on the street. You also have the option of commanding the dog to sit.

Start from the sit position, heel the dog and, as you are walking, switch the leash to your left hand. Next, give the command to "Stand!" Immediately follow the command with a hand signal: put your right hand, palm down, close to the dog's nose. Repeat the command "Stand!" If he moves, tap him on the nose with your hand. He'll soon learn to stop and stand.

Jumping up on people

Correcting the pup when he jumps up on people requires a reverse technique from the one you have been using in the basic commands. You now have to teach him *not* to do something.

There are several methods for convincing the pup he shouldn't jump up. One is to take the psychological approach. The reason the dog jumps up is simply that he wants to reach your face. So, remove the attraction— bend down to him every time he comes to you. When your face is down near his level, he has no reason to jump up. But you will have to get the other members of the family to cooperate on this one. If they encourage the dog to jump up and you discourage it, there's going to be a confused pup. While some dog owners don't mind the dog jumping up, strangers (particularly those in clean or white clothes) will not take too kindly to such an effusive greeting by your dog.

The dog may try to jump up when you least expect it. If you are quick enough, you can stall him by grasping his front paws, waltzing him back and away from you, then pushing him down. Another method that can be used on a large dog is to plant your knee on his chest as he leaps up. The impact will usually throw him back. When he drops down, immediately tell him "No!"—then give him the command to sit. Praise him when he sits.

Car chasing

This is a habit that has to be stopped before it becomes chronic. Car chasers are difficult to rehabilitate. Prevention is worth a pound of cure in this case. If you are out with the dog and he suddenly gets the urge to chase a car or bicycle, make him come to you and give him the command to sit-stay. Release him and have a friendly tussle with him to get his mind off the car or bicycle. If he tries to dash after another car, give him a severe reprimanding and make him sit-stay. A full discussion on this bad habit is given in Chapter 9.

TRAINING HINTS

Set regular sessions, ten to fifteen minutes twice a day. Keep the lessons short and don't run overtime.

Don't feed the pup before his lessons, he'll work better on an empty stomach. Avoid giving him a tidbit every time he performs to your satisfaction. You want the dog to learn that when he performs his lessons correctly, you will be pleased. When he errs, you will be displeased. You *don't* want him to perform like a trained seal; for every trick, a tidbit. He's anxious to please you, tidbit or no tidbit.

Always give the dog a warm-up before going on to the next lesson. This will get both you and the dog in the mood.

Keep your temper and the pup's interest. Build his confidence, don't tear it down. Don't blow your top when the dog makes a mistake. This will serve only to ruin the lesson. If you find yourself getting angry or edgy, stop the lesson. You can resume when you've cooled off.

Be liberal with your praise when the dog does his job. Mete out the reprimands with good judgment. When he errs or omits a movement, reprimand him right away. Follow up the reprimand with a pat on the head or a word of praise, letting him know that you and he are still good friends but that you do expect performance.

Stay away from distractions. The pup will be hard pressed to concentrate on his lessons without having to cope with other dogs, cats or people. Clear the classroom and keep visitors away.

Finally, resist the temptation to show off your dog. The basic commands are not meant to be circus or vaudeville tricks. Each of them has a definite purpose and should be used only when the need arises.

Part Four

RESPONSIBLE DOG OWNERSHIP

7. Raising a Dog in the City

In Chapter 1, we mentioned that his willingness to serve man has put the dog in a position of dependency. The degree of dependency varies according to where the dog lives. And this leads us to the often-asked question: "Should dogs be kept in the city?"

The subject of keeping a dog in the city has many supporters and objectors. The supporters say dogs don't mind where they live, just so long as they can be with their masters. And to back up their claim, they point to the thousands of dogs that seem to enjoy urban life. When it comes to the objectors, the arguments range all the way from cruelty to animals to the statement that dogs are sanitary nuisances. Pro or con, both sides have convincing arguments.

There is no question but that city life imposes restrictions on people and dogs. Neither the space nor freedom of movement found in the country is available in the city. The modern city is a conglomeration of steel, glass, concrete, brick and asphalt; all formed into buildings, sidewalks and streets—all erected in limited space. Ground and floor space are costly commodities in the big cities. There are no "wide-open spaces" in the cities, except in the parks. And these are usually out-of-bounds for dogs. Unfortunately, very few backyards remain in the cities, and empty lots are turned into parking places until the owners decide to erect another apartment house or skyscraper.

True, some apartment houses have spacious grounds, beautifully landscaped. But they also have NO DOGS ALLOWED signs. While you may keep a dog in the apartment house, you cannot take him into the grounds. The alternative, of course, is to walk and exercise the dog on the sidewalks. But even here you run into restrictions. In most cities, you must keep your dog on a leash. He may not run loose. If he does, he runs the risk of being picked up by the dogcatcher. Or, if he manages to elude the dogcatcher, he faces the ever-present danger of being struck by a car or truck.

All of this appears to strengthen the arguments of those who think dogs shouldn't be kept in cities. However, there is a middle-of-the-road aspect to this matter of raising a dog in the city. It can be done and successfully if you will recognize the limitations imposed by city life.

If you plan to raise your dog in the city, you must take three important factors into consideration. They are 1) the selection of a suitable breed or mixed breed, 2) proper training for the dog in how to get along in the city and 3) providing the dog with adequate exercise as an outlet for excessive energy.

SELECTION OF A SUITABLE BREED

A comparison of the various breeds, including size, weight, disposition, has been covered in the chapter on selecting your dog. In general, the very large dogs, such as the St. Bernard, Irish Wolfhound and Great Dane, are not recommended for city life. Nor are the Sporting Dogs, such as the Irish or English Setters, Pointers and Retrievers. Both the very large and sporting dogs need plenty of space and exercise, usually more exercise than the average city dweller can or will give them.

You will see these breeds in the city. People keep these dogs for various reasons: to scare muggers and burglars away, as a symbol of status (the biggest car, apartment, television, etc.), and simply because they like big dogs. We have no quarrel with the reasons for wanting a big dog, only the impracticality of the project. Unless you are the rugged type, willing to take long walks in the rain and snow, forget about the big dogs.

Boxers, German Shepherd Dogs, Doberman Pinschers, Collies and dogs containing mixtures of these breeds are popular in cities. They are not small dogs, but manage to adapt to city life providing they get enough exercise and what we're going to call "survival training." And by "survival training," we don't mean defense against the atom or hydrogen bombs or disease. We mean survival against the forces that work against the dog's chances of getting along in the city.

Every year, hundreds of city dwellers get a puppy of a large breed or mixture and attempt to raise the pup in the confinement of a cramped city apartment. It works out well while the puppy is young and small. But when he grows up, races around the apartment to the annoyance of everybody, the luster of owning a dog soon rubs off. Eventually, the dog has to go and the owner frantically look around for a new home for the dog or else turns him over to the local humane society.

The above is not an extreme example. When the writer was manager of the Bide-A-Wee Home for Animals in New York City, he saw many dogs brought into the shelter because they were too big for city apartments. And from reports, Bide-A-Wee is still getting these unwanted dogs. Since Bide-A-Wee has the policy of never destroying any animal unless incurably ill, these big dogs that were evicted from city apartments spend their days in the Bide-A-Wee shelters. Some of them may be lucky enough to get a home in the country.

The small, medium-sized and toy dogs make the best city pets. These dogs take up less space and don't need the lengthy and vigorous exercise periods required by larger dogs. Regardless of breed or size, all city dogs need to be taught how to get along in the city. There is more to city living than getting enough exercise. If that was all that was necessary, city dogs could get exercise on portable treadmills. But city life has more complex problems.

TEACHING YOUR DOG HOW TO GET ALONG IN THE CITY

The threat to the city dog's survival comes from non-dog owners, property owners and dog haters. In some cities, feelings run high between those who own dogs and those who do not. Civic organizations (the "Keep-Our-City-Clean" kind) constantly agitate for more anti-dog legislation. More and more landlords refuse to rent their apartments or houses to people who own dogs (it used to be children), and the places where dogs can live are becoming scarce. If dogs can adapt to city life, why all this prejudice and discrimination?

Basically, it all narrows down to the irresponsible dog owner. He's the type who gets a dog for himself or family, doesn't bother to train the dog and then, when the novelty of owning a dog wears off (or the work involved in the care of the dog is too much), lets the dog shift for himself. There are many of these irresponsible dog owners. And by their neglect and nonfeasance, they provide ammunition for the dog haters and property owners. By continuing to disregard the laws and the rights of their neighbors, these irresponsible dog owners bring disrepute down on the heads of all dogs.

The only way for you and your dog to escape the labels of irresponsibility and nuisance is for you to teach your dog how to get along in the city. You will not be able to convert dog haters into dog lovers, or convince them that dogs should live in the city. But you can help reduce the number of complaints that might eventually lead to more and more anti-dog laws.

When you've taught your dog obedience and good manners, you've already taken a major step in his city survival training. An obedient dog is rarely a nuisance, *as long as he is under your control.* But the average city dweller is not home all of the time. And this is when the city dog gets into trouble. Barking, howling, racing up and down the apartment—these are some of the objections to keeping dogs in the city.

A noisy dog in an apartment may be living on borrowed time. The chronic barker and howler will bring quick and loud complaints from irate neighbors. Very often these complaints will be followed by a letter from the landlord asking you to please keep your dog quiet or get rid of him. Or you may get a summons from the police or local S.P.C.A. When this happens, you can hardly blame the neighbors.

Dogs that bark or howl when left alone are the result of poor training or the lack of it. They may also be special behavior problems. Oddly enough, many people neglect to teach their dogs to stay alone. Their dogs will be models of efficiency when it comes to heeling, sitting and fetching the newspaper. But when the owners go out for even a half hour, their dogs soon let the whole neighborhood know they have been left alone. One thing is certain, noisy dogs can have a very short stay in the city!

Our dogs have come to crave human company. They have become so attached to people that when left alone, they are miserable and discontented. See this in action the next time you visit a supermarket parking lot. Observe the dogs left in the cars while their owners are shopping. These dogs keep looking anxiously out the car windows, sticking their noses out through the crack of an opened window and in general showing signs of agitation. They may also bark, howl or climb all over the car seats. Part of the trouble is being cooped up in the car, part is from being left alone. Fortunately, the shopping trip is comparatively short. But for a dog shut up in an apartment, time creeps along.

Put yourself in the dog's place. He sleeps all or most of the night. Then comes morning and his owner goes out to work. The dog tries sleeping some more, then wakes up full of energy. He will not get any outdoor exercise until you come home, so he tries to work off his excess energy by loping around the apartment or vocalizing.

You will have to make every effort to get your dog to stay alone without making a fuss. Start when he's a pup. Teaching him to sleep in his own bed, and not in yours, is a step in the right direction. However, asking the pup to stay alone at night and most of the day is a big request. In time, he may get used to it.

The best approach to teaching the pup to stay alone is when you are home. Put him in another room for an hour or so each day. Give him one of his favorite toys or a shinbone, then leave him alone. When he howls or whimpers, ignore him for awhile. Then, if he persists in howling, go to him and tell him "No!" Be stern about it and let him know that you are displeased. From this point on, reprimand him every time he cries. Gradually increase the time the pup is placed in a separate room and when you let him out, make a big production and praise him. That way, he'll get the idea that when he stays alone without making any noise, you will be pleased. When he howls or whimpers, you will be displeased. Be patient and don't expect the pup to learn this lesson in one or two fifteen-minute lessons.

Teaching the older dog to stay alone is more of a problem. A bad habit is difficult to break. But you've got to do something about it. In training the older dog to be quiet when you are out, you will have to use some subterfuge. You've got to fool him into thinking you've gone out. Put him in another room and close the door. Give him a toy or bone. Next, slam the front door, then tiptoe over to the room where the dog is waiting. The minute he barks or howls, rap sharply on the door and give him a loud, stern "No!" or "Quiet!"

You might as well brace yourself for a long session. Teaching the confirmed barker or howler to stay alone is going to take plenty of patience. You will spend a lot of time outside the room, ready to rap on the door. If it cures the dog, it will be worth all of the time and effort. Remember, your alternative is giving up the dog.

Some dogs cannot be trained to stay alone, no matter what technique you use. These are problem dogs and their handling is discussed in Chapter 9. If you want to keep such a dog in the face of complaints (and other than moving to the country), you will have to make special arrangements to have the dog walked. Have a neighbor (a sympathetic one) or a friend come and take the dog out several times, if you plan to be gone all day. In some cities, professional "dog walkers" are available. The cost of keeping the dog adds up, but you are faced with a choice of keeping the dog quiet or getting rid of him.

Loud and excessive barking while you are home can also lead to complaints. Your dog should be taught when and when not to bark. The dog that keeps barking long after he's alerted you to the ringing of the telephone or doorbell is a pest. Once he's alerted you, his job is done. Teach him this fact. When the telephone or doorbell rings, give the dog a pat on the head or a word of praise. Then tell him to be quiet. He'll soon learn to bark a warning until you've been alerted, then stop.

By using the basic obedience commands and teaching your dog to be quiet in the apartment, you will have improved your dog's chances of surviving in the city. Disobedient, unmannerly and noisy dogs are a prime reason why people object to dogs being kept in the city.

DOG SANITATION

Another vital part of your dog's city-survival training is to see that he doesn't create a sanitary nuisance in the apartment or street. This matter of dog sanitation in the city has given the dog haters and those opposed to dogs being kept in the city plenty of ammunition. It is also a reason why dogs are banned from most apartment houses and hotels. Soiled sidewalks, streets and other public places have been the cause of violent arguments between dog owners and non-dog owners. In some cities, the dog sanitation problem has precipitated some strong laws governing dogs in the city.

Soiled sidewalks, streets and park paths cannot be blamed entirely on stray dogs. In most cities, the strays are kept to a minimum, the minimum being those dogs wily enough to escape the nets of the dog catchers. But as a rule, strays are promptly rounded up and impounded. No, the great majority of sanitary nuisances are committed by dogs with homes, aided and abetted by their irresponsible owners.

Despite laws requiring dog owners to take their dogs into the streets, many dogs are allowed to use the sidewalks and cross-paths. Not long ago, New York City's Sanitation Department received more than 8,000 complaints of dogs soiling the sidewalks, streets and other public thoroughfares. Sanitation inspectors issued summonses to the owners of offending dogs (when they could catch them), but these failed to alleviate the problem. The Sanitation Department soon found itself in the middle of a big squabble. On one side were the dog owners who claimed they were being persecuted. On the other side were irate civic organizations clamoring for a clean city. The Commissioner of Sanitation was faced with a contretemps: he liked dogs, yet it was his duty to keep the city clean.

The Commissioner called a conference of interested parties. He invited the civic organizations to present their views. And he invited dog authorities, dog owners, dog organizations and anyone else with an interest in dogs.

All were asked to help solve the problem without resorting to stringent legislation.

All kinds of corrective measures were tossed around at the conference, from imposing stiffer fines to erecting "dog comfort stations" around the city. One of these dog comfort stations was set up outside the A.S.P.C.A., but failed to attract any dogs or owners. The idea was impractical to begin with and the resulting structure was poorly designed and costly. Most dogs objected to using it and owners were too lazy or indifferent to take their dogs to the station. Furthermore, in a city the size of New York, with more than 350,000 dogs, the number of these comfort stations needed would send the taxpayers' blood pressure skyrocketing.

There was one valuable observation that came out of the conference, one that everybody present agreed upon. It was this: if the city dog owners wanted to prevent a mass exile of their dogs, it was up to them to control their dogs in public places and to clean up the mess when an accident occurred.

Accidents will happen and dogs are not always able to get to the street in time. This is especially true of dogs that are confined all day in an apartment. They "hold it in" and then can't make it to the street. If this happens to your dog, clean up the mess. Nobody would object to this. But when people looked the other way when their dog commits a nuisance of this sort, tempers boil.

When you take your dog out for a walk, take him into the street and make him walk there until he has had a bowel movement. Keep him in the street and close to the curb, not on it! After he's done his business, you can let him up on the sidewalk or take him for a romp in the park (if allowed). It wouldn't be a bad idea to take the dog out armed with a disposable plastic bag and scoop. Or, if you prefer, there are elongated tongs on the market made especially for this purpose. Some of the dog magazines carry advertisements on these gadgets.

The dog sanitation problem in the city is not confined to the outside. Poor sanitation within the apartment house can also be a source of complaints. Soiled newspapers should not be rolled up and put out in the hall to permeate the atmosphere with odors. Nor should they be thrust into open boxes or cans. Get a metal can with a tight lid and use it just for the dog's soiled papers. If the apartment house has an incinerator, make frequent trips and dispose of the soiled newspapers. A liberal use of deodorants will help keep down objectionable odors in your apartment and the hall. When you take these precautions, the neighbors can have no cause for complaints.

EXERCISING THE CITY DOG

The city dog, unless he is ill or very old, needs to be taken out at least twice a day. This exercise period is a must and it should not be offered as a reward for being good while you are out. Dogs are affected mentally and physically by their confinement and will store up excess energy. Unless you give the dog ample exercise, he'll get rid of this energy by chewing the rugs, gnawing on the furniture, racing up and down the apartment, and other erratic behavior.

Toy and small dogs do not require the vigorous exercise needed by the larger dogs. But they still need to be taken out, if only to "shake a leg." Otherwise, these small dogs will become fat, lazy and may develop into behavior problems.

A ride down in the elevator and a quick trip out to the street to evacuate his bowels is not exercise for the dog. It might be for an old or infirm dog. But for the average healthy dog that has been penned up all day, this quick trip wouldn't even get him out of breath. You dog should have an outing of at least a half hour each trip, longer if possible. During these outings, the dog should have a chance to run and jump. Admittedly, there may not be much of an opportunity to allow the dog to run in the average city. Running him on the leash will help, but he'll have to keep his speed geared down to yours. If there's an empty lot nearby and you can use it, take along a ball or stick and let the dog chase it. He'll get plenty of exercise this way and he'll enjoy the game. Or, if the roof of your apartment house has a guard or parapet, and you have permission, take the dog on the roof and exercise him.

In the absence of a roof playground or empty lot, you

can still exercise the dog by getting him to jump. Hold a stick or ball over his head and encourage him to leap for it. This is good exercise and will help release his pent-up energy. Be sensible about the form of exercise. Select a game or exercise that is well within the dog's ability to perform. Don't tax his strength or yours. There's no point in forcing an old or obese dog to run and jump to the point of collapse. Nor should a pregnant female be made to play rough or hazardous games.

Make the exercise period a time of fun. It can also be a time when you and the dog momentarily forget the restrictions of city life. When you do make them pleasant, the dog will look forward to these outings. He will learn to save his energies for the exercise or play periods, instead of squandering them by raising a rumpus in the apartment while you are at work.

There is a place and need for dogs in the city. Some dogs adapt very easily to city life, others never do adapt and are misfits. As long as you recognize that there are restrictions in raising a dog in the city and try to compensate for them, the chances are you will be successful as a city dog owner. The city dog is totally dependent on you. In your hands are the means to help him to adjust to or become a casualty of urban living. To answer the question posed at the beginning of this chapter: it all depends on *how* you keep a dog in the city.

8. The Suburban and Country Dog

THE SUBURBAN DOG

Suburbia (called "disturbia" by its critics) is a land of gracious living. Thousands of ranch and split-level houses are set on quarter- and half-acre plots. Communities have materialized in an astonishingly short time on former pasture land or farm wasteland. People who once lived in cramped city apartments now live in style. They own a car, a patio and maybe a plastic swimming pool. And they keep dogs.

The suburbs seem a likely place to keep a dog. There is more space and the dog has more opportunity to get outdoors and run off his excess energy. True. The suburban dog does have more space and freedom than his city cousin. Some suburban dogs have too much freedom.

Unfortunately, many suburban dog owners mistake the suburbs for the open country. Quarter- and half-acre plots are not farms. Unless the plot has a fence around its perimeter, the suburban dog strays over the boundary lines and gets into mischief. This is the major problem among suburban dog owners. If a neighbor happens to be a gardener who love his hobby with a purple passion, the dog owner can expect some hostile sessions when his dog decides to dig or sleep in the neighbor's flower bed.

CANINE DELINQUENTS

The number of canine delinquents in suburbia is steadily increasing. Their owners turn them out several times a day—or what is worse, put them out all day. The dogs are left to their own devices. They band into teams, gangs and packs that roam the neighborhood. All kinds of nuisances are committed by these errant dogs. They run over newly seeded lawns, tree the community cats, urinate on shrubbery and trees, dig in flower beds, chase cars, knock over and root in garbage cans, and engage in various other forms of mischief. Ironically, many of these wayward dogs have been well schooled in basic obedience and are models of deportment when in the house or with their masters.

You cannot expect your dog, no matter how obedient he is, to behave properly when out roaming the neighborhood in company with other dogs. The old saying, "Out of sight, out of mind," is very apropos. Basic obedience is no cure-all. The efficacy of the basic obedience depends on your presence. The commands are control measures, not conscience guides. No dog is going to pause when faced with temptation and say to himself, "No!" If your dog is off your property and spots a female in heat, he's going to run after her, even if it means cornering her in your neighbor's flower bed. Likewise, if you turn your dog outdoors and he sights the neighbor's cat, he'll run her up a tree. When you are present in situations like these, you can bring the dog under control with a stern "No!" When he's out on his own and out of your sight, anything can happen.

Then what's the use of having a dog in the suburbs if you can't let him outside without having to accompany him? There's no getting around it, if you want to avoid having a problem dog and steer clear of the law, you will have to control the dog. And it is possible to control him and still give him the advantages of the outdoors. You do this by making use of the big advantage you have over the city dog owner—space. In short, you either fence the property or build a kennel area. By alternating between walks on a leash and free play and exercise in the kennel area, the suburban dog can have a happy environment and stay out of trouble.

HOME KENNELS

The ideal situation would be to enclose the entire property with a four- or five-foot chain-link fence. You would keep other dogs out and your dog would have the freedom of the place. When you are too busy to take him for a walk, you simply turn him outdoors in the enclosure. Later, you can put on his leash and take him for a walk or romp in the fields or woods. But erecting a chain-link fence around a quarter- or half-acre plot is a costly project. Not many suburbanites can afford this kind of luxury.

Wood-and-wire kennel

There are some satisfactory substitutes, however. One is to build a wood-and-wire kennel area. By using wood and galvanized or other treated heavy-gauge wire, you can construct a sturdy and roomy kennel for your dog. Poultry or livestock wire fencing will make a good enclosure when fastened to wooden posts and top and base boards. Most fence or lumber companies carry this type of heavy-gauge wire fencing. Or you can order it from Sears Roebuck and Company or Montgomery Ward.

The wood-and-wire kennel needn't take up much space. An area measuring six by twelve feet (and at least five feet high) will make a suitable kennel run. Set the kennel upon a spot that will not be too hot in summer. If you can locate it where it will be partially shaded by trees, so much the better. Also, take care that the kennel is not exposed to the wintry winds. When equipped with a snug doghouse, this wood-and-wire kennel makes an excellent place to keep the suburban dog. You can turn him out for short periods, all day or leave him out overnight. When he's in the kennel, you know that he's out of mischief.

Snow-fence kennel

If you are not handy with tools or don't want to spend the time and money in building the wood-and-wire kennel, you can use snow fencing and studded-steel posts. A fifty-foot roll of snow fencing (it usually comes in this size) will make a kennel ten by fifteen feet, or any variation limited to the fifty feet of fencing. This will give your dog one hundred and fifty square feet of space, which is ample room for him. If you use the side of the house or other building as one side of the kennel, you can make the kennel larger. But ten by fifteen feet will do.

Snow fencing, composed of prefabricated wood and wire, is relatively inexpensive, costing from $10 on up for a fifty-foot roll. Steel posts are available at extra cost. They come in six-, seven- and eight-foot lengths. The snow fencing is made of rough wooden slats fastened together by strands of twisted wire. "Farm" red is the standard color, but white is available at a higher cost. While it is not as sightly as a chain-link or wood-and-wire kennel, the snow fence has the advantage of being semipermanent or portable. When you want to move the kennel, just unhook the snow fence from the posts, pull up the posts and relocate the kennel.

You can make a gate into the snow-fence kennel by placing two posts about three feet apart and using the fence material that will span this space as a gate. One post is used as a hinge post, the other as the latch post. The three-foot piece of snow fence serving as the gate will swing open or closed on its own wires. It will not work as easily as a gate on hinges and you will have to fasten the bottom of the gate with wire when closed, else the dog can push under it.

Setting up a kennel area may seem like a lot of trouble. But in the long run, it will keep you and the dog out of trouble. A kennel will come in handy if you have a female dog, especially during her heat periods. When she is in heat, put her out in the kennel. While it is true that some desirous and enterprising male may leap over the kennel fence, you will at least know where your female dog is at all times. Keeping a female in heat in the house until she gets over her period can be a trying and frustrating experience. You have to watch her all the time and you never know when someone will leave the door open. Once she gets out, she'll be gone.

The main problem, then, in raising a dog in the suburbs is the matter of proper control. Granted, it's a big temptation to just turn the dog out when he gives you that "I've got to go" look. But turn your back on this temptation. Take him out on the leash or build him a kennel. By doing this you will avoid ending up with a problem dog and hostile neighbors.

THE COUNTRY DOG

The country dog leads a more natural life than either his city or suburban relatives. He has plenty of space and opportunity to run off energy. Most of the time, the country dog can be turned outdoors with small risk of his getting into trouble. All in all, the country dog enjoys an existence that is fairly close to that of his early ancestors. But it must not be supposed that all one has to do with the country dog is to turn him out and forget about him. The country dog owner still has responsibilities toward the dog and neighbors. Country dogs should certainly be taught the basic commands. If a country dog is to serve a special purpose on the farm, such as a herd or stock dog, he will need specialized training.

MOLESTING LIVESTOCK

The major source of trouble for the country dog owner is the chasing, injuring or killing of livestock by his dog. Many dogs, since they are fundamentally hunters, take great delight in chasing poultry and livestock. Others make it a more deadly game and injure or kill livestock and poultry, especially sheep. Your country dog must be taught that he cannot molest livestock. Farmers and the law have no sympathy for the problems of an owner of a livestock-killing dog. And the law exacts severe penalties from the dog owner. A full discussion on livestock-killing dogs and the law will be found in Chapter 10.

Training the dog not to molest livestock

When you have taught your dog basic obedience, you can take steps to teach him not to molest poultry or livestock. Prior to this the pup should be kept in a kennel or the house and not allowed to roam the countryside.

Introduce the pup to poultry and livestock while he is on the leash. If you have your own poultry or livestock, so much the better. You can let the pup accompany you while you do your chores. If you don't have any poultry or animals, you will have to get the cooperation of a neighboring farmer in helping you train your pup.

Naturally, when the pup gets near any livestock or poultry, he's going to be curious and playful. But keep him under control and be on the alert for any sudden lunge to grab a chicken or nip at the heels of an animal. The pup may only have playful intentions, but he can inflict serious or mortal injury on poultry. All he has to do is puncture a bird with his teeth and if it happens to be in a vital spot, the bird is in trouble.

By all means, let the pup satisfy his curiosity. He'll only accomplish this when he has had a chance to move close to and sniff the bird or animal. Lead him over to the cow, sheep or horse and let him sniff the animal. If he tries to dash at the animal or begins to bounce around, barking all the while, correct him. This is the time to set the dog straight about livestock. They are his friends and he is not to molest them. Be stern with him.

You will have to work differently when introducing the pup to poultry. Most poultry are very flighty and skittish, especially White Leghorns, which will fly in all directions when disturbed or frightened. And very few of the other poultry breeds will stand still and permit the pup to sniff them. At his approach, they will usually squawk and run off. The best method of bringing the dog and poultry together for the first time is for you to get a bird and bring it to the dog. Give him the command to sit-stay and then let him sniff the bird. Be on the alert for any sudden moves. Also, make sure that you have a tight hold on the bird; if it gets away from you, the dog will be after it before you can issue a reprimand. Let him smell the bird all over. If he tries to grab or nip the bird, reprimand him with a sharp rap on the nose.

Later, after the dog has been introduced to the bird, you can lead him on the leash around and among the other poultry. Keep him under control and curb any tendency to run or dash or bark with a jerk on the leash or vocal reprimand. Eventually, the pup will learn to accept the poultry and livestock. But don't expect this to happen after one or two lessons; you will have to keep working with the pup. When a chicken can stroll past the pup without his giving chase, you can consider the job done.

Possible encounters with skunks, poisonous snakes and porcupines are to be expected if the country dog is not confined. There is nothing you can do about them, except keep the dog in a kennel. First aid for your dog when he does meet a skunk, snake or porcupine is given in Chapter 17.

SPECIAL ADVANTAGES OF HOME KENNELS

A kennel, such as described for the suburban dog, is also practical for the country dog. The need for a country dog kennel is not so much for the purpose of keeping the dog confined all the time, but rather for special occasions —for example, to confine a female in heat or as a safe place to keep a hunting dog during the hunting season, when the possibility of theft is likely. A strong kennel run is also a good place in which to keep a dog when there is a rabies epidemic among wildlife or stray dogs. Finally, a run will prove a handy place to keep your country dog when you have to leave the farm or ranch for any length of time. At least you will know the dog is not out chasing wildlife or molesting the neighbor's poultry or livestock.

9. Problem Dogs

Since our domestic animals are usually confined or restrained, they are susceptible to abnormal behavior. And the dog is no exception. We've taken the dog and forced him to live under all kinds of unnatural conditions. Many of these conditions lead to abnormal behavior or neuroses. You have learned in the early chapters the importance of environment in the early development of the puppy. Environment is also a vital factor in the mature dog's behavior.

While it may not have been difficult for you to provide the puppy with the proper socialization and environment, you may find when he's grown older that the situation and environment have changed. You now notice that your dog is developing certain unfavorable tendencies. He is showing signs of abnormal behavior and will, unless curbed, develop into a problem dog.

CAUSES OF ABNORMAL BEHAVIOR

Let us delve lightly into the background of abnormal behavior. It may be functional or organic. A dog that is confined all day to a small apartment and seeks release from his stored-up energy by chewing the rugs or furniture is showing signs of functional abnormal behavior. When a rabid dog runs through the streets, snapping at people and animals in his path, he is suffering from a disease that affects his behavior. This would be organic abnormal behavior. In many cases, the trend of functional abnormal behavior can be altered. Functional abnormal behavior can also be prevented. But the outcome of organic abnormal behavior depends on the prognosis of the disease. In the case of rabies, there is no cure and the abnormal behavior ends with the death of the dog.

Dr. J. P. Scott, who has been responsible for shedding considerable light on the abnormal behavior of dogs, points out that there are four factors that produce abnormal behavior in the dog. These are *overexcitement, lack*

of escape, lack of adaptation, and *genetic susceptibility.*
All four of these factors must be present at one time. The
presence of one or two will not produce prolonged or
harmful effects.

Overexcitement

Any situation or stimulus that tends to overexcite the
dog will contribute toward abnormal behavior. For example, the ringing of a doorbell or telephone may overexcite
the dog.

Lack of escape

When the dog cannot escape from the situation or stimulus that is causing his overexcitement, he takes another
step toward abnormal behavior. Let us go back to the dog
in the apartment who hears the doorbell or telephone
ringing. Since he is confined, he cannot escape from the
sound of the bells. Lacking a means of escape, the dog
may bark, scratch at the door or howl.

Lack of adaptation

If the doorbell and telephone rang continuously, the
dog would more than likely adapt to them. But these are
sporadic stimuli and the dog cannot or will not adapt to
them. In some situations, the dog has no opportunity to
adapt. In others, the opportunity may be present, and the
dog fails to adapt and resorts to abnormal behavior.

Genetic susceptibility

You will remember that dogs are sensitive to sounds
and touch. Some of them are oversensitive and may be
said to have a genetic susceptibility. This susceptibility is
usually related to a metabolic disturbance in the dog's
nervous system. This is the one factor contributing to
abnormal behavior that cannot be controlled. You can do
something about the other three.

It should be pointed out here that we are not trying to
make a "dog psychologist" out of you, if there is such a
profession. Rather, our intention is to acquaint you with
the causes of abnormal behavior and what—if anything—
can be done about it. Diagnosing the *exact* cause of your
dog's abnormal behavior may often be beyond your abili-

ties. But by knowing what contributes toward abnormal behavior and some of its examples, you can take steps to prevent it. Or you can at least see to it that your dog is not placed in a situation or environment that will ultimately lead to abnormal behavior.

Fortunately, you can do quite a bit about most cases of abnormal behavior. You have control of the dog's environment and may often be in the position of rearranging it if it is contributing to your dog's abnormal behavior. In many cases, you can provide a means of escape from the stimuli that are causing overexcitement. For instance, if the telephone overexcites the dog, you can tone down the bell or change over to a signal light while you are away from home. In general, you can work toward decreasing or eliminating overexcitement, providing a means of escape and offering substitutes, whenever possible.

Now, let us examine some of the types of abnormal behavior that may occur under city, suburban and country conditions.

THE CHRONIC BARKER OR HOWLER

It's normal for your dog to bark a warning or greeting. It's abnormal for him to keep on barking long after the reason has ceased to exist. Yet many dogs do just this. In the chapter on raising a dog in the city, we gave some instructions on how to teach your dog not to bark after he's alerted you. Perhaps, despite your efforts, your dog still keeps up an abnormal barking after he should have stopped. Or, what is worse, he barks continuously when you are away from home (which you learn from angry neighbors when you come home).

If we apply the social psychologist's yardstick to the chronic barker, we have all four of the factors needed to produce abnormal behavior. The door and telephone bells, knocks on the door, loud voices in the hall and other noises are all overexcitement factors. Since the dog is confined in the house or apartment, he cannot escape. He can't or will not adapt to the sounds and noises, and he doubtless has a genetic susceptibility. The result of all of this is abnormal barking.

Or look at it this way. The dog hears a noise in the hall or the doorbell rings. It strikes the dog's ears the wrong way and overexcites him. He'd like to get at whatever is causing the noise, but he can't. So he does the next best thing, he barks. He can't get used to the noises, since they are infrequent or sporadic. And because his nervous system is on the minus side, he develops abnormal behavior and keeps barking long after the noise has stopped.

We should make it clear that you are not out to make your dog a *barkless* dog. You want him to bark an alert, even when you are not at home. But you want him to quiet down after his warning has been acknowledged or the cause of the warning has gone away.

As for therapy for the chronic barker, you will have to provide some form of escape. You can't very well stop people from coming to the door or noises in the hall. And unless you decide to move to the country, you can't take the dog out of the offending environment. But you can try to substitute some action that will take his mind off the noises.

In an actual case of this type, one owner found a novel solution to his barking dog problem. He was obliged to leave the apartment all day. While he was out, his dog barked whenever anyone walked past the apartment door. This was normal, since the dog was barking a warning. But he kept it up long after the person had moved on and no noise existed. Neighbors complained and the harassed dog owner tried all the standard remedies, without success. Faced with the possibility of having to give up his dog, he sought professional advice. The problem was discussed and a possible solution suggested. It was this: teach the dog to go fetch something from another room whenever he heard a noise. In a short time, the dog was trained to bark a warning, then go to the shelf, take a book and disappear into the room containing his bed. Ridiculous? Maybe. But it solved the problem for this dog owner.

There is, however, a tale of how a dog owner contributed to his dog's abnormal behavior. This owner was more concerned about his dog getting enough exercise than in keeping the dog out of trouble. Dog and owner lived in a city apartment. The owner worked all day and became worried about his dog getting enough exercise. He hit upon what he thought was a brilliant idea to get the dog exercising while he, the owner, was at work. It was simple. He knew the dog barked and ran around the apartment whenever the telephone rang. So the owner merely rang his own number three or four times a day, thereby getting the dog to race around the apartment. The finale to this little tour-de-force is not difficult to imagine. Both dog and owner were evicted.

What about the dog that howls when you are not at home? He is definitely a problem. He howls because he is confined and lonely. You can try to cure him by teaching him to stay alone without making a noise. (See Chapter 7) Or, if this fails, have someone come in and take the dog out for a walk several times a day. There is a third possibility: give the dog some company by adding a kitten to the ménage. Another dog would be just the company he would want, but you might find yourself with a howling duet, instead of a solo!

The suburban dog that barks indiscriminately at friend and stranger is well on his way to becoming a problem. While a barking dog does not necessarily mean a biting dog, there's always the possibility that the barker will follow up his noise with a bite. Milkmen, mailmen, newsboys and utility servicemen are the frequent targets of the barker (and biter).

Barking at people who come into the yard or house, especially servicemen, usually starts from the dog's protective instinct. He barks a warning. But it can go beyond the mere warning for various reasons, among them being a fear of the mailman's bag, the clattering of the milk bottles, a rolled-up newspaper tossed onto the porch or into the yard by the newsboy, the uniforms of the servicemen and others. Regardless of the cause, you will have to take measures to break the dog of this overzealous barking. Later, he may take to biting and you will then have a more serious problem on your hands.

There is no single step in breaking the dog of the barking habit. Your main course of action is to make a "formal" introduction between the dog and servicemen. To do this, you will have to get the cooperation of the servicemen. When one of them arrives, ask him to stand still and not move his arms, bottles or bag. Have the dog on the leash and make him heel as you walk out to meet the serviceman. Remind the man to stand still, speaking to him in friendly tones. The dog will probably bristle and bark. Cut him short with a stern reprimand. Then let him smell the man. Remember, it is with his nose that a dog identifies a person or object; he never will accept the mailman or anyone else unless he can satisfy his nose. Keep reassuring the dog (and maybe the man). Don't, under any circumstances, let the man hand you a letter or bottle of milk. The dog may misinterpret this as an attack on you. Just let the dog see that nobody is going to harm him or you. Later you can pick up the mail or bring in the milk. You'll have to go through more than one of these sessions, but it will be worth it. Once the dog gets used to the servicemen, he will accept them.

The matter of the newsboy flinging a rolled-up newspaper is somewhat different and requires special handling. First of all, there are two factors that cause the dog to get overexcited: the newsboy on his bicycle (the bicycle excites the dog), and the boy's act of throwing the newspaper (which the dog interprets as being thrown at him). This means that you have two hurdles to overcome; three, if the newsboy is a lad who takes great delight in throwing the paper and watching the dog go berserk. But overcome them you must, if you want to avoid having the dog turn into a biter.

You can try introducing the dog to the newsboy, but this involves risk. The newsboy is one person the dog would like to grab, since the boy makes a threatening gesture to the dog when he throws the newspaper. If he hits the dog, there is all the more reason for wanting to get at him. Your safest procedure is to have the boy park his bicycle away from the house (the bicycle is part of the problem) and put the newspaper into a special container outside the fence. You can also keep the dog indoors at the time when the newsboy makes his daily delivery. As a last resort, cancel your newspaper delivery and pick up the paper at the store.

THE BITING DOG

When a dog wants to show his displeasure, he'll growl, snarl or bite. He will also bite from fear and in self-defense. These are natural reactions and *normal* behavior. But from our standpoint, any of these traits constitute undesirable behavior. It makes no difference if psychologists and animal behaviorists state that from the dog's viewpoint there is just provocation for him to bite—a biting dog is proscribed.

It is estimated that 600,000 people are bitten by dogs every year in the United States. The U. S. Post Office Department reported an average of 6,000 mailmen bitten each year. Furthermore, more than 76 percent of the dogs involved in these bites had owners.

The dog bite situation as a national problem rarely gets the attention it deserves. Dog food companies, breeders and others engaged in selling or promoting dogs and dog products are reluctant to bring up the problem. In fact, it's considered bad publicity for dogs. Consequently, the subject is ignored, glossed over or pigeonholed. Nevertheless, dogs *do* bite, and an ostrichlike attitude will not help reduce the number of bites.

The number of dog bites can be reduced. But only when dog owners train their dogs and keep them under control, and the public learns more about dogs and their habits and how to act around a strange dog. The two go hand-in-hand; advising the dog owner to control his dog without instructing the public in how to meet a dog will never ease the situation. It is at best a half measure.

You, as an intelligent dog owner, will teach your dog basic obedience. As we have pointed out several times before, basic obedience is a fine control measure when you are present. When you are not, your dog is under no obligation to behave. Some dog authorities stoutly maintain that an obedient dog is rarely, if ever, a biter. Of course not, if you are around to stop him. Many dogs involved in bite cases have had obedience training. In fact, dog show judges are occasionally bitten by dogs that are supposed to have had the ultimate in training and handling. Maybe your dog has never bitten anyone, maybe he never will. If you've given him obedience training and discouraged nipping and biting when he was a pup, you will probably avoid a chronic biter. But as far as we're concerned, nobody can say with certainty that his dog will never bite. When forced into a situation where he is overexcited and provoked, *any* dog will bite.

Chronic biters more or less fall into five classifications: shy dogs, resentful dogs, vicious dogs, overly protective dogs and "unbalanced" or mentally ill dogs. You will no doubt recognize that the first three dogs are probably the result of poor handling during the early socialization period of puppyhood. The overly protective dog is the result of genetic susceptibility and the mentally ill dog may be the result of genetic susceptibility, disease or injury.

All of the above groups of dogs are potential chronic biters. When provoked, they can usually be relied upon to retaliate by snapping or biting. Now, let's see what provocation will trigger these biters into action. (We're excluding dogfights.) Here are some of the common triggering devices of dog bites:

Keeping dogs on chains, ropes, cables or in close confinement. When kept this way, the dogs become overly aggressive and when teased or merely approached, they bite. Fastening a dog on a short chain and teasing him was one of the methods used to make military dogs "vicious."

Sudden movements and wrong way of approaching dogs by strangers. The dog may be downwind from the person, he may be sensitive to touch, or be suddenly awakened out of a sleep by the approach of a person—all of which cause him to snap or bite.

Teasing or rough handling by children or thoughtless adults. The dog may get overexcited or be oversensitive to touch.

Irrespective of what is triggering your dog into biting, the fact is you will have to do something about it. The practical approach would be to remove those factors causing the dog to get overexcited and bite. Or to provide him with a means of escape. You can't very well eliminate the servicemen. Although, if you don't restrain your dog, these men will remove themselves.

The Post Office Department has been searching for

vays to solve the dog bite problem among its employees. So far, the Department hasn't come up with any method to make dogs stop biting the mailman or a device to prevent the men from being bitten. (They have tried metal trousers, handouts of dog candy, etc.) The Department also has what it calls the "anti-dog bite policy," which requires the local postmaster to send a letter to the offending dog's owner, advising him that his dog is interfering with the delivery of the mail. The letter goes on to state that the dog owner is requested to take steps to control his dog by leashing or penning the animal.

This rule looked good in writing, but was difficult to put into practice. The main objection is that the letter of complaint has to be delivered to the dog owner's mailbox. Thus, the mailman must run the gantlet of hostile dogs once more. Now the Post Office Department is considering the idea of having the local postmaster telephone the dog owner and issue the ultimatum: keep your dog away from the mailman or face discontinuance of mail. But there's one big snag: not all dog owners with offending dogs have telephones!

All levity aside, the dog bite problem is a serious one. In the suburbs where dogs are roaming loose, it becomes more than just the problem of the individual dog owner. It is a community problem. You and every other dog owner should make every effort to reduce the number of dog bites, even though your dog, as yet, is not an offender.

If you know that your dog bites, try to eliminate any factors causing overexcitement and look for ways to help him escape or adapt. Talk to the servicemen, solicit their cooperation and introduce them to the dog while you have him on the leash. Instead of keeping your dog on a chain or rope, where he will build up energy and possibly release it by attacking the first person or animal that comes near him, put a fence around the yard. Or, if this is not practical, at least make a kennel.

Should your dog be shy or sensitive to touch, let this fact be known to all who come to your house. Make it very clear to children that they must not touch or tease the dog. Some dogs, especially older dogs raised in homes where there are no children, are often resentful of young-

APPLYING EMERGENCY MUZZLE

Make a loop large enough to fit over dog's muzzle.

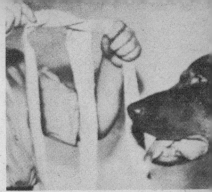

(*Right*) Quickly slip noose or loop over dog's nose and tie on top.

(*Below, left*) Bring ends down under dog's lower jaw and tie.

(*Below, right*) Tie both ends around behind the dog's ears with a bow-knot.

RESTRAINING DOG
FOR EXAMINATION OR TREATMENT
Just keep a firm grip—don't wrestle with him.

TAKING DOG'S TEMPERATURE
Dip bulb end of rectal thermometer in vaseline or baby oil.
Insert and keep in for at least three minutes.

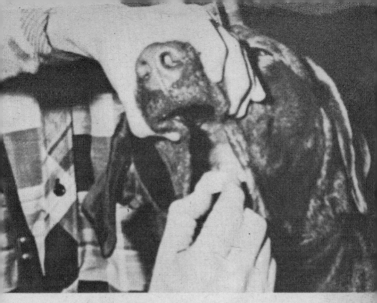

ADMINISTERING PILLS, TABLETS, AND CAPSULES
Place well back in dog's mouth.

GIVING LIQUID MEDICINES
Make a pouch in the side of the dog's mouth and pour in liquid medicines from a small bottle or syringe.

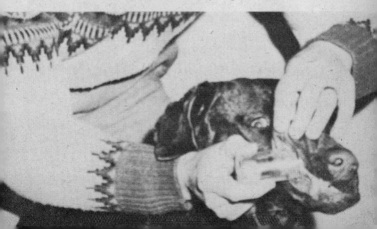

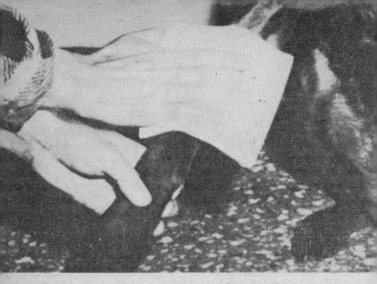

SERIOUS BLEEDING

Control serious bleeding by direct pressure with a clean compress, towel, handkerchief, etc.

SNAKE BITE

Constriction, incision, and suction! A bottle from which the air has been drawn can be used as emergency suction apparatus (see text on snake bite).

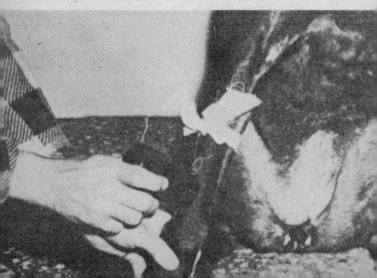

GROOMING

Grooming makes your dog look and feel good. Brush with and against the lie of the hair.

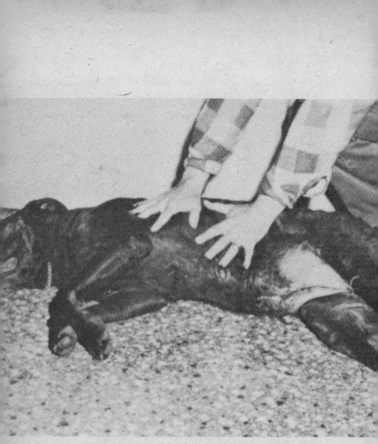

ARTIFICIAL RESPIRATION
Press hands down on dog's rib cage—release—wait—then press
down again. Keep at it!

WALKING WITH DOG

An obedient dog in the city is a pleasure—a disobedient dog is a nuisance and a pest. Keep your dog under control when taking him for a walk.

SITTING AT CURB

Teach him to stop and sit while waiting for the traffic light.

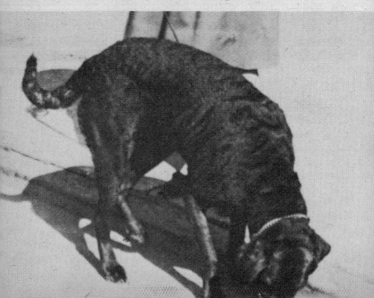

LEFT TURN
Use your right knee to urge the dog into a left turn.

CURB YOUR DOG!
Don't be an irresponsible dog owner. If you live in the city, curb your dog!

All photographs: Claire von Buchwald MacNeill's Chesapeake Bay Retriever; Grainger Studio.

sters and will snap at them. In brief, take every possible step to control your dog and alert people to the problem. This is not to advocate your keeping a vicious dog that is a menace to all who come near him. Such a dog will keep all people away from your home, and this not not what you want with a house pet.

While this is a book on the care and training of *your* dog, we do not think it amiss to set down some rules for meeting another dog. You may be out for a walk and encounter a strange dog. Or your neighbor may own a problem dog that bites. By knowing how to act and what to do when you meet a strange dog, you will be able to prevent what otherwise may be a very unpleasant or dangerous experience.

HOW TO MEET A STRANGE DOG

For the sake of simplicity, we'll divide dogs into friendly and unfriendly dogs. You can usually tell the friendly dog by the way he approaches you. He'll come up to you openly, his nose sniffing for your scent, his tail wagging and held high, and he may give out with a friendly bark. His whole approach is, you might say, aboveboard.

Most of us would say that any dog that bars our path with a growl or show of teeth is an unfriendly one. This may be an injustice to the dog, since he may merely be guarding his master or property. But until you know he is just being protective and is a friendly dog when "off duty," treat him as an unfriendly dog. And consider unfriendly dogs as unsafe.

Recognizing the unsafe dog

Proceed with caution if you meet a dog that fits any of the following qualifications:

Standing with body rigid, tail stiff and held at "half-mast."

Barking shrilly or hysterically.

Going into a slink or crouch, with his body and tail rigid, teeth bared.

Coming at you with head lowered, nose held close to the ground.

Standing with a staring expression, ears laid flat.
Attempting to circle and get behind you.

Safety rules for meeting a strange dog

When a strange dog approaches you, STOP.

Stand still and do not move your hands or body.

Speak softly. Always speak to any dog that has not seen you approach. Make sure the dog knows you are around.

Wait to see what the dog is going to do. Look for signs of an unsafe dog.

If the dog tries to circle and get behind you, *pivot slowly*, so that you are always facing him. Do not move your arms, legs (except to pivot) or make any threatening gesture.

Never turn your back on a dog that is moving toward you. *Do not panic and run.* Admittedly, it takes courage to stand still, but it is your best defense tactic. Wait until the dog stops moving before you move, and then move slowly. *Stop* when he moves again.

Never touch any strange dog. And never strike or kick at any dog.

Do not hand a person a package or shake hands when that person's dog is close by. The dog may misinterpret your move as an attack on his master.

Finally, never accept a dog owner's suggestion that you "make friends" with his dog by touching or feeding the animal. Remember, the dog should make the first overture of friendship, not you. And he will not do this until he smells you.

What to do if attacked by a dog

The safety rules will help you to avoid being bitten in most situations. Study and remember them. Pass them along to your family and neighbors. However, there may come a time when it is too late to apply the safety rules. This will be when you've reached the point of no return. For example, you might stumble over a dog asleep in the bushes, or a dog suddenly leaps at you before you can stop or back away. These are serious situations and the most you can do is to protect yourself from being severely bitten.

If a large dog attacks you

Quickly fold your arms and hold them across your face. Twist your body to the right or left (depending from which direction the dog leaps) as the dog jumps at you. The upper arm or shoulder should strike the dog and knock him off balance. Repeat this maneuver if he attacks again. Call for help. If the dog tries to get behind you, pivot with him. Stand still when he stops attacking and move only when he has retreated to a safe distance. You may get bitten, but your defensive tactics will reduce the severity of the attack and save your life.

If a small dog attacks

Lift one knee as the dog leaps. The knee will perform the same function as the arm and shoulder block on the big dog. Lift your knee *straight* up, not forward and up. If properly executed, the lifted knee will knock the small dog off balance. Repeat if he tries to attack again. Call for help. Pivot with the dog if he tries to circle and get behind you. Stand still when he stops attacking and move only when he's gone off.

Some common sense

In any meeting with a strange or hostile dog, remember that dogs instinctively chase motion. Stand still. Don't turn and run, although your knees are shaking and you want to get away fast. Your entire plan of defense against a possibly dangerous dog is to eliminate motion until the dog wanders off.

There are some situations in which no safety rules or defensive tactics will work. These are usually the result of ignorance of the nature of dogs and the dangers involved. For example, many people do not know that dogs are very protective about their food. Many dogs will snap or attack anyone trying to take away their food. Yet people still try to do this and are severely bitten. Children should be warned not to touch a strange dog's food or try to offer him any. Very often, a child will hold out a piece of candy and when the dog moves to take it, the child pulls back. This is extremely dangerous.

THE CAR CHASER

The car-chasing dog is a real problem. He's both a nuisance and a potential cause of an accident, since many drivers instinctively swerve away from the dog. This may be all right when the road is clear. When it isn't, the swerving driver may strike another car or a pedestrian.

One of the theories advanced as to why dogs chase cars is their instinctive reaction to motion. You will recall the dog is an animal of the chase, a running hunter, and chasing a car is an extension of the hunting instinct. But there are other factors contributing to car chasing. The pup may have been badly frightened by a car and his reaction is to get back at it (he can't tell one car from another, so he chases any car). He may also have had an experience where some people drove past in a car and threw something at him or made loud noises. Or perhaps a passing car contained another dog that barked out of the window. And finally, certain car motors and exhausts make a noise that strikes the dog's ears the wrong way.

The writer has observed an example of this reaction of a dog to motor and exhaust noises. While commuting to New York City, two cars were used alternately. The writer owned an American car with the motor up front. A neighbor had a foreign car with the motor in the rear.

Along the route to the city was a house with a male Springer Spaniel. The house had no yard or fence and the dog usually stayed on the porch. When we drove past in the American car, he paid no attention and went on with his scratching or napping. But when we drove by in the foreign car, the dog went berserk. He dashed down off the porch, raced after us and snapped at the rear tires, gradually giving up as we sped away.

Now, it might be argued at this point that the dog had some grudge against a foreign car, other than its noise. But we varied the experiment. We pushed the car fast enough to make it coast down the hill past the dog. While the motor was off, the dog took no notice of the car and went on with his nap. But when we started the motor, he came tearing down off the porch and took up the chase. We were satisfied that it was the noise of the motor or exhaust that irked the dog.

Despite careful training and restraint, dogs do develop the car-chasing habit. This is especially true if, when they are turned out of doors, they join a gang of canine delinquents. Once your dog has the car-chasing habit, you will have to take drastic steps to break it. Keep him in a yard or kennel, take him outside only on the leash, and reprimand him severely if he so much as takes a step toward a moving car. If he races along the inside of the fence as a car goes by, take him to task for this too.

Several techniques for breaking dogs of the car-chasing habit have been developed by trainers. None of them is guaranteed. Car chasing is a tough problem. There have been cases where dogs were struck and severely injured, only to resume their old habit upon recovery. While being struck by a car may cure some dogs, it only seems to aggravate the habit in others. They now have a stronger reason to chase a car.

Even though the car-chasing deterrents are not guaranteed, they are worth a trial. One of the techniques is a variation of the old saw, "Give him enough rope and he'll hang himself." We're not interested in hanging the dog, just in stopping him from chasing cars. Put him on a long rope, about twenty feet long, and take him out on the street or highway. When he bolts for a car, give him plenty of rope, brace yourself, and when he gets to the end of the line—dump him hard. Don't be afraid to upset him. The jolt you give him will be nothing compared to what he'll get if hit by a fast-moving car. After a few of these sessions, the dog will think twice about taking off after a car.

Another method is to fling a heavy chain at the dog's feet when he chases a car. This flung chain works similar to the South American gaucho's bola which he hurls at an animal to entangle it. Have someone drive past in a car and hold the chain ready. When the dog sails after the car, throw the chain at his feet. If your aim is good, the chain will tangle around his feet and either throw or stop him. A chain with links the size of snow chains will be satisfactory. Don't try to break the dog's legs; the entanglement plus the surprise will usually do the trick. If this seems like harsh treatment, consider what may happen to him and the occupants of a car that may strike him or crash trying to avoid him.

There are some other methods aimed at breaking the car-chasing habit. One is the water pistol treatment. This consists of having two people drive past the dog, one of them armed with a water pistol loaded with an ammonia-and-water solution. The "ammunition" should not be too strong, just powerful enough to make the dog's eyes water when hit. The trouble with this method is that you have to be a marksman. Some dogs are wily enough to dodge the spray. The other method is to hang a lead or steel pipe from the dog's harness or collar, so that it dangles across his front legs. When he runs, the pipe bangs against his legs, impeding his progress, or at least discouraging him. This trick has worked, but again, some smart dogs simply take the pipe in their teeth and go after the car. But, as we said before, try anything to break the car-chasing habit.

If you are bothered by dogs chasing your car, here's a tip that will help. When a dog charges out to chase your car, simply stop (but make sure that you signal your intention to stop to any cars behind). Since the dog is chasing motion, your stopping will eliminate the motive for the chase. Dogs rarely attack a standing car. You merely have to stop the car and wait a few minutes. No need for shouts, oaths or insults. Once you stop the car the dog will either stand barking at you or will walk away, confused or baffled. But if he happens to be a confirmed car-chasing addict, he'll probably resume the chase when you start up again. But keep repeating the process and even the most dedicated car chaser will give up. Also, when driving along and a dog suddenly races out to give chase, *don't swerve*. Keep a straight course. The dog knows enough to stay clear and will run along the side or to the rear of the car.

THE TRAMP DOG

Some dogs, particularly males, get the wanderlust and are gone from home for days. Others will go off for short periods, either to explore the neighborhood or try their luck with a female in heat. But the true tramp dog is the one that takes off and is gone for a long time, returning home only to eat and rest his sore feet. He finds no affection or security at home and he seeks it elsewhere. Or he just happens to be a "lone wolf."

If we were able to psychoanalyze the tramp dog, we would probably discover some deep-rooted cause for his wanderlust. And the cause would no doubt extend away back to the dog's puppy days. Some of the causes of wanderlust are lack of attachment to human beings during the important socialization period, rivalry between children and the dog, and rejection when the dog grows up. On the other hand, the tramp dog may be the kind of dog that can get along without human companionship. Let's call him a semi-tame dog, a throwback to the wolf.

The tramp dog that heads for the open road because he isn't getting enough attention at home can usually be rehabilitated. You'll have to make him feel that he belongs. Spend more time with him, take him out for long walks and play games with him. Let him see that you care about him and that he's not just something to keep fenced in or chained up all day. When possible, take the dog with you on car trips. And if you are working around the house or yard, let him tag along. In short, show him that he's wanted.

The "lone wolf" is something else again. He can take you or leave you, and it's doubtful if he can be rehabilitated. Penning him up will do no good; on the contrary, it will make matters worse. The dog will wait and when he gets the chance, he'll be gone. If you've got such a dog, you might as well resign yourself to his wanderings. Or get another dog.

THE "PIDDLER" OR WETTING DOG

Some dogs will frequently urinate from fear, excitement, and disease or injury to the kidneys and bladder. The very shy or timid dog often wets when scolded or spoken to in a harsh voice. Urinating is also an act of submission to authority. For example, a puppy will urinate when an older male dog exerts his authority. When an older male meets a young male puppy, certain preliminaries take place. The dogs sniff each other, determine the sex of each and then the older dog exerts his authority. There is a brief scuffle, usually ending with the pup upside down on his back. While in this position, he will urinate. He thus acknowledges the superiority of the older male.

In a sense, this behavior is carried on when you scold or speak harshly to a pup or timid dog. You are the symbol of authority and the dog submits by urinating. The timid dog takes it to extremes, of course, and never quite outgrows this juvenile trait.

If your dog is a piddler, he should first be examined for any disease or injury involving his kidneys or bladder. If he is free from disease or injury, then the problem is a behavioral one. Speak gently to the timid dog that piddles, and avoid sudden movements or threatening gestures. Pass the word along to the family and visitors. You may not be able to eliminate the tendency to urinate, but you will be able to reduce the frequency.

THE SEXUALLY FRUSTRATED DOG

The sexually frustrated dog is a common problem in the city and suburbs, especially in areas where the dog population is predominantly male. This sexual segregation leads to abnormal behavior, such as aggressiveness and homosexuality (or its canine equivalent). Also, dogs reared from puppyhood, with close attachment to human beings, will often respond to human attachment with sexual overtures. Housedogs are the group most affected by this behavior.

Most of the time it is the male dog that is sexually frustrated, although females are affected (but for shorter periods of time on account of their regulated heat periods). Males that are sexually frustrated will mount the leg of a child or adult and go through the sexual-act motions. Such behavior may be embarrassing and dangerous. An overly aggressive and sexually frustrated male can cause both physical and mental harm to a child. A sexual attack by an otherwise friendly dog may leave a child emotionally shocked and bewildered.

There are those who say that dogs don't have to be mated to be content. Nonsense! The world is full of sexually frustrated dogs and people. And it is the rare house-dog that hasn't at one time or other grabbed hold of someone's leg and simulated the sex act. The sexual urge is a powerful drive in man and beast.

Discourage your dog from mounting. This will not eliminate the sexual urge, of course, but it will save some embarrassment and avoid possible injury. A sexually frustrated Great Dane, for example, could inflict some harm just from his weight alone. Mate the dog if possible. Plenty of exercise will help to release some of the energy, and will at least reduce some of the agressiveness. Hormones and surgery help many cases, but are not 100% sure.

TRANQUILIZERS

What about using tranquilizers to help problem dogs? There's no doubt about it, tranquilizers are useful in easing fear and excitement in dogs. But they are not cure-alls and should not be used as substitutes for training. Nor should they be expected to atone for a faulty environment.

The tranquilizers are, you might say, a last resort. There is no sense in keeping a dog that has to be narcotized or tranquilized to make life bearable for him and his master. You'll be better off getting another and more stable dog.

However, there is no harm in an occasional use of tranquilizers. They will be helpful when you ship the dog in a crate, when he has to be quieted down because small children are coming to the house, or when riding in a car. Tranquilizers are also valuable for minor surgery and postoperative care. When you want to use tranquilizers, have your veterinarian prescribe the proper kind and dosage. Don't use human tranquilizers.

REHABILITATING PROBLEM DOGS

It should be apparent by now that prevention is your best defense against abnormal behavior in your dog. And that prevention includes early socialization, training and compatible environment. However, despite your efforts to prevent abnormal behavior, it may occur. In many instances, you will be able to rehabilitate your dog. In others, the problem may be too much for you and you will want to seek professional advice. A word about professional advice: so far, there are no objective tests that allow for a differential diagnosis of the dog's neuroses. Each case must be evaluated on an individual basis. It isn't possible to reach the dog by psychoanalysis. The best that can be done is to review the problem and try to work out a rehabilitation program that fits the case.

Professional dog trainers, handlers and some veterinarians are expert in handling and rehabilitating problem dogs. They can take a problem dog to their kennel and work wonders with him. They can work their magic because they take the dog out of the environment or away from the stimuli that cause his abnormal behavior. In other words, they provide the escape factor. But when the dog returns home to the same environment and stimuli, he may regress. Therefore, you will have a better chance of rehabilitating your dog if the work is done at home.

There have been cases where dogs have regressed when brought home from a kennel. For example, a childless couple with a small Scottish Terrier lived next door to a family with four children. The dog was confined to a yard and the house. Every day, as the children went past the yard on their way to school, one or more of them teased the Scotty by rubbing a stick along the fence. This infuriated the dog and he snarled, barked and raced along the fence. One day he got out and nipped one of the children. Later, he became suspicious of all people and the owners became worried that he would bite someone again. They tried various methods to discourage the dog and they scolded the children. The children still teased the dog and the dog still tried to get at the children. Finally, in desperation, the owners sent the dog off to be rehabilitated. At the trainer's kennel, the Scotty quieted down and became very docile. There were no children at the kennel and the dog had no problem. But when he came back to the yard and the children, he started all over again.

Eventually a do-it-yourself rehabilitation program was worked out and the problem resolved. This is what the owners did: they supplied the children with candy for themselves and with dog candy for the dog. Instead of rubbing a stick and watching the Scotty run amok, the children tossed him dog candy while they munched on theirs. It took several sessions before the Scotty calmed down and realized that the children were not going to get him stirred up. But he soon stopped his tantrums and learned to sit up for his candy.

We do not mean to disparage the work of the trainers and handlers. What we are saying is that *you*—and we said this before—are the expert on your dog. You should do the rehabilitating, under the supervision of an expert if you wish. By all means, seek professional help. The trainers and handlers know a great deal about dogs and can offer practical help. But they can't change the dog's environment; you can. In the final analysis, your degree of success in rehabilitating your dog depends on your removing the offending factors and offering him a means of escape.

10. Your Dog and the Law

Your dog doesn't recognize any man-made laws. As far as he is concerned, he is subject only to those natural laws dealing with food, mating and self-preservation. Therefore, you are responsible for his actions. As a dog owner, you are liable for any damage done by your dog to a person, property or the welfare of the community.

In general, most of the laws involving dogs are restrictive and very few favor the dog. Under the law, your dog is regarded as a piece of property or chattel. But he is a unique property. Like a house or car, the dog has monetary value; unlike them, he is alive and has emotional value. Yet the dog laws often ignore both the monetary value and emotional aspect of owning a dog. In some sections of the country, your dog can be seized or shot on sight without your permission or without your being compensated for the loss of the dog. And this happens in spite of the fact that the Constitution of the United States specifically states that no person can be deprived of property without his consent. It further provides that a person must receive due compensation for his property. Obviously, the law is a bit lopsided when it comes to dogs.

Most of the dog laws are vested in the states and are considered "police powers." Each state, in turn, can job out the dog laws to the various counties, towns, villages or hamlets. This is usually done by the state legislature passing laws permitting the counties or towns to control the licensing and keeping of dogs in their baliwicks. It is a delegation of authority by the state to the county or local government.

There are so many state, county and local laws governing dogs that it is impossible to give them here. We can only generalize and make you aware that dog laws exist and that you are liable for your dog's action. The old legal cliché, "Ignorance of the law is no excuse," still has teeth and can result in a big bite.

DOG LICENSES

There is hardly a community that doesn't require dogs to be licensed. Dog licenses serve several purposes. They are a means of identification, serve as a checkup or census of the local dog population, contribute toward the operation of shelters or "pounds," and provide funds for indemnities for livestock injured or killed by dogs.

In the big livestock-producing states, the indemnity fund is very important. Marauding dogs injure or kill a considerable number of livestock, especially sheep. But such a fund is rarely used in cities and suburbs that have license fees, but no livestock. These areas do have people bitten by dogs. There is, as yet, no provision in most dog license laws to pay medical expenses of people bitten by dogs.

The need for such a provision has been recognized by various county and township governments. Some municipal governments have already taken steps to provide payment for medical expenses for injuries resulting from dog bites. New York's Westchester County Board of Supervisors considered such protection, stating: "It's time that we recognize that a human being is worth as much as a cow or hog." More county and township governments should petition the state legislatures to permit the use of dog license fees to defray medical expenses of people bitten by dogs. With the increase in the number of dogs kept comes a corresponding increase in the number of dog bites. Some victims of dog bites have had extensive treatment; one girl was bitten so severely that her wounds required 300 stitches.

Dog licenses vary in cost according to the locality and the sex of the dog. In some areas, there is a flat fee for all dogs regardless of sex. In others, there is a fixed fee for males and spayed females, and a higher fee for unspayed females. When obtaining a license for a spayed female, you will have to produce a certificate from a veterinarian stating that the dog was spayed.

Inquire about your local license laws and get a license for your dog. This is advisable not only because it's the law, but as a protection for your dog. If he is lost and is wearing his license tag, your chances of getting him back are better. A license tag is very important in those states that allow dogs to be used for vivisection. Usually unclaimed and unlicensed dogs may be used for medical research. But a dog that is currenly licensed may not be sent to a laboratory.

The age at which dogs must be licensed is also variable. Some localities say all dogs, regardless of age, must be licensed. Others require all dogs over the age of six months to be licensed. Inquire at your local police station or town clerk as to the age requirements. Failure to get your dog licensed may result in the seizure of your dog or a fine or both.

LEASH LAWS

While many communities have laws requiring dogs to be on the leash when taken out, they are not strictly enforced. Very often this laxity in enforcing the leash law is due to the fact that there is no "pound" or place to keep any dogs picked up when off the leash. The authorities will, however, pick up and find some place to keep a dog that is off the leash, providing a complaint is filed. Thus, the local authorities shift the onus of impounding a taxpayer's errant dog onto his neighbor, even though their dog laws state that dogs must be kept on the leash. If your dog is running off the leash and annoying your neighbor, then the neighbor must go before a judge and file a complaint. Then he might get what the lawyers call an abatement—a cessation of the nuisance—and the dog will be picked up and impounded.

LIABILITY FOR DOG BITES

Bite cases are a frequent source of lawsuits. The common law (the unwritten law of a country that is binding because of long usage and acceptance) generally allows a dog to have one bite. After that, the owner can be held liable. Usually, the dog owner must be aware that his dog is a biter. If your dog bites someone and you are so informed, then you automatically become aware of the fact and can be held liable for any future bites.

If you keep a vicious watchdog, you should realize that he is a potential danger. Anyone injured by the dog— through no fault of his own—can probably get damages. On the other hand, you are not at fault if a person is bitten through his own negligence. For example, if you posted BEWARE OF THE DOG or VICIOUS DOG, WATCH OUT signs in conspicuous places and kept the dog confined, you would be exercising proper care. Anyone who trespasses or teases the dog and gets bitten, does so through his own negligence.

Dogs bite other dogs. Your dog may tangle with your neighbor's dog and inflict injuries. Your neighbor brings suit. What's the law here? Well, there are many factors to consider, such as leash laws, trespassing, negligence, etc. It often takes a modern Solomon to adjudicate these cases.

INJURING OR KILLING LIVESTOCK

The law allows severe penalties against dogs that injure and kill livestock. Large numbers of livestock and poultry are injured or killed each year by dogs. Sheep are particularly helpless against dogs and sheep raising is a poor risk in certain areas where there are many roaming dogs. Sheep-killing dogs are proscribed in most states.

Every state and community has some kind of livestock protection laws. Generally, these laws afford legal protection to farmers whose livestock or poultry are injured or killed by marauding dogs. As mentioned elsewhere, indemnities for injuries or destruction of livestock are usually paid out of the license fee funds. The maximum indemnity for injury or destruction of a cow, horse, sheep, goat, hog or poultry is fixed by law.

Most states permit the livestock farmer to take steps to protect his livestock against dogs. When a dog is not accompanied by his owner, the farmer has the right to chase or kill such a dog if the animal is in the act of molesting, injuring or killing livestock. In some states the farmer is permitted to set traps or use poisoned bait against livestock-killing dogs. But the farmer must use reasonable care when he resorts to these tactics, so that he doesn't injure or kill innocent animals. Owners of livestock-killing dogs are liable for damages, and the farmer has the right to instigate action.

RABID DOGS

Rabid dogs cause loss of livestock every year, as well as endanger human beings. Most states have very stringent laws aimed at the eradication of rabies. (For the cause and mode of transmission of rabies, see Chapter 12.) Illinois, for example, has a compulsory rabies vaccination law requiring all dogs to be inoculated against this disease.

Rabies control in most states is under the supervision of the Department of Agriculture. State rabies laws usually provide for the quarantine of all animals in an epidemic area. The laws may also require all dogs to be inoculated and muzzled.

The owner of a rabid dog may be held liable for any damage done or spread of the disease. However, if he is unaware that his dog has rabies, he may be held liable only for the *direct* damage or destruction. This would include any bite wounds and noninfectious injuries, but no condition resulting from the rabies virus. The expenses for any action taken by the state against an owner of a rabid dog is usually paid for by the owner.

SHIPPING YOUR DOG BY PUBLIC CARRIER

You may want to ship your dog by public carrier to another city, state or country. Trucking concerns, railroads, airlines and steamship lines will accept your dog for transportation, subject to certain rules. These carriers are considered to be semipublic agencies and are obliged to take your dog, *providing he is in good health and free from infectious disease*. You are required to produce a certificate stating the dog is in good health, free from infectious disease, and inoculated against rabies.

The carriers also have certain obligations. They must see to it that the dogs shipped on their conveyances are fed and watered. They must also take ordinary precautions against injury, suffocation, drowning, etc. But it is up to you to provide a strong crate or carrying box for the dog. The public carrier has the right to refuse to take a dog if he is not in an unbreakable and escape-proof crate or case. You cannot hold the carrier responsible if your dog gnaws his way out of the crate.

Rates for shipping animals interstate are customarily fixed by federal law. Transporting animals by public carriers within a state is regulated by a state agency. Since certain diseases are communicable from dogs to human beings and other animals, the various states and foreign countries control the movement of dogs into and out of their jurisdiction. If you plan to take your dog into another state or country, inquire in advance as to crating, inoculations, health certificates, etc. By doing this, you will save yourself disappointment. England, for example, has very strict rabies laws, especially against dogs coming from the United States. There is a six-month quarantine period in the British Isles. If you plan to visit the British Isles for two or three months, there would be no point in taking your dog, since he would be quarantined all the time you were there.

CRUELTY TO ANIMALS

All states have laws governing cruelty to animals. Some states have humane laws based on the principles set forth by Henry Bergh, founder of the American Society for the Prevention of Cruelty to Animals, a little more than one hundred years ago. Bergh stated that every animal should have adequate food, water, and shelter and be free from "malicious abuse." A number of states go beyond the so-called Bergh Law and specify what constitutes cruelty— *e.g.*, abandoning any animal, striking an animal with a car or truck and then leaving the scene of the accident, failure to provide veterinary attention, keeping a dog on a short leash or chain all day or night, transporting animals in the trunk compartments of cars, setting out poisons for stray dogs and other animals, cropping of ears and docking of tails, and other inhumane treatment of animals.

Many dog owners violate anticruelty laws simply because they are unfamiliar with the laws. Play safe and spare your dog some possible misery: Find out what your state anticruelty laws require in the way of treatment. Your local humane society will be glad to advise you on this important matter. You can also obtain information on humane laws from your justice of the peace, magistrate, or police department.

BREEDING FEES

Breeding fees and the rights of both owners are often the subject of arguments and litigation. If you own a purebred male or female and want to breed the animal, you should insist on a written agreement. It is customary for the owner of the male to set the stud or breeding fee. It may be a cash fee or the choice of a pup from the resulting litter. Whatever the method of payment, get it in writing.

The certificate of service or breeding should also state what constitutes a litter. Is it one puppy or five? If you are asking a puppy as payment for the stud fee, specify whether you want a male or female, and at what age you will claim the puppy.

If you or the other party is to pay cash for the stud fee, the certificate should state the manner of payment; for example, cash at time of mating or part down and the balance at whelping. You should also stipulate on the certificate that a return service or mating is not mandatory. After all, you cannot guarantee conception; you merely agree to mate your male with a female. When they copulate, your part of the bargain has been fulfilled. Be businesslike and have a written agreement, no matter how well you know the other party.

You can't expect a stud fee if your male roams the neighborhood and mates with your neighbor's female. Not even if he's just won the Best-in-Show at the Westminster Dog Show! Under the common law, the feeling is that the owner of a female is the loser by her pregnancy. Any puppies resulting from this pregnancy belong to the owner of the female. This holds true if your neighbor's female trespasses on your property and is bred by your male. You can't demand a stud fee or pup. You are supposed to control your dog.

LEASES AND DOGS

If all the squabbles between landlords and dog-owning tenants were brought into court, there would be a backlog of cases that would take years to hear. Most leases state whether you can keep a dog on the premises and you'll be wise to examine your lease before getting a dog.

In some cases, landlords have allowed dogs to be kept by tenants, then later changed their minds. If this occurs, the chances are that you could keep the dog. The fact that he permitted you to have the dog in the first place will be in your favor. But the landlord can prevent other tenants from getting dogs.

The writer was embroiled in many of these landlord-tenant disputes when he was manager of the Bide-A-Wee Home in New York City. On one occasion he was subpoenaed as a witness in a case where the landlord claimed a tenant brought in a dog after the landlord had issued his edict about no dogs being allowed in the apartment house. The tenant had adopted the dog from Bide-A-Wee. And the date on the adoption certificate proved that the tenant had brought the dog home *before* the landlord posted his notice.

Unfortunately, not all the landlord-tenant disputes are that clear-cut. At any rate, you would be wise to notify your landlord that you intend getting a dog, even though your lease has no anti-dog clause. Very often the landlord has the last word about dogs in the apartment house. If he can get enough neighbors to complain that your dog is a nuisance, you're out of luck.

OWNERSHIP

Occasionally, the ownership of a dog is contested. Since dogs are property, the rightful owner can reclaim his dog if lost or stolen. Such reclamation would be subject to stray or license laws, in addition to the costs of feeding and sheltering the animal. When you sell a dog and sign the bill of sale, you relinquish all rights in the dog. The purchaser becomes the owner.

One certain way to prove ownership of your dog is to

have the animal tattooed and registered in one of the dog identification services available on a nationwide basis. One of these services bases its identification of dogs on the Social Security number of the owner; the Social Security number is tattooed in one of the dog's ears and on the inside of a flank (rear leg). Some of the dog identification services operate through veterinarians and humane societies, sending mobile units into cities and suburbs.

A dog tattoo number is a permanent identification mark (especially the tattoo inside the flank); a license tag or personal identification tag on the collar can be lost or removed, accidentally or on purpose. Furthermore, research laboratories using dogs will rarely accept a dog with a tattoo number unless the animal is actually signed over by the owner. Thus, a registered tattoo number will not only establish your ownership to a dog, but may very well save his life.

WARRANTY OF QUALITY

You can't get any warranty of disposition when you buy a pup. But you can get protection against his being diseased. Since some diseases have a long incubation period, your pup may appear healthy at the time of purchase, then come down with a disease one or two weeks later. Regardless of the time lapse, if you can prove the disease was probably incubating at time of purchase, you can get a refund or another pup. You must, however, promptly report the discovery of disease to the seller.

If you buy the pup under an express warranty that states the seller will refund your money or replace the pup within a certain time limit, you have to abide by the time limit. If the pup gets sick after the specified time limit, you have no claim.

PUPPIES AND REGISTRATION

The seller (or breeder) of purebred puppies should register the litter with the American Kennel Club. He should furnish you, the buyer of a puppy, with an application for registration. This application should be signed by the breeder. If the puppy is already registered, you should have the seller deliver to you the individual registration certificate, properly signed over to you.

PUBLIC NUISANCE

Noisy dog may be a public nuisance

There's no doubt that a noisy dog may be a public nuisance. What's more, he may get you entangled with the law. For example, Pennsylvania courts have ruled that owners may be restrained from keeping noisy dogs. In most communities, however, it's a matter of a dog making an unreasonable amount of noise (more than the average, normal person can tolerate). Few persons would object to the dog that barks a warning when some danger threatens the house or family. But the dog that barks or howls all day and night—getting on the neighbors' nerves—is a public nuisance. And the neighbors probably can do something about him in court.

Federal and state game laws are very explicit when it comes to the dog that molests or kills game birds and mammals. Most states allow any person (who need not be a game protector or police officer) to kill any dog caught attacking or molesting protected birds and mammals. In addition to the killing of the attacking dog, the owner of the dog can be fined.

If your dog has a tendency to chase birds and other wildlife, keep him under control. Bear in mind that even though squirrels and raccoons may be declared pests in your state or county, these mammals are considered game in other states and as such are protected by law. Also, it is possible that the status of these mammals may change in your region. Scarcity may move them from the unprotected status to that of protected mammal.

Much of what we have outlined here is probably applicable to your community. But you should be interested in getting more specific information about your local dog laws. You can avoid a brush with the law by keeping your dog under control, getting him a license, and conducting any transactions involving breeding or buying in a businesslike manner.

Part Five

YOUR DOG'S HEALTH

11. The Dog's Body and How It Functions

A general knowledge of your dog's body and how it functions will prove helpful in his daily care. It will also be useful in giving the location of wounds or symptoms to the veterinarian over the telephone.

First, let us consider the nature of the dog. He is a hunter and scavenger. He comes from a long line of carnivorous animals, tracing back more than 40 million years to the Eocene epoch. His earliest ancestor was a civetlike animal named *Miacis*, a meat eater that lived in the prehistoric forests. The dog is related to the wolf, coyote, fox, jackal, dingo, raccoon, dhole and fennec. All of these, including the domestic dog, are geared for the hunt. They are all predators and scavengers and all show the same wolf- or doglike appearance.

Nature has endowed the dog with a body to help him perform his role of a hunter. His nervous and muscular systems are designed to make him tops in his trade of hunter. He has adequate nervous energy, speed and muscular control—all vital assets to the hunting animal.

In developing the dog, Nature practiced "natural" selection, producing an animal that is adaptable to a variety of climates and conditions. Among all the animals, the dog is the most cosmopolitan in this respect. There is hardly an area on earth that does not have some member of the dog family.

Man, however, has taken a hand in the development of the dog. He has practiced what is known as "selective breeding." For centuries, men have developed dogs for specialized purposes, for hunting, herding livestock, police work and as draft animals. But so far, nobody has been able to radically change the basic nature of the dog or his body. The dog is still a dog. And despite all the fancy coiffures—the custom-made sweaters and blankets—the dog remains a hunter and scavenger.

Even though the dog is a specialized animal, there is not a wide variation between his body and that of other mammals. Or man, for that matter. Your dog has all the vital organs found in other mammels: heart, lungs, liver, pancreas, spleen, stomach, intestines, kidneys, bladder, etc. He does have some variations in the functions of these organs. And he differs somewhat in his skeletal and muscular structure. But, in general, we can make many comparisons between the dog's body and organs and those of other animals and man.

HAIR AND SKIN

Hair

The dog's hair and its condition are very important to his well-being. It serves as an insulator against both heat and cold. If the dog's hair is in poor condition—thin, patchy or dry—it cannot perform its function as insulator. Therefore, it's imperative that you keep your dog's hair in top condition. A fancy trim, while it may be stylish, is of no value to the dog if his hair is sparse and unthrifty, exposing him to cold or heat.

Normally, the dog sheds his hair twice a year, in the spring and fall. During shedding, the old hair is replaced with new. Nature does this to keep the dog in a more or less standard coat, protecting him at all times. Excessive shedding of hair, caused by disease, parasites or faulty diet, defeats this purpose. The result is the dog is uncomfortable.

The dog's hair has another protective function besides serving as an insulator. When angry or aroused, the dog's hair "stands on end." This rising of the hair or feathers is a very common reaction in animals and birds. It's also found in certain reptiles. The puff adder snake, for instance, will puff up or elate when aroused. It's all done to scare or impress the enemy. Watch your dog the next time he's aroused or frightened. His reaction to being startled or sensing a strange person or animal is to growl and raise the hairs along his back. The reaction is controlled by many small muscles along the dog's back. Human beings sometimes experience a similar reaction when faced with the unknown or eerie.

Skin

There is a wide variation in the color of the skin among dogs. Some dogs have pink skin, some dark and others mottled. But the color of the dog's skin has no bearing on its function.

The dog's skin can be visualized as a binder or wrapper to cover the skeleton, muscles, nerves, viscera, etc. It has more or less the same glands as human skin. But the dog's skin glands do not function the same as those of human beings. Take, for example, the dog's sweat glands. At one time we were told the dog perspired only through the pads of his feet and his tongue. He does use these outlets for cooling, but his skin also helps out. His sweat glands help to some extent, but not as much as those of human beings. Instead of regulating the internal body temperature—as our sweat glands do—the dog's cooling system regulates only his skin or surface temperature.

When heat builds up in the human body, the sweat glands go to work and cool the body by evaporating the perspiration given off by the sweat glands. Not so with the dog; he cools off by radiation, without any evaporation. Thus, only the surface of the dog's skin is cooled. This is a big reason why the dog often has difficulty adjusting to overly hot days. It's also a reason why dogs become heat-exhaustion victims when locked up in automobiles with little or no ventilation on a hot day. In a hot car, there is simply no place for the dog's heat to go—and without any evaporation, he is in trouble.

Dog skin has great powers of regeneration. It can quickly repair damage to tissues. Minor cuts, tears or abrasions usually heal with little trouble. The dog has an additional healing aid in his saliva. The saliva contains a "built-in" germicide. If the dog has an opportunity to lick his cuts or wounds, he speeds up the healing process. But there is always the possibility of infection and it's best to apply an antiseptic, especially to deep or large wounds.

THE SKELETON

The dog is a quadruped. He can stand on his hind legs, but he does so with difficulty. His normal position is on all fours. His whole skeletal formation is constructed with that end in view. And while circus or other trick dogs seem to be very nimble and at home on their hind legs, the average dog prefers to stand on all fours.

There is not much difference between the dog's skeleton and that of other mammals. Nature has made some changes here and there, depending upon the animal's mode of life. But, except for these minor changes, most mammals, including man, have a common skeleton. When the prehistoric forerunner of man walked on all fours, his skeleton approximated that of the dog. And even though we walk upright today, that similarity of skeleton still exists.

What variations do exist between our skeleton and that of the dog are minor. The dog, for example, has more caudal or tail bones than we do. We have collarbones or clavicles; the dog does not. His shoulder blades are fastened directly to his skeleton. We also have opposable thumbs. These are lacking in the dog and most mammals.

While we don't need to know every bone in the dog's skeleton, we should be familiar with the main bones or sections of the skeleton. The "body" part of the dog's skeleton consists of the skull, ribs and spinal column (atlas, axis, cervical vertebrae, thoracic vertebrae, lumbar vertebrae and the caudal vertebrae). The skull is attached to the spinal cord at the atlas. The front or fore legs consist of the shoulder blade or scapula, humerus, radius, carpus (knee) and the metacarpus or pastern. The hind quarters consist of the pelvis, femur, tibia, fibula, tarsus (hock) and the metatarsus.

The dog's skeleton is a strong framework and under normal conditions offers good protection to the vital organs. Unfortunately, domestic dogs don't live under normal conditions. Too many dog skeletons are cracked by automobiles. Automobile injuries account for the majority of dog bone fractures or breaks. The bones most frequently broken are the ribs, bones of the fore and hind legs, and the pelvis. Fractures of the pelvis are far more common than you would suppose. A large number of dogs hit by cars manage to get the front part of their bodies clear of the car, but are struck in the hindquarters or pelvis. (See Chapter 17, under CAR AND TRUCK ACCIDENTS)

Canine hip dysplasia

Some dogs, notably the large breeds, may be born with abnormalities of the skeleton, particularly the hip joints.

Canine hip dysplasia—or badly formed hip joints—is a common abnormality found in large dogs, such as the German Shepherd, Great Dane, and even the Foxhound. The condition rarely occurs in small dogs that weigh twenty-five pounds or less at maturity; it is also less common in the small breeds with short legs (Dachshund, Basset, and Beagle).

The cause of canine hip dysplasia is complex, with both heredity and environment playing important roles. Dr. Wayne H. Riser of the Orthopedic Foundation for Animals, Philadelphia, Pennsylvania, considers hip dysplasia to be of man-made origin, at least in dogs. He points out that the condition is rare in wild mammals. Man's responsibility for the condition stems from the intense breeding practices followed in developing large dogs. The original wild dog of prehistoric times has been estimated to weigh less than forty pounds at maturity. In developing large dogs quickly, undue stress and strain have been placed on the bones and muscles.

Hip dysplasia is not to be confused with arthritis or other bone conditions. It is an entity in itself. The condition is progressive and results in varying degrees of lameness, which vary with individual dogs. Some dogs show no outward signs of the condition, while others may be severely crippled. Nevertheless, every dog affected by hip dysplasia, according to Dr. Riser, has restricted hip joint movement because of excessive scarring of the joint capsules.

Although hip dysplasia can seriously interfere with the abilities of a working dog (police work, hunting or livestock herding, for example), it does not rule out the keeping of a lame dog as a house pet, provided the owner understands the dog's limitations and does nothing to aggravate the condition. The pet dog can tolerate a mild degree of hip dysplasia, just so long as he is not required to perform violent exercise or tricks that will intensify the condition or cause the dog pain. Since there is no cure for hip dysplasia, it may be humane to euthanize the dog severely crippled by the ailment.

A positive diagnosis of canine hip dysplasia can be made only upon a radiographic examination of the pelvis. Also, the condition usually cannot be diagnosed until the dog is about one year old.

Dog breeders, especially the German Shepherd breeders, are trying to reduce the incidence of hip dysplasia in their dogs. Hip dysplasia is a hereditary condition of polygenic origin—that is, it appears in a dog's offspring with no specific pattern of inheritance. The defect is influenced by a combination of genes and is determined by the genetics of the sire and dam, as well as the environment. Using this knowledge, breeders are working to control and eliminate canine hip dysplasia by breeding only from dogs with normal hips.

THE MUSCULAR SYSTEM

In keeping with his role as a hunter, the dog has a well-muscled body. His muscles are tough and well coordinated. In some dogs, certain muscles are highly developed. Draft dogs, such as the Husky and Newfoundland, have powerful chest and back muscles. But all dogs have good muscles that help them run, jump and spring.

As with human muscles, those of the dog can be strained, stretched and otherwise injured. This is a point to keep in mind when you try to get your dog to jump too high or drag something that may be too heavy. He can get a charley horse just as easily as you can.

THE NERVOUS SYSTEM

Like all mammalian nervous systems, that of the dog is complex. Basically, the dog's nervous system is composed of the peripheral and central nervous systems. The peripheral system consists in part of sensory fibers and motor neurons. These are gathered together in bundles and are called *nerves*. The central system has segregated neurons and lies within the skull and spinal cavities. The central nervous system is divided into two main parts: the brain and the spinal cord. The brain has an important role in complex behavior, since it governs learning, motivation, perception, etc. The function of the spinal cord is twofold: it acts as a conductor to and from the brain and it effects reflex actions.

All of the above are true for other mammals, including man. It is in the area of reflex action that the dog's nervous system differs from man. The dog has a highly developed reflex-action mechanism. His reflexes are very important to his daily life. They play a major part in his everyday behavior. For example, reflexes are responsible for the dog's blinking when something strikes his eye, for scratching when he has an itch, for making his hair stand up on end when he sights or smells something strange, and for making his ears twitch when he hears various sounds. These and many other reflexes are well developed in the dog.

The dog's reflexes have been the subject of study for many years. Much of the information obtained from studying the dog's reflexes can be applied to man. Perhaps one of the most publicized experiments involving the reflexes of the dog was that done by the Russian scientist Ivan P. Pavlov (1849-1936). Pavlov introduced the concept of the conditioned reflex. The conditioned reflex involves a simple response to a particular action or stimulus.

In a very simplified version, Pavlov's experiment went something like this: He set a pan of food in front of a dog. At the sight of the food, the dog's saliva began to flow. This act of salivating at the sight of food, Pavlov called an *unconditioned response or reflex*. He next varied the experiment by ringing a bell before setting down the pan of food. After a time, the dog salivated when he heard the bell ring and without seeing the food. Pavlov called the ringing of the bell a *conditioned stimulus* and the dog's flow of saliva at hearing the bell, a *conditioned response or reflex*.

The dog's nervous system can be damaged by disease. Distemper and rabies are diseases that involve the central nervous system. The majority of dogs that recover from distemper are usually left with an impairment of the central nervous system. In the case of rabies, there are no survivors.

THE DIGESTIVE SYSTEM

None of the dog's digestion takes place in the mouth, as it does in human beings. It starts in his stomach. But the main process of digestion occurs in the dog's small intestine.

The dog's digestive apparatus consists of the mouth (merely a passageway for food), esophagus, stomach, pylorus, small intestine, large intestine and the rectum. The liver and pancreas are also involved in the digestive process.

Very often, the dog's manner of eating surprises and startles a new dog owner. The dog is not what you would call a dainty eater. He bolts or wolfs his food, swallowing whole chunks or masses. This bolting down of food is a hangover from the wild state, the days when the dog's ancestors had to eat their food fast or else have it taken away. It was purely a question of the wild dog getting his food "while the getting was good."

As a prevention against acute indigestion, Nature has supplied the dog's stomach with strong juices. He also has a good reverse action and can regurgitate food that may be too large. The stomach juices are capable of dissolving large chunks of food and bones. By the time the food reaches the small intestine, the juices have broken it down to a state where it can be easily processed and assimilated.

At one time it was believed that the dog's digestive system could not handle starches. Dog owners were cautioned not to feed dogs starchy food in any form. Today, we know that this is not true, that dogs can tolerate starch in their diet. Dogs having a disease or malfunctioning of the pancreas, however, have difficulty in utilizing starch and must be put on a special diet. It was also a common belief that fat should not be fed to dogs. This, too, has been disproved. The no-starch, no-fat dictum forced dogs into being strictly protein eaters. As a result, many dogs were suffering from malnutrition.

THE URINARY SYSTEM

The dog's urinary system is similar to that of other mammals. Its purpose is to process and get rid of liquid wastes. The main parts of the urinary tract are the kidneys (used to excrete urea, uric acid and other wastes), the bladder (a receptacle for fluid), and the urethra (the canal that carries the urine from the bladder).

Urinary-tract ailments are more common in older dogs, although puppies may have urinary-tract infections. These infections may exist as part of a major disease, such as leptospirosis, or as a primary condition. (For the symptoms of urinary tract ailments, see Chapter 13.)

THE REPRODUCTIVE SYSTEM

The male dog reaches sexual maturity at between 6 to 8 months. He can then mate at any time of the year and for a large part of his life. Some males seem to be more sexually active in the late winter and early spring. This could be a throwback to his wild ancestors and the modern wolves and coyotes that breed in late winter and early spring.

The reproductive organs of the male include the penis, testicles and the prostate gland. Males, to be efficient breeders, must be in good health and not overly fat. Adequate exercise is very important in keeping the male sexually potent.

Females can mate and produce offspring twice a year. Successive matings are not usually recommended. Also, a female entering her heat period or estrus cycle for the first time should not be bred. Rather, she should be permitted to reach maximum growth. When bred in the second heat period and thereafter, the bitch will produce healthier and more vigorous puppies.

The reproductive organs of the female include the vagina, ovaries and uterus. The bitch has a reproductive cycle that is divided into four phases: 1) a nine-day period in which the external genitals are enlarged, swollen and emitting a bloody discharge; 2) another nine-day period during which ovulation occurs and the bitch has a strong desire to mate (she can be mated during this stage); 3) the anestrum period lasting 2 months; and 4) the metestrum period lasting 3 months. The anestrum and metestrum periods are post-heat periods during which the female cannot be mated. The average female reaches sexual maturity or the first heat period at 6 to 8 months of age.

Some individuals and breeds vary from this rule, not coming into heat for as long as 12 months.

Domestic dogs will mate with wolves and coyotes and produce hybrids. They will also breed with jackals. The reproductive similarity between the dog, wolf and jackal has received considerable study. The duration of pregnancy in the dog and wolf is the same—60 to 63 days, and the wolf-dog puppies are fertile. Coyotes are small wolves and the same breeding similarities exist between them and dogs.

A more detailed coverage of the dog's reproductive cycles, whelping and rearing the puppies will be found in Chapters 19 and 20.

12. The Four Major Dog Diseases

Dogs, like human beings, are susceptible to various bacterial, viral and protozoan diseases. There are four major dog diseases that are capable of reaching epidemic proportions and resulting in a high mortality rate. They are distemper, rabies, leptospirosis and canine infectious hepatitis. These diseases are the "Big Four"—the scourges of dogdom. Of the four, distemper is the most widespread.

As a dog owner, you should be familiar with these diseases. By knowing the causes, modes of transmission and symptoms, you will be better equipped to help prevent your dog from becoming a victim. There are those who believe the average dog owner doesn't need to know anything about dog diseases, that at the first sign of something wrong, the dog should be rushed to the veterinarian. This is faulty thinking. It assumes that every dog owner can afford to take his dog to the veterinarian at every itch or burp and that the veterinarians can handle the traffic such a policy would entail. After all, there are about 20,-000 veterinarians in the United States and more than 25 million dogs, not to mention millions of cats, birds and other pets. Furthermore, a large percentage of these veterinarians are engaged in treating livestock.

In setting down the background of the dog diseases and giving their symptoms, we are not trying to qualify you as a diagnostician or dog doctor. Diagnosing and treating major diseases are in the domain of the veterinarian. But you should have a "working" knowledge of the dog diseases. It's up to you to bring your dog's health problems to the attention of the veterinarian. He's not going to telephone and inquire about your dog's health. He's too busy. You will have to know when to take your dog to him. And to do this you will have to know how to recognize the difference between serious and minor conditions. A knowledge of dog diseases will help you make that distinction.

Finally, there's the matter of your being an informed dog owner. Today, Americans have a much better knowledge of their general health, diseases and treatments. They have acquired this knowledge by reading books and magazines, watching television and listening to the radio. You, as a dog owner, should become informed about your dog's health and what can be done for him if he should contract a serious disease. If your dog should become a victim of a major disease, you will have a large part in nursing him back to health. A working knowledge of the diseases will help you to understand the treatment and the dog's chances of recovery. It will also enable you to assist the veterinarian.

DISTEMPER

Despite the tremendous amount of research being done on distemper, it still continues to be a major dog killer. It is an acute, highly infectious disease caused by a virus. Young dogs, especially puppies, are the most frequent and numerous victims. Nursing puppies, however, are rarely affected, since a certain degree of immunity is passed to them from their mother by way of colostrum-milk. But to get this natural immunity, the pups must partake of the colostrum-milk during the first 8 to 24 hours of life.

While distemper is basically a puppy and young dog disease, older dogs can become victims. This is particularly true of those older dogs that have led sheltered lives, with little or no opportunity to become exposed to the virus and build up an immunity. The writer has seen dogs 7 and 8 years old with distemper.

The distemper virus is known as the virus of Carré. It is an airborne virus; that is, it is transmitted chiefly through the air. But it can also be transmitted by direct contact with the saliva, urine, feces or nasal discharge from an infected dog. Human beings are often unwitting carriers of the distemper virus, bringing it home on their hands, shoes and clothing.

The incidence of distemper has seasonal peaks, with the disease reaching its most virulent form in the early spring, fall and winter. Warm weather has an adverse effect on the distemper virus, forcing it to become dormant. The prevalence of distemper is at its lowest point during summer. The incubation period for distemper ranges from 3 to 21 days or longer. It is a very serious disease and one that requires prompt attention.

Basically, distemper is a disease of the epithelial tissues. All of the visible mucous membranes—mouth, gums, nostrils, etc.—become inflamed as the virus intrenches itself. The distemper virus is the vanguard for secondary bacterial invaders. After the virus has set the stage, bacteria move in and cause such symptoms as tonsillitis, diarrhea, pneumonia and skin eruptions. The chief bacterial invaders are members of the staphylococci, streptococci and brucella groups. It is this combination of bacteria and virus that makes distemper so difficult to treat.

One of the earliest symptoms of distemper is what we might call general cold symptoms: running nose, weeping eyes, sneezing, a dry, hacking cough, poor appetite and diarrhea. The dog's temperature will fluctuate between 103° and 104° F. All of these symptoms become worse as the disease progresses.

The failure to start treatment when these early symptoms appear contributes toward a high mortality rate for this dreaded dog disease. Too many dog owners dismiss the early symptoms as "just a cold" and are later stunned when told the dog has distemper. Granted, recovery from distemper is the exception rather than the rule, but some dogs have recovered when promptly treated.

As the virus and bacteria continue their devastation, the dog becomes more and more emaciated and dehydrated. The discharge from the eyes and nose changes from a colorless fluid to a thick, ropey and often bloody discharge. When the discharge dries on the nose or eyes, it cakes and interferes with breathing and vision. The dog has an increased thirst and will try to drink great quantities of water. His bowel movement changes from a soft stool to a watery or bloody movement, with a highly objectionable odor. He may vomit and go into fits or convulsions, with muscular twitching or champing of the jaws. Eventually, the dog succumbs from an overwhelming infection.

The distemper story is not a pleasant one. It's rather grim and dismal. Your dog's chances, once he's contracted the disease, are very slim. There is no specific cure; the best that can be done is to treat the various symptoms.

Those dogs that do recover are usually left with nervous disorders, such as tics or chorea.

Immunization

Fortunately, your dog can be immunized against distemper. The veterinary profession has made great strides in the immunization of dogs against distemper, as well as hepatitis, rabies and leptospirosis. But it must be made clear now that there is no such thing as a permanent inoculation. A few years ago, veterinarians gave a series of injections against distemper and called the final shot "permanent." We know today that no inoculation can be considered permanent. Some types of inoculations are just more lasting or durable than others.

Before we discuss an immunization program for your dog, let's see how the distemper immunization theory is supposed to work. First of all, as stated before, newborn puppies receive varying degrees of immunity in the form of antibodies in the colostrum-milk. Tests taken on puppies 48 hours after birth at the Cornell Virus Research Institute reveal that the pups have the same level of immunity as their mother. Likewise, if the mother is not immune, the pups will not be immune. It was also found that immunity was passed from the mother to the pups during the first 8 hours of life. No immunity was passed after the pups were one day old. The point to remember here is that every pup should get colostrum-milk during the first 8 hours of his life. The immunity passed through the colostrum-milk can last from 1 to 3 weeks up to as long as 3 or 4 months.

On the other hand, while the immunity passed through the colostrum-milk is vital to the protection of the nursing pup, it presents some problems after the pup is weaned. Drs. James A. Baker and James Gillespie of the Cornell Virus Research Institute found that natural immunity passed by the mother later interfered with the vaccination of the weaned pups. Those puppies with natural immunity simply could not be vaccinated. In other words, the natural antibodies prevented an immune response in vaccinated pups.

This was an important discovery. Prior to it, veterinarians customarily gave puppies injections of distemper serum spaced 10 to 14 days apart until the pup was 9 to 12 weeks of age. After this, the puppy was given an injection of distemper vaccine, the so-called "permanent shot." Yet, despite this prophylaxis, many pups came down with distemper. The veterinarians gave reasons for these distemper "breaks." The pups probably were exposed to the disease before being vaccinated, they were in a poor state of nutrition and had intestinal parasites. In many cases, this was true. But in others, no. Hindsight, of course, shows us that many of these distemper "breaks" could be ascribed to the presence of natural antibodies that interfered with the vaccination.

Drs. Baker and Gillespie further learned that puppies with natural immunity passed along to them from the mother could not be artificially infected with distemper. In short, they just could not get distemper until their natural immunity wore off and they were ready to catch the disease.

Working from this basis, Dr. Gillespie developed a test whereby the degree or level of immunity passed from the mother to the pup could be determined. By blood-testing the mother during pregnancy and using a chart called the Nomograph, it is now possible to tell how much immunity a pup will inherit. It is also possible to predict when the pup will lose that natural immunity. The blood test can be used for dogs of any age and will show the state of their immunity. It is easy to see the great value of such a test. There is no longer any need for guesswork or hit-or-miss immunizations.

The blood test and Nomograph indicate when a puppy should be vaccinated against distemper or when an older dog should be given a booster shot. Effective distemper immunization depends on the kind of vaccine used, the health of the dog, and the overall immunization program. The use of a standardized vaccine would be ideal; however, not all vaccines are standardized, and several types are in use. Cornell University veterinarians are now conducting research with the view toward producing or perfecting a standard distemper vaccine.

Variations in vaccines and immunization techniques led to a symposium on canine distemper immunizations, jointly sponsored by the American Kennel Club and

American Veterinary Medical Association. This symposium was held a few years ago. The combined AKC and AVMA panel proposed the following guidelines for effective distemper immunization: 1) the use of an attenuated live-virus vaccine of chick embryo or tissue culture origin (an attenuated live-virus vaccine is one that has had the virulency or potency of the virus modified or reduced; chick embryo origin means that the virus was propagated in a fertile egg; tissue culture origin means that the modified live virus was grown on tissue cells [e.g., ferret, pig, etc.]); 2) when feasible, use of a Nomograph to determine the age at which puppies should be vaccinated; 3) a blood test for vaccinated dogs within thirty days after the initial vaccination and then revaccination if the blood test so indicates; and 4) in the absence of a blood test and Nomograph reading, a booster shot for distemper each year for all dogs.

The symposium panel also recommended that puppies of unknown immunity status (that is, when there is no veterinarian's vaccination certificate or other record of immunity) should be given a dose of live-virus vaccine if the pups are older than three months. If the puppies are younger than three months, they should be given two or more doses, the first dose to be given at the time the pup is weaned and the last dose administered when the pup is twelve to sixteen weeks of age. The panel proposed that an ideal distemper immunization program would consist of a dose of vaccine at two-week intervals until the puppy was twelve to sixteen weeks of age, with an annual booster shot thereafter. Orphan puppies that do not receive any colostrum-milk (because their mother died before colostrum-milk—with protective antibodies—could be passed on to them) can be vaccinated as early as two weeks of age with attenuated live-virus distemper vaccine.

Now let's translate all this research data into a practical distemper immunization program for your dog. We'll start when you get your puppy. Unless the seller or person who gives you a dog can produce certification that the dog has immunity against distemper as shown by a blood test, start from scratch. It will cost you some money for vaccinations, but the alternative is gambling with your dog's life.

Forget about "temporary shots," "puppy shots," or "permanent shots." Without supporting data, such as the kind of vaccine and dosage, they are unreliable; without a blood test and Nomograph, they are worthless.

Take the puppy (or older dog, as the case may be) to a veterinarian and let him set up an immunization program for your dog. Most veterinarians are using attenuated live-virus distemper vaccine of either chick embryo or tissue culture origin. If you really want to be sure your dog has immunity to distemper, have a blood test taken thirty days after the last vaccination. Then be certain to get the dog a booster shot each year.

All this may sound like overcaution. But the old adage "It's better to be safe than sorry" still holds up. Many dogs die needlessly from distemper because owners fail to have the animals vaccinated or do not allow the veterinarian to complete the immunization program. Since protection against distemper is available, it seems foolish or negligent for the dog owner not to make use of it.

Many dog owners have asked how soon can a new puppy or dog be brought into a home or kennel in which another dog has died from distemper. Estimates of just how long the distemper virus survives in air or on objects varies considerably. Certainly all objects (dishes, water pan, toys, etc.) with which a dog ill with distemper has come into contact ought to be removed and destroyed. No new puppy or dog should be brought into the area of possible exposure without immediate vaccination with an attenuated live-virus vaccine of chick embryo or tissue culture origin, unless the dog has been vaccinated with such a vaccine within the past ten or twelve months.

RABIES

First, it should be pointed out that rabies is a relatively rare dog disease. Very few veterinarians or dog breeders have ever seen a case of rabies. Yet no other disease of man or animal has been surrounded with as much superstition, fear or fiction as rabies. It is one of the oldest diseases, dating back to several centuries before Christ. Rabies is basically a disease of canines; i.e., the domestic dog, coyote, wolf, dingo, and pariah dog. But it is transmissible to other animals, including man, squirrel, fox, skunk, rabbit, mink, horse, cow; even the bat. Some birds are susceptible to the disease. However, the chief victims are members of the dog family. And since the dog lives close to man, the disease assumes a position of great importance.

Rabies is caused by a virus that affects the central nervous system. The virus is found in the saliva of infected animals. The method of transmisson is through the bite of a rabid animal. When a person or animal is bitten by a rabid animal, the saliva containing the rabies virus is passed into the bite wounds. The incubation period for rabies ranges from two weeks to several months, with the average time at thirty to sixty days. The important fact to remember is that a person or animal must be bitten by a rabid animal before there is any danger of contracting the disease.

Not every person bitten by a rabid animal necessarily contracts rabies. According to the United States Bureau of Animal Industry, Pathological Division, approximately 15 percent of all human beings and 35 percent of all animals bitten by rabid animals contract rabies. Several factors determine whether a bite victim will become infected. Since the rabies virus attacks the central nervous system, it follows that the closer the bite to that system, the greater the danger. Bites on the hands, face or neck are the most dangerous from this standpoint. The depth of the bite is also an important factor; the deeper the bite, the greater the chances of contracting rabies when bitten by a rabid animal. Finally, the amount of bleeding from the bite wounds must also be considered. If the bite wounds bleed profusely, the rabies virus may be washed out. But this chance should not be taken and all wounds should receive prompt medical attention.

Generally, the symptoms of rabies are complex and only a close observation of a suspected animal can determine if the animal is rabid. The only positive test is a microscopic examination of the dog's brain. When the rabies virus attacks the brain it causes the formation of what are known as "Negri" bodies. These are visible under a microscope and are positive signs of rabies.

One of the first rabies symptoms to appear is a very

noticeable change in the dog's behavior. A friendly dog may become irritable, snappy, or ferocious. Or the opposite may occur: a snappy, surly dog may become docile and dull. However, most rabid dogs are very restless and easily excited. The only positive case of rabies observed by the writer was a dog that would fly into fierce rages when a stick was thrust at him through the cage door. The dog had been confined as a suspected case of rabies after having bitten three people and another dog. He became increasingly worse and died four days after being confined. A microscopic examination of his brain revealed the Negri bodies that are associated with rabies. This is the only case of proven rabies seen by the writer in more than twenty years of experience with dogs. The rarity of the disease, however, does not lessen its danger.

There are two forms of rabies: 1) a highly excitable, raging type, in which the dog runs amok, snapping and biting any person or animal in its path, and 2) a dumb type, in which the dog appears to be stunned or in a state of shock. In the dumb form of rabies the dog shows no inclination to roam or bite. A classical symptom of the dumb form of rabies is what may be called "fallen jaw." The dog's mouth hangs open several inches. Now, any dog that has something stuck in his mouth or throat will usually open his mouth. But if an obstruction is the main trouble, the dog will paw and scratch at his mouth. In the case of "fallen jaw" associated with rabies, the dog makes no attempt to dislodge anything or paw at his mouth. He just sits staring, with his mouth hanging open.

Other symptoms of rabies are convulsions, foaming at the mouth, a change in the voice pitch and paralysis of the throat muscles. The rabid animal becomes very thirsty, but because of the throat paralysis, cannot drink water or other liquids. This inability to drink has given rise to the erroneous name of hydrophobia—a fear of water. It is not a fear of water, it is an inability to drink water.

There is no known cure for rabies, either in human beings or animals. If you suspect rabies, *do not touch the dog*. While there is no need to get panicked just because your dog has a fit or foams at the mouth, it is wise to proceed with caution. Call your veterinarian, police, board of health or local humane society.

If you are bitten by a strange dog, here is the procedure to follow: Get the name and adress of the dog's owner or a description of the dog. Next, thoroughly wash the wounds with soap and warm water, making sure that you work the soap down into the bites. Tincture of green soap is best. Work up a good lather and keep it in the wounds for at least 20 or 30 minutes. This is no guarantee that you won't contract rabies if the dog was rabid, but it may help. Have the wounds treated by a doctor. Under the law, he must report treating dog bites. When a dog bite is reported to the authorities, the usual procedure is to confine and isolate the offending dog. The dog is observed for a period ranging from 10 to 14 days. Rabies works quickly on the dog; if he is still alive and his general behavior and symptoms improve after the observation period, he didn't have rabies. If the dog dies during confinement period, his head is sent to a diagnostic laboratory where the brain is examined for Negri bodies.

It's to your advantage to have the offending dog confined, otherwise you will be subjected to a series of antirabies injections. If you were bitten by a stray dog, try to give as complete a description as possible. Circulate the description around—to the newspaper, radio station and any other public communication source. Ask friends and neighbors to be on the lookout for the stray dog.

If your dog bites someone, see that the victim receives prompt medical treatment. Next, report the bite to the police or board of health and surrender your dog for observation. Don't argue about it. Someone's life may be at stake. Give complete information as to rabies vaccination.

Immunization

Your dog can be immunized against rabies. Usually the rabies vaccination is given when the dog is six months old, since the disease affects mostly older dogs. Currently, two types of rabies vaccinations are given: one type of vaccine confers immunity for one year, the other type confers immunity for three years. Consult your veterinarian as to a rabies vaccination for your dog. If your dog receives the vaccine good for one year, see to it that he gets a yearly shot.

INFECTIOUS CANINE HEPATITIS

Not too long ago, infectious canine hepatitis was confused with distemper or at least considered to be part of what many veterinarians called the "distemper complex." Today, hepatitis is considered to be a separate disease.

Canine hepatitis is another virus disease. The virus is spread by direct contact with the nasal discharge, saliva or urine of an infected animal. Affecting the liver and usually running a short course of a few days, hepatitis can be fatal if treatment is delayed. The canine hepatitis virus is not the same one that infects human beings.

Hepatitis has distemper-like symptoms, especially in the early stages of the disease. Listlessness, inflamed tonsils, increased thirst, discharge from the nose, diarrhea and vomiting are all symptoms of hepatitis and distemper. Unlike distemper, the dog usually has a high temperature, above 104° F. There is also abdominal tenderness, blood in the vomit or stool, and inflammation of the inner surface of the eyelids and front part of the eyeballs. An opacity or bluing of the eyes may also be present, although this is usually present after the acute stage of the disease has subsided.

The hepatitis virus gains entry into the dog's gastrointestinal tract when the dog comes into contact with or ingests infected matter or comes into contact with urine or saliva from an infected dog. It has been shown that the hepatitis virus remains in the urine for as long as six or more months after a dog has recovered from the disease. If your dog has hepatitis symptoms, see that he gets prompt veterinary attention.

Immunization

Your dog can be immunized against canine hepatitis. Most veterinarians give a combination injection of distemper and hepatitis vaccine. The blood test developed by Dr. Gillespie can be used to determine the level of immunity against hepatitis. Consult your veterinarian for hepatitis vaccination.

LEPTOSPIROSIS

The last of the "Big Four" is leptospirosis, a bacterial disease of dogs, human beings and other animals. It occurs in two forms: 1) canicola fever, and 2) Weil's disease. Both types are transmissible from animals to man. The organisms causing leptospirosis belong to the spirochete group of bacteria.

Leptospirosis affects the kidneys and liver. It is marked by a yellowish discoloration of the dog's skin and mucous membranes (gums, palate, nostrils, etc.). Distemper-like symptoms appear in the early stages. These are weakness, no appetite, vomiting, increased thirst, nasal discharge and general emaciation. The temperature rises to 103° to 105° the first day, then *drops* sharply to as low as 97° F. the next day. There is also muscular stiffness, especially the hind legs; a heavy, dark urine, abdominal pain; a watery and bloody bowel movement; and jaundice. Leptospirosis requires immediate veterinary attention.

Rats are known carriers of the organism causing leptospirosis and the flea, louse, tick and fly are suspected as being carriers. The mosquito is also suspect. Your prevention program should include the elimination of fleas, lice and ticks from the dog. Insect and rodent control should be practiced, both for human and animal protection. Since rats often get into dog food and other supplies, discard any stale or loose dog food. Avoid damaged packages of dog food in the food stores.

Immunization

Leptospirosis vaccine is available. It is important to keep in mind that while the leptospirosis vaccine affords long-lasting protection, it will not last for the dog's lifetime. You will be wise to have the dog revaccinated from time to time, especially if there is an outbreak of leptospirosis in the neighborhood.

13. Other Diseases and Ailments

While the Big Four diseases are the most important and dangerous, there are other diseases and ailments that require prompt attention. Some of the diseases and ailments in this chapter are chronic and affect older dogs; others may be acute or chronic and affect all dogs. In some cases you can help clear up the condition, while in others both you and the veterinarian will work as a team to cure the dog.

KENNEL OR HOUSE COUGH

Kennel or house cough (tracheobronchitis) is a common ailment of dogs of all ages. The cause is unknown, although keeping a dog in a hot, dry and stuffy kennel or house is thought to pave the way for the condition. Highly infectious, the disease usually runs a course of 2 to 4 weeks.

The most noticeable symptom of kennel or house cough is the cough itself. It's a deep, gagging cough that hangs on for weeks. When the cough first appears, you may think the dog has something stuck in his throat. He'll keep gagging and retching, as if he's trying to bring up something. Very often all he brings up is some foamy matter.

The pharynx, larynx and trachea become inflamed and contribute toward the cough and gagging reflex. Later, bronchitis sets in. There may be a slight rise in the dog's temperature, otherwise he will show no other marked symptoms. Exercise or excitement will aggravate the cough.

House cough by itself is not serious, but if left untreated, complications, such as pneumonia, may result. Any cough that lasts for more than two days should receive veterinary attention. Antibiotics have proved helpful in clearing up kennel or house cough.

While there is no immunization against kennel or house cough, you can take some preventive measures. Since the condition reaches its highest peak during the

175

late fall, winter and early spring, you will have to regulate the heat and humidity in the dog's sleeping quarters. If possible, turn off the radiator in the room where the dog sleeps. Or put a pot of water on the radiator to help humidify the air.

PNEUMONIA

Bronchopneumonia is the type most often encountered in dogs. It may exist as a symptom of distemper or other disease or be present as the primary disease. Pneumonia can also be caused by bacteria, viruses, and mechanical factors, such as liquids or other foreign matter in the lungs.

The symptoms of pneumonia include a grating, rasping cough; heavy nasal discharge that may be bloody or greenish-yellow; poor or no appetite; listlessness; and a temperature range of 103° to 105°F. or higher.

Pneumonia requires prompt veterinary attention. Fortunately, with the antibiotics, pneumonia is not as dangerous as it used to be. There is always the danger of complications and the quicker you get the dog to the veterinarian, the better his chances of recovery. At the first signs of what you consider to be pneumonia, keep the dog warm with a blanket or heavy sweater. As with all diseases, make every effort to keep up the dog's strength. Give him easily digested food, such as bouillon, warm milk, egg custard or Pablum. Keep him out of drafts and dampness. (For more detailed instructions on home nursing of the sick dog, see Chapter 18.)

BABESIASIS

Babesiasis or canine piroplasmosis is a disease of the blood. It is caused by a protozoan, *Babesia canis*, which is carried by the brown dog tick. The disease is relatively rare, but is always a potential hazard in areas that are heavily infested with the brown dog tick.

The symptoms of babesiasis include listlessness, weakness, little or no appetite, pale gums and eyelids, staggering and a temperature above the normal range (101° to 102°F.). The positive diagnosis of babesiasis requires a microscopic examination of a blood sample.

There is no immunization for the disease. Preventive measures should include the elimination of all ticks from the dog and area. Control ticks in the area by spraying or cutting down weeds and brush. Also, eradicate the intermediate hosts of ticks, such as field mice and other small rodents. (See Chapter 15)

DIABETES

Diabetes, a chronic disorder affecting carbohydrate metabolism and involving the pancreas, is usually seen in dogs over five years old. The symptoms include increased thirst, heavy urination, weakness, emaciation and eventually coma.

Diabetes requires veterinary attention. The usual treatment is an adjustment of the diet and insulin injections.

FITS

Ordinary fits or convulsions

Ordinary fits or convulsions have a rapid onset and usually last for a short time. They may be caused by disease, parasites, teething, faulty diet, overexcitement and poisoning. Fits may recur.

The symptoms are a general uneasiness, champing of the jaws, foaming at the mouth (also a symptom of rabies), stiffened muscles, collapse, kicking of the feet and eventual unconsciousness.

There isn't much you can do for the dog when he has a fit, except to see that he doesn't injure himself. A dog in a fit will thrash around, possibly striking sharp objects. If there is such a danger, you can throw a coat or blanket over him and drag him out of danger. When he recovers from the fit, feed him sparingly. A mild laxative such as milk of magnesia may be helpful. If the fit recurs, consult your veterinarian.

Running fits or canine hysteria

Running fits or canine hysteria are nervous attacks characterized by running, yelping and general confusion on the part of the dog. The cause is unknown, although a faulty diet is suspected of playing a major role. Other symptoms are restlessness, excitement, staring expression, fear and aimless running back and forth.

It should be mentioned at this point that running fits are very often mistaken for rabies. The mistake is easily made if you will compare the symptoms of the two conditions. In both rabies and running fits the dog is easily excited, foams at the mouth, has a staring expression, shows fear and runs amok. However, rabies and running fits differ in their progress. Running fits eventually pass away and all symptoms disappear. In rabies, all symptoms become increasingly worse, ending with the death of the dog.

Since you have no way of knowing with certainty whether your dog is suffering from rabies or running fits, treat all fits in which the dog runs as suspected rabies. Try to confine the dog without being injured or handling him. Call your veterinarian. Admittedly, confining the dog without handling him may be difficult. But do what you can without endangering yourself, even if it's just penning the dog in the yard.

While the cause of running fits is unknown, the addition of fresh meat and cooked eggs to the diet may help prevent a recurrence. Also, include a vitamin and mineral supplement, such as Pervinal, in the dog's daily diet. Regularity in bowel movements is also considered important for the dog that is subject to running fits.

URINARY TRACT AILMENTS

Ordinarily, we associate urinary tract ailments with older dogs. But disease or injury to the kidneys or bladder may also occur in young dogs or puppies.

Inflammation of the kidneys may be caused by infection, injury, stones or improper diet. The symptoms include pain in the kidney region, excessive thirst, difficult urination, vomiting and little or no appetite. Kidney ailments require veterinarian attention. Very often a dog with a kidney ailment will have to be put on a prolonged special diet.

Infection or the formation of stones may cause inflammation of the bladder. A dog suffering from infected bladder or stones will have difficulty in urinating. He may have blood in the urine, pain in the bladder region and little or no appetite. He will also have an increased thirst. A complete blockage of the urinary tract may occur. Immediate veterinary attention is recommended for all urinary tract ailments. Neglect can lead to complete stoppage and death of the dog.

PYOMETRA

Pyometra is a disease of the female dog. It is caused by ovarian dysfunction and increased hormone (progesterone) secretion, with the accumulation of pus in the uterus. Pyometra usually affects maiden or unbred females over five years old.

The symptoms are loss of appetite, increased thirst, vomiting after drinking water or milk, increased urination, distended abdomen and possibly pain in the abdominal region. There is a rise in the temperature in the early stages of the disease; a drop as the disease progresses. A female with pyometra gives off a "sweetish" odor. Pyometra requires veterinary attention.

METRITIS

Metritis is another "female" disease. It is an acute or chronic inflammation of the uterus. Metritis may result from injury or infection during whelping. Or it may occur shortly after the pups are delivered. The disease or condition may also be present as part of another disease.

The symptoms for metritis are vaginal discharge (may be bloody), increased thirst, vomiting, abdominal pain and little or no appetite. Metritis should receive veterinary attention.

PROSTATITIS

So far as it is known, only three animals suffer from prostatitis: the dog, the lion and man. Prostatitis is an acute or chronic inflammation of the prostate gland. It is common in old male dogs.

The symptoms include frequent and painful urination, difficult bowel movements (resulting from an enlarged prostate pressing on the rectum), restlessness, reluctance to sit down, and a rise in the temperature. Some cases of prostatitis are helped by chemotherapy, others require surgery. Consult your veterinarian for the best treatment for your dog.

ANAL GLANDS

Many of us have seen a dog drag his rear end over the floor or ground, his two hind legs pointing up or straight ahead. The common reaction to this scene is to say the dogs has worms. Yes, he could have worms. But he might also have swollen and infected anal glands.

The anal glands are small glands situated inside and just below the anus. There are two glands, one on either side of the anus. Normally, the anal glands secrete a yellowish fluid. Just what the purpose of the anal glands is has never been fully ascertained. It might be that the anal glands once functioned like the scent glands of the skunk. At any rate, these glands become swollen, infected or abscessed. When they do, the dog is in misery. This is the time when he sits on his anal glands, trying to ease the pressure. When your dog starts to drag his rear end, it's time to have him checked for worms or swollen anal glands.

Most of the time, the dog's anal glands simply become overloaded with fluid. And all that is required is to empty the glands. This is a relatively simple chore. But it's an odoriferous one. You can do it yourself or have the veterinarian perform the job. If you want to do it, here's the procedure to follow: First, place the dog on a table or bench and have someone restrain him. Next, see if you can feel the swollen anal glands on the outside of the dog's rectum. Look to the side and just below the anus. You may be able to detect small lumps or nodules. If you can feel the anal glands, you can exert pressure to empty them. But first place a handful of cotton or several layers of gauze over the dog's anus. This will help prevent the anal gland fluid from spraying all over you. Exert pressure on the glands in an upward direction so that the fluid will be forced out of the glands, up into the anus, and then out onto the cotton or gauze. Keep the cotton or gauze up tight against the anus.

If this external pressure fails to empty the glands, you will have to squeeze the glands from inside the anus. Put on a rubber glove and apply Vaseline to the finger being inserted. When your finger is inserted, feel to the right and left, and downward from the anus. After you locate the anal glands, hold some cotton or gauze against the anus. Now you can exert gentle pressure on each anal gland.

After you've emptied the anal glands, keep an eye on the dog for a week or so. If the glands fill up again or the dog shows signs of being in pain, consult your veterinarian. Quite possibly, the anal glands may be infected or abscessed.

ASCITES

Ascites is another condition usually seen in older dogs. It is caused by fluid collecting in the abdominal cavity. Ascites may be the result of kidney, liver or heart disease. The visible symptoms of ascites are a swollen, pendulous abdomen and a shortness of breath. Ascites requires veterinary attention.

EAR TROUBLES

Ear troubles are common in dogs, especially the long-eared varieties, such as the Dachshund, Setter, and Cocker. Minor cuts, insect bites, ear cankers and hematomas are common ear ailments. Prompt attention to ear conditions, no matter how trivial they seem, will prevent serious trouble that may lead to deafness.

Ear canker or otorrhea

Ear canker may be visible on the outer parts of the ear or just down inside. Both inner and outer ear cankers are caused by infections or parasites.

The symptoms of ear canker are ulcerations, constant shaking of the head, pawing at the ears and presence of scabs or crusts. Some dogs are very irritable when they are suffering from ear cankers and will resent having their ears touched.

You can help relieve the dog's discomfort by washing the canker with mild soap and warm water. Use absorbent cotton and wash away the scabs and crusts. After you've cleaned the canker, apply some mineral or sesame oil on a cotton swab and gently coat the affected part. A dusting with an antiseptic powder, such as BFI powder, will help. If the canker persists, consult your veterinarian.

Hematoma

A hematoma is a swelling containing blood. It usually occurs between the skin and the ear cartilage and often follows an injury to the ear. The condition is common in long- or floppy-eared dogs.

The symptoms are a soft swelling inside or outside the ear, pain or sensitivity when the spot is touched, and heat in the affected part. A hematoma requires surgical drainage, so take the dog to the veterinarian.

EYE AILMENTS

Your dog's eyes are very vulnerable to disease, parasites and injury. Weeping and inflamed eyes are common symptoms in many dog diseases, including the Big Four—distemper, rabies, hepatitis, and leptospirosis. But your dog's eyes may weep, become inflamed or ulcerated from causes other than disease. Country doges often get small seeds, bits of grass and other foreign objects in their eyes. They also get whipped across the eyes by brush or weeds. The city dog is often exposed to smoke, fumes, coal dust and chemical irritants that affect his eyes. All of these factors can contribute to acute or chronic eye ailments.

Conjunctivitis

Conjunctivitis is an inflammation of the mucous membrane that lines the inner surface of the eyelids and the front part of the eyeballs. It is marked by redness, weeping and sensitivity to light (photophobia).

If the condition is caused by a foreign object in the eye, remove it by using the twisted corner of a clean handkerchief. Next, wash the eye with warm water. Use an eyedropper and place a few drops of water in the corner of the eye. When the dog blinks, the water will wash over the eyeball. An eye ointment, such as butyne sulfate or mercuric oxide, will help ease the dog's pain. Again, place a small amount of the eye ointment in the corner of the dog's eye and let him blink it over the eyeball. If the inflammation persists for more than a day or two, consult your veterinarian.

Keratitis

There are two forms of keratitis: 1) a simple inflammation of the cornea, and 2) an ulceration of the cornea. The cornea is the transparent part of the eyeball coat which protects the iris and pupil. In simple inflammation of the cornea, the affected part is red and the eye waters. A photophobia may be present. In the ulcerative type of keratitis, small craters or depressions may be visible on the cornea. There may also be a bluish-white clouding of the eye. You will recall that this is also a symptom of hepatitis. (See Chapter 12)

You can give the dog some relief by applying eye ointment. Keep him out of direct sunlight or brightly lit rooms. The ulcerative form of keratitis should receive veterinary attention. Simple inflammation of the cornea can be treated by applying eye ointment. However, if the inflammation persists, take the dog to the veterinarian.

HERNIAS

Hernias are not unusual in dogs. They are protrusions of parts of internal organs (usually intestines) through a rip or break in the abdominal wall. There is also a hernia of the diaphragm in which the upper visceral organs are pushed upward through a tear in the diaphragm. Diaphragmatic hernias are often the result of a dog's being struck in the middle of the body by a car. Umbilical hernias, in which the intestines push through the navel, are often seen in puppies.

The symptoms of a hernia are soft, springy swellings that vary in size from time to time. These swellings may disappear when pressed with the fingers or when the dog sits or lies down. They usually reappear when the dog shifts his position or rises. Hernias require veterinary surgery.

ABSCESSES

Abscesses are swellings on the skin caused by a collection of fluid, such as blood, serum, vaccine, etc. They may occur as the result of an animal or insect bite, sting or faulty vaccination. The symptoms include swellings on the skin, pain or sensitivity when touched, and loss of appetite. The dog may also run a fever. Dogs with abscesses may be very irritable and snappy. Ice packs sometimes help, but surgical drainage is often necessary to completely clear up an abscess.

CYSTS

Cysts are swellings caused by capsulized fluids in the tissues. They may be external, appearing under the skin, or internal, forming on organs such as the ovaries or uterus. The symptoms of external cysts are swellings with a more or less movable core. They require surgical attention.

TUMORS

Tumors are caused by the excessive growth of tissue. They may be malignant or nonmalignant (benign), and may appear on any part of the body, internally as well as externally. Most tumors have a tendency to increase in size and are seen mostly on older dogs. Prompt veterinary attention is necessary.

DIARRHEA

Diarrhea is not a disease, but a symptom of a disease or infestation of parasites. It may also be caused by a malfunction of the intestinal tract, triggered by faulty diet or the swallowing of foreign matter. While functional diarrhea is more common in young puppies, older dogs are also affected. A soft bowel movement is not diarrhea; a watery or bloody, loose movement is diarrhea.

To clear up ordinary diarrhea, you will first have to determine the cause. Check the dog's diet. It's possible that his food is too laxative. Dog foods containing liver are apt to be on the laxative side. Eliminate them. Add cooked starchy foods to the diet. Boiled rice, macaroni or barley will help solidify bowel movements in ordinary functional diarrhea. If you feed the dog milk, boil it. The commercial diarrhea medicines, such as Peptobismol, will bring ordinary diarrhea under control. For a 7- to 10-week-old puppy, 1 teaspoonful every 4 hours will bring quick results. In the case of bloody diarrhea or when the condition persists for more than a day or two, take a specimen of the dog's bowel movement to the veterinarian. The dog may have worms or intestinal parasites. (See Chapter 14)

CONSTIPATION

Constipation is common in older dogs. It may be caused by disease, improper feeding, lack of exercise and mechanical obstruction. If you look back over the symptoms of prostatitis, you will see that constipation is one of them. However, faulty diet and lack of exercise account for the large portion of constipation in older dogs. Swallowing foreign objects, such as sponge balls, soft rubber toys and the like, often results in constipation and vomiting among puppies. The swallowed objects lodge in the intestines and obstruct passage of waste matter.

Your treatment of constipation will depend on the cause. If you suspect the pup swallowed a toy or ball, give him some milk of magnesia. If this fails to produce results, give him an enema. (See Chapter 17) If the enema does not dislodge the obstruction—and it may be too high to reach—you will have to take the dog to the veterinarian. The older dog with a chronic case of constipation will need a diet change. Add more bulk, such as leafy vegetables, to the diet. Also give him more exercise. If the old dog has prostatitis, this condition will have to be cleared up before you can expect any improvement in the constipation.

COPROPHAGY

Coprophagy, or the eating of feces, is not a disease per se. Nobody is sure just what causes a dog to eat his or other feces. One theory advanced is that the dog suffers from a mineral deficiency. Another is that the dog is infested with parasites. Some animal behaviorists think dogs eat their own feces out of boredom. Their idea is that dogs confined to a cage or kennel have little diversion, so they start playing with and eating their feces.

We'd like to put forth our theory on coprophagy. It's quite possible that the eating of feces is a leftover instinct, a carryover from the time when the dog's ancestors were hunters and scavengers. Life for the early canids was one of feast or famine. When the hunting was good the wild dogs ate heartily; when the game was scarce, they were forced to scavenge and eat whatever they could find, even if it was the feces of other animals. That way, the wild dogs managed to survive.

With all due respect to the animal behaviorists' theory of coprophagy, we think the true reason lies elsewhere. When the writer was managing a large dairy farm in Connecticut some years ago, he had ten dogs that had the run of the 235-acre farm. These dogs were fed a high-quality dog meal, supplemented with milk from the farm. They were free from worms 90 percent of the time and received a vitamin and mineral supplement. The dogs were not penned up all day and night, but were allowed the freedom of the farm, since there were many rodents and other vermin in the area. Yet these dogs never failed to eat each other's feces or that of the cows and horses. Our main point in telling this tale is that these dogs were certainly not bored. They had freedom, helped round up the cattle, and chased game and vermin.

It's doubtful if you can cure the dog that eats feces. You can try giving him vitamin and mineral supplements. And by all means you should get rid of worms and other intestinal parasites. The best measure is to remove temptation: don't leave feces lying around.

FLATULENCE

Some breeds of dogs, such as the Bulldog, Boxer and Boston Terrier, seem to have more gas than others. But this is not to say that other dogs can't be bothered with excessive gas. Flatulence may be caused by improper diet.

If your dog is an offender, try eliminating eggs from the diet. Beans, peas and cheese often produce gas and should not be fed to the dog with this problem. Charcoal tablets added to the daily ration sometimes help to reduce gas. Some veterinarians recommend the daily addition of meat tenderizer to dog food as a means of reducing flatulence.

VOMITING

Most dogs have a good reverse digestive action and will vomit very easily. Vomiting may be caused by disease, overloaded stomach, obstruction, worms, overexcitement, poisoning, and poor liver or kidney function.

If your dog vomits, skip his regular meal. Give him warm beef bouillon. Restrict his water intake and let him lick an ice cube instead. Since vomiting may be a sign of serious disease or poisoning, you should consult your veterinarian.

BAD BREATH

Bad breath can be caused by a faulty diet, intestinal disorders, and infections of the teeth and mouth. Certain foods will, of course, produce strong breath odors. A diet high in meat or fish would be an example of this.

A sour breath usually means that the dog has a digestive disturbance. The smell of urine in the breath is an indication that the dog has some trouble with his urinary system.

Your handling of strong breath odors will depend on the cause. If the dog has a smell of decayed meat or fishy odor, eliminate or at least reduce these items from his diet. Check over his teeth and mouth for sores, ulcers, cavities, etc., and have them treated. In the cases of sour and uremic breaths, you should take the dog to the veterinarian. These could lead to more serious trouble than bad breath.

BLOAT

Many animals are subject to bloat and the dog is no exception. Bloat may be defined as excessive gas in the stomach. It is usually more common in the very large dogs. Great Danes seem to be the most frequent victims of bloat.

Bloat appears very quickly and usually in the warm season. Right after eating a large amount of dry dog food, followed by plenty of water, aided and abetted by vigorous exercise, the first symptoms of bloat appear. They are excesive energy, excitement, swelling of the stomach, shallow breathing and ultimately shock.

Bloat can be fatal. Immediate veterinary attention is necessary. If you have a large breed of dog, avoid feeding him large quantities of dry dog food. The dry-feeding or cafeteria system is not for him.

14. Internal Parasites

All animals harbor internal parasites. Some of these parasites, such as the intestinal flora, are beneficial. Others, such as the protozoa and worms, can cause severe damage and even death, if left unchecked. Dogs come in for a share of these internal parasites. Of the two major types of internal parasites infesting dogs—worms and protozoa —worms are by far the most common and troublesome.

Every dog owner should know something about the life cycles of the various worms and protozoa and how these parasites enter the dog's body. While there are treatments and drugs to expel these parasites, your dog can become reinfested at any time. Only by breaking up or destroying the life cycles of these parasites can reinfestation be prevented. Prevention, then, is your best weapon against internal parasites.

WORMS

Worms can be very damaging to your dog's health. They are particularly dangerous to young puppies. Worms sap the dog's strength, make him irritable, and open the door for more serious conditions by lowering his resistance.

Ascarids

The most important ascarid infesting dogs is the large ascarid (erroneously called roundworm), *Toxocara canis*. This worm measures from 1 to 7 inches and is found in the small intestine and very frequently in the stomach. It is widely distributed throughout the United States and in some sections of the country presents a serious threat to the health of dogs.

Ascarids are passed from infected dogs into the feces as unsegmented eggs. Other dogs pick up the eggs by coming into contact with the feces containing the eggs. The eggs enter the dog's body by way of the muoth. When the eggs reach the dog's small intestine, they penetrate

189

the intestinal wall and move into the bloodstream. Next, they are carried to the lungs, where they go into the air passages and migrate up to the trachea and into the esophagus. From the esophagus, they are swallowed and move down again to the intestines where they mature into worms. This migration from small intestine and back again takes 10 days. The entire life cycle, from egg to mature worm, is completed in 75 to 90 days.

Young dogs and puppies are the most frequent victims of ascarids. Many ascarids in young puppies are the result of prenatal infestation of the mother. Intrauterine infestation by T. canis is common. Even though older dogs can become infested with ascarids, such infestations are usually light and rarely cause any serious damage. But the situation is very different in puppies; ascarid infestations can be devastating and lethal.

In most cases where pups have become infected with ascarids in the uterus, the larvae localize in the liver of the newborn pup. Some of the ascarid larvae may move to the lungs. Within 24 hours after the puppies are born, the immature ascarids begin to move along their way to the intestines where they will mature. Eggs of ascarids may appear in the feces of puppies 21 to 24 days after birth.

As the pup grows older, his susceptibility to ascarids lessens. Females are more immune to ascarids than males. They arrive at this immunity at a much earlier age, too. Females reach immunity at six months and males at 36 months. However, this immunity is not absolute and older males and females can have infestations.

The most noticeable symptoms of ascarid infestation in puppies are a distended abdomen, poor hair, diarrhea and a "sweetish" breath odor. Vomiting often occurs and mature ascarids are seen in the vomit. Since the ascarid larvae migrate to the lungs, pneumonia is always a danger and frequently accounts for the sudden death of infected pups. Once the ascarids mature in the pup's intestines, they can cause various complications ranging from persistent diarrhea to complete blockage of the intestinal tract.

Although the larvae of T. canis do not ordinarily mature in the human intestinal tract, children are sometimes infested with these ascarids. Immature *T. canis* larvae have been found to cause a disease of children known as *visceral larval migrans*. Somehow or other, children manage to ingest the *T. canis* ova and become infected. The ascarid larvae are also suspected of causing other diseases and allergic reactions in human beings. Research is now being conducted to determine the extent of human infestations by canine ascarids.

Since ascarids are passed to puppies while still in the uterus, most dog breeders worm the pups shortly after birth. But the age at which puppies are wormed for ascarids is very important. If it's too early, very few ascarids will be expelled. Remember that infectious larvae can still be migrating from the lungs. These would not be affected by worm medicine. At 4 weeks of age, most of the inherited ascarids will be in the intestinal tract and can be expelled. The job may take more than one worming, though, and you should be prepared to do follow-up wormings.

If your dog is infested with ascarids, the veterinarian may prescribe a series of wormings at 2-week intervals. This series may continue until your pup is 3 months old, after which the worming may be reduced to a once-a-month basis until the pup is mature. If you have a female, treatment for ascarids can be stopped when she reaches 7 to 8 months of age. If a male, he will have to be wormed at intervals until he is 2 or 3 years old. Such prolonged treatment is not intended to "pad the bill." It is the most practical course to follow for the *total* elimination of ascarids until the dog has the natural immunity of age.

Fortunately, the process of removing ascarids is a simple one. There are a number of worm compounds or vermicides that are safe and effective. The main problem in treating for ascarids is not which compound to use, but when to use it for the best results. Remember that your pup can become reinfected with ascarids at any time. Sanitation then becomes an extremely important measure in eradicating infectious ova. You should concentrate on destroying the life cycle. Treating the soil with chemicals is of little value, since *T. canis* ova are resistant to chemicals ordinarily used for this purpose. But the ova are highly susceptible to drying or direct sunlight. So, if your dog lives in a doghouse and kennel, expose the house to sunlight and fresh air.

As we outlined in the chapter on the new puppy, the best procedure to follow if you suspect worms is to take a specimen of his bowel movement to the veterinarian. The veterinarian will take it from there. But if you decide to worm the pup yourself, do so with care. There are a number of vermicides ón the market that will expel *T. canis*. Follow the directions explicitly. Vermicides are given on the basis of the dog's weight. Don't guess at his weight, weigh him. Use a bathroom scale and first weigh yourself. Next, hold the dog and step on the scale. Subtract your weight from the new reading and the result will be the weight of the dog. If you have a large dog, such as a Great Dane, you will have to find a platform scale. Coalyards, lumberyards and other concerns dealing with heavy materials usually have platform scales. Perhaps the owner or manager will let you weigh the dog.

Hookworms

Hookworms derive their names from the toothlike structures in the cheeks or mouth cavities. With these hooklike structures, the hookworms fasten onto the dog's intestinal walls where they feed on blood.

Several species of hookworm infest dogs, but the most common is *Ancylostoma caninum*, found throughout the southern United States. A "northern" hookworm, *Uncinaria stenocephela*, while infesting dogs, is not as significant as *A. caninum*. On the small side, *A. caninum* measures ⅛ to ¾ of an inch in length when straightened out. Hundreds of these hookworms may be found in a single dog. And all of them will be firmly hooked onto the intestinal walls.

The female hookworm is capable of producing thousands of eggs each day. Hookworm eggs are passed in the feces, but usually they will not start to develop until certain optimum conditions exist. These optimum conditions include plenty of oxygen, moisture and warmth. The eggs thrive in sandy soil and a damp, shady spot. Exposure to direct sunlight, wind or freezing temperatures will kill the eggs.

When the hookworm eggs get the optimum conditions,

they develop into infectious larvae within 5 days. After being ingested by the dog, the larvae mature into hookworms in the alimentary tract. Dogs can be infected through the skin and this is a very common mode of entry for hookworms. Prenatal infection is also common with hookworms.

Upon entering the dog's bloodstream, the larvae move to the lungs where they soon find their way to the trachea. From the trachea, the larvae are coughed up and swallowed, thus gaining entrance to the intestinal tract. The larvae mature in the small intestine and very often in the cecum. The migratory phase, from bloodstream to trachea to the small intestine or cecum, takes approximately 3 days. The complete life cycle, from egg to mature hookworm, requires 21 days.

As with ascarids, young dogs and puppies are the most frequent victims. Many puppies born with hookworm larvae have very little chance of survival. The early symptoms of hookworm infestation include anemia (pale gums, eyelids, etc.), listlessness, bloody bowel movements, and loss of weight. In the later stages of hookworm infestation, many distemperlike symptoms appear: nasal and eye discharge, coughing, temperature above 103°F., and others.

The treatment or elimination of hookworms can be long and drawn out. Furthermore, the outlook is often discouraging. Many pups with hookworm infestation suffer from malnutrition and are in a very weakened state. An overdose of worm medicine can be fatal. The problem becomes one of having to build up the puppy and eliminate the hookworms. In many cases, the pup has to be built up before worming can be attempted. There are specific worm medicines for hookworms, but many of them are toxic in the wrong dosages. Your safest procedure would be to have the veterinarian handle the hookworm problem. If the pup is run-down, the veterinarian can prescribe a special diet to bring the dog back to health, as well as the correct type and dosage of vermicide.

You will have to practice rigid sanitation to prevent any reinfestation of hookworms. Keep the kennel run and doghouse clean. Sodium borate will help to kill hookworm eggs and larvae. It is toxic to dogs and cannot be left where the dog can eat it. Work it into the soil; do not scatter it on the surface. Feed the dog a diet high in protein; this will help give him resistance to strength-sapping hookworms.

Whipworms

Whipworms are small whip-shaped worms that infest the colon and cecum. The whiplike part of the worm's body—the long esophageal section—makes up three-quarters of the overall body length, which is roughly 3 inches. Whipworms are widely distributed throughout the United States. Only one species is known to infest dogs, *Trichuria vulpis*. Whipworms are often difficult to eradicate, since they bind or sew themselves into the lining of the colon or cecum.

The eggs of the whipworm as passed in the feces of an infected dog and begin to divide within 24 hours. This division or fission is the first stage in the development of the larvae. No further change takes place until the eggs are ingested by the dog. Once inside the dog, the whipworm larvae work their way to the colon or cecum where they mature.

The complete life cycle of the whipworm takes from 90 to 100 days. Since the life cycle is a long one, puppies under 3 months of age do not have mature whipworms. While whipworms are often found in the colon, they prefer the cecum. Inflammation of the colon and cecum, accompanied by pain and tenderness in those regions, loss of weight, and diarrhea are symptoms of whipworm infestation.

Heavy infestations of whipworms are usually found in dogs that are over two years old. Whipworms, of course, lower the dog's resistance to other disease. Dual infestations—hookworms and whipworms—are not uncommon and have been found in old, but otherwise well-cared-for dogs.

Not too long ago, surgery was the only way to get whipworms out of the dog's colon and cecum. But now several whipworm compounds have been developed that are effective in eradicating whipworms. One of these compounds, Whipcide, manufactured by the Pittman Moore

Company, Indianapolis, Indiana, has shown great promise in the elimination of whipworms. Inasmuch as whipworms are difficult to eradicate, the job is best left to the veterinarian. You can help break up the whipworm life cycle by practicing rigid sanitation in the dog's house and kennel run.

Tapeworms

Two species of tapeworms infest dogs. These are *Dipylidium caninum* and *Taenia pisiformis*. Both species are similar in that they have a head, neck and numerous body segments. There is a wide variation in the size of tapeworms, but the ones infesting dogs usually measure from 1 to 2 feet in length. *D. caninum* and *T. pisiformis* are widely distributed throughout the United States.

Fleas and lice are carriers of tapeworm eggs. Your dog can ingest tapeworm eggs when he bites and swallows fleas or lice. Tapeworm eggs are also found in fish, reptiles or small mammals that are secondary hosts for these parasites. After gaining entry into the dog's intestinal system, the tapeworm eggs mature in 3 to 4 weeks. At maturity, the segments of the tapeworm below the neck get larger and wider, with the last few segments longer than the rest. These rear-end segments contain the eggs. The eggs pass out of the intestinal tract with or without a bowel movement. If they are not passed out in a bowel movement, the eggs work out of the anus and adhere to the hair around the dog's anus. Here they dry up until they resemble small brown-rice kernels. This is another method by which the tapeworm eggs are spread. Dogs always sniff each other's rear ends and it is more than likely that tapeworm eggs can be passed this way.

Tapeworms feed on the dog's intestinal walls. But the damage they cause is nowhere near as much as that done by hookworms or ascarids. The most common symptom of tapeworm is an irritation of the anus. This causes the dog to drag or slide his rear end over the ground or floor. But, since this is also a symptom of anal gland trouble, a positive diagnosis of tapeworms should be made only when actual segments with eggs are seen. Or by an examination of the bowel movement under a microscope. Occasionally, dogs infested with tapeworms will show signs of being nervous or "jumpy." Most of the time, the tapeworms will cause a chronic enteritis. Now and then, they will block the intestinal tract. *T. pisiformis* is the tapeworm most apt to cause a blockage.

Tapeworms are easy to expel. Various tapeworm compounds are on the market. When using any of these patent worm medicines, do so with caution. There is always the danger of overdosing the dog. The prevention of tapeworm infestation is largely a matter of sanitation. Keep your dog free of fleas, lice and ticks. (See Chapter 15) Also, eliminate rodents that may be secondary hosts for tapeworms. If you give the dog fish, see that it is well cooked.

Heartworms

The dog heartworm, *Dirofilaria immitis*, is more prevalent than originally suspected. Infesting the dog, cat, fox and wildcat, the heartworm was discovered in 1856 by Dr. Joseph Leidy. At first thought to be a tropical parasite, canine heartworms have been located in dogs in more than thirty states. The heaviest infestations of heartworm are in dogs that live in the Gulf States and the Eastern Seaboard to as far north as southern Maine.

More cases of heartworm are found among the working and hunting dogs than in house dogs. This is readily understood when we consider the fact that the mosquito and flea are carriers of the heartworm eggs. The mosquito is responsible for spreading the parasite more quickly than the flea. And since the Gulf and Seaboard states are plagued with mosquitoes, the incidence of heartworm infestation is highest in these areas. The heartworm is comparatively unknown in the dry inland states that have little or no mosquito problem.

The adult heartworms locate in the right ventricle of the heart and in the pulmonary artery. But they may also appear in other areas. Heartworms are round, slender and longish worms, measuring from 5 to 14 inches. They have a diameter of less than ⅛ of an inch. The female heartworm is ovoviviparous; that is, she produces eggs that are hatched within her body. When the eggs are hatched, they produce numerous living microfilariae that swim in the bloodstream of the infected dog. These microfilariae are removed from the bloodstream by sucking intermediate hosts, such as the flea and mosquito. In the flea and mosquito, the microfilariae develop into infective larvae.

After undergoing several changes inside the mosquito or flea, the microfilariae are ready for the true host, the dog, cat, fox or wildcat. They are transferred to the dog or other susceptible animal by the bite of the flea or mosquito as it feeds. Once inside the dog's bloodstream, the microfilariae develop into mature heartworms in approximately 8 months.

The symptoms of heartworm infestation are varied. In hunting dogs, the first noticeable symptom is that the dog tires very quickly. He may also gasp, cough, breathe with great difficulty and go into a fit or convulsion. There may be abdominal dropsy or a swelling of the lower chest region. Pustular lesions between the toes and on the dog's head are occasionally seen as a result of an allergy to dead or living heartworms. Many dogs infested with heartworms become depressed and are usually nervous, starting a fight with other dogs at the slightest pretense. Dogs with heartworms will also seek out dark or shady corners of the kennel or house. They show a marked aversion to light. This tendency to seek dark corners and aversion to light are also symptoms of rabies and distemper.

A positive diagnosis of heartworms will have to be made by the veterinarian. The treatment is also his job. Prevention is your problem. The destruction of the primary hosts —the flea and mosquito—should be your main objective. If you live in a heavily infested mosquito region, screen the dog's kennel. Keep him well covered with insect powder and give him a weekly dip in an approved insecticide. Cut down any weeds, brush or other foliage that might act as a resting place for mosquitoes. While the dog will need shade in summer, trees can be the resting places for heartworm-carrying mosquitoes. Provide shade in the form of awnings. The soil and wooden parts of the doghouse and kennel can be treated with spray containing lindane, chlordane or methoxychlor. Also, you can mix a pound of 25% lindane or chlordane with sand and work it into the soil. Concrete or asphalt runs will, of course, offer the most protection against parasites. If you live in the heartworm region and have a hunting dog, you will be wise to have him blood-tested for heartworm microfilariae several times a year.

Esophageal worms

These parasites are found in the dog's esophagus. The esophageal worm requires an intermediate host to complete its life cycle. The intermediate host is the dung beetle. Dogs pick up the parasite by eating dung or manure containing the infected beetle.

Esophageal worms cause lumps in the esophagus, vomiting and extreme difficulty in swallowing. Remember, however, that difficulty in swallowing is also a symptom of rabies or an obstruction in the throat. The lumps caused by esophageal worms may exert pressure on the windpipe, which, in turn, brings about coughing, labored breathing and—in extreme cases—suffocation.

Esophageal worms require veterinary attention. Help prevent your dog from becoming infected by restricting him to a kennel, except when taken out for walks. Keep him away from dung or manure piles.

Other worms

While not as common as the ascarids, hookworms, etc., the lungworm, kidneyworm and eyeworm are found in dogs. The diagnosis and treatment require veterinary knowledge.

Flukes (Trematodes)

Flukes or trematodes infest the dog's small intestine. They are dangerous parasites because they may be carriers of a rickettsia-like organism that causes a condition known as "salmon or fish poisoning." Flukes are small, flattish parasites. They require two intermediate hosts: the snail and fish. Dogs fed raw fish, especially salmon or trout, may ingest the fluke and the disease organism. So far, "salmon or fish poisoning" is localized in northern California, Oregon, Washington, and southwestern Canada.

The symptoms of "salmon or fish poisoning" include a discharge from the eyes and nose; bloody diarrhea; swollen face and sunken eyes; no appetite; increased thirst; subnormal temperature—below 101°F.; and prostration.

The condition is extremely serious and requires immediate veterinary attention. Do not feed your dog raw fish; if you feed fish, bone and boil it.

INTESTINAL PROTOZOA

Next to worms, the intestinal protozoa are the most troublesome of parasites. The common protozoa infecting dogs are the coccidia. There are four species of coccidia capable of infecting dogs and other animals, including poultry. Usually, however, each of the four species prefers its own specific host, such as the dog, cow, or chicken. But it is possible for a dog to become infected with the poultry-type coccidia if he eats raw chicken viscera that are infected.

Coccidia fasten onto the cells that line the small intestine and the tissue under the intestinal lining. They reproduce and develop into what are known as oöcysts. These oöcysts are oval-shaped cells with a membrane and one or two granular bodies floating within the cell. Oöcysts are highly infective. They are eliminated from the dog's intestinal tract with the feces. Your dog can become infected, therefore, by coming into contact with the infected feces of other dogs. It is also possible—if your dog has coccidia—for him to reinfect himself by eating his feces that contain oöcysts.

Coccidiosis has distemper-like symptoms: nasal and eye discharge; soft bowel movement (changing to a watery or bloody diarrhea); weakness, emaciation and a rise in temperature. There is also a progressive weight loss. Puppies are very susceptible to coccidia. Very often they become infected as early as 3 to 4 weeks of age. If left untreated, puppies deteriorate very rapidly, ending with convulsions and death.

A positive diagnosis of coccidiosis is easily made by a microscopic examination of the feces for oöcysts. Both the diagnosis and treatment should be left to the veterinarian. You can take preventive measures that include keeping the dog's sleeping and living quarters clean. Keep out strange dogs and avoid an accumulation of feces in the yard or kennel.

Other protozoa

For many years, it was believed that the coccidia were the main protozoa affecting dogs. Now we know that others are responsible for intestinal troubles. Among these are organisms belonging to the Entamoeba, Giardia and Trichomona groups. The symptoms caused by these organisms are similar to those of coccidiosis. Diagnosis and treatment are jobs for the veterinarian.

INTERNAL PARASITE CONTROL

It may not be possible for you to achieve 100% control or elimination of internal parasites. The best you can hope for is to minimize or reduce the dog's chances of infection. This you do by trying to prevent your dog from coming into contact with infected matter, and by breaking up the life cycle of internal parasites.

Veterinary parasitologists are constantly working on methods to eradicate and break up the life cycles of parasites. Recently, a medicated dog food containing a vermicide for ascarids was developed and placed on the market. This medicated dog food is in the form of a meal and is manufactured by Best Foods Division, Corn Products Company, New York. It is dispensed only through veterinarians.

In the initial tests with this medicated dog food, 7-week-old puppies were put on a diet of the food. A second group of puppies the same age was fed a regular dog food. After six weeks of continuous feeding, the two groups were compared as to eradication of ascarids and general health. The results showed that the pups on the medicated dog food had a marked decrease in ascarid infestations and were in better health than the other group. The medicated dog food definitely proved effective in controlling ascarids. Studies were also done on mature dogs infected with *Toxocara canis*. At the completion of a three-week trial, those older dogs fed the medicated food were almost free of ascarids.

You will recall that the main problem in eliminating ascarids is that they migrate in the dog's body. The principle of the medicated food is that the daily feeding will eliminate ascarids as they appear in the intestines. The theory is a sound one, since ascarids do migrate. However, the possibility of ascarids developing resistance—or mutations—to the medicated dog meal must be taken into consideration. This has happened in the case of antibiotics and bacteria. Certain bacteria, notably *Staphylococcus aureus*, developed resistance to most antibiotics. The same is true for certain insects. During World War II and shortly thereafter, DDT was the wonder insecticide. It was used to control all kinds of insects, from gnats to ticks. Eventually, the insects developed mutations that were resistant to DDT. Consequently, other insecticides had to be developed.

KENNEL SANITATION

Until these new methods of eradicating and preventing internal parasite infection have been proven by the test of time, you will have to stick to old-fashioned sanitation.

Thoroughly clean the doghouse and kennel at least twice a month. Choose a good detergent and disinfectant. Compounds containing both a detergent and disinfectant are available. Pick one that is nontoxic and with a high degree of efficiency against the major organisms. The compound should be soluble in water. Follow the directions on the label—don't guess at the amounts to be used. Also, allow enough time for the compound to work; germs are not killed in a minute.

If possible, hose down the doghouse and kennel before using the detergent and disinfectant compound. This will wash away any feces or solid matter. Next, scrub all walls, floors and wooden bases with the compound. Work it into the cracks and corners. Take out any movable fixtures and wash them. Let the solution remain for about a half hour. Afterwards, you can rinse off any excess compound. Follow up the housecleaning by spraying with an insecticide containing lindane, chlordane, pyrethrum or rotenone. Dirt kennels can be sprinkled with lime which is then worked into the soil. Concrete or asphalt runs can be flushed, treated with the detergent and disinfectant compound, then rinsed.

To sum up the situation on internal parasites and their control: in most cases the diagnosis and treatment should be left to the veterinarian; prevention is largely your responsibility. Practice rigid sanitation in the doghouse and kennel. A periodic examination of the dog's bowel movement for internal parasites is good management and good sense. It will prevent serious complications and it will enable you to keep the dog in top condition.

If you have a hunting dog and work him in mosquito-infested country, have a blood test for heartworm filariae done every three or four months. Finally, if you decide to do your own worming for ascarids and tapeworms, adhere to the instructions on the label. A puppy can be seriously harmed, possibly killed, by an overdose of worm medicine. Remember, worm medicines are poisons, that's why the worms are killed. If in doubt, better let the veterinarian do the job.

15. Fleas, Lice and Ticks

Some wag once remarked that the best way to keep a city dog from becoming bored in an apartment was to load him with fleas. That way the dog would be so busy scratching, he wouldn't have time to complain about being lonesome. The person who made the remark didn't know much about dogs or fleas. Nor did he know that fleas are not adverse to congregating on and taking bites out of human beings.

In addition to causing skin irritations and irritability, fleas, lice and ticks may also be carriers of disease organisms. In the previous chapter, we mentioned that the flea is a carrier of tapeworm eggs, as well as microfilariae of heartworms. The flea is also the carrier of organisms causing bubonic plague and endemic typhus fever in man. Lice, while not as common as fleas, are just as dangerous to dogs. Severe infestations of lice have been responsible for the destruction of entire litters of puppies. They are also known carriers of the organism causing typhus fever, trench fever and relapsing fever in human beings. Ticks, once regarded as strictly rural pests, are now well distributed throughout the United States, in cities and suburbs as well as rural sections. Ticks are known carriers of organisms causing piroplasmosis in dogs and Rocky Mountain spotted fever and tularemia in man.

This is an impressive array of diseases carried by these pests, not to mention the misery and cost of eradication. Fortunately, fleas, lice and ticks can be controlled. Your main efforts should be directed toward destroying the life cycle of these parasites, as well as eradicating them from the dog.

FLEAS

Most dogs owners are quickly introduced to fleas. Just let your dog come into contact with another dog harboring fleas and you are in business.

Four species of fleas are associated with dogs and human beings. These are the human flea, dog flea, cat flea and the dog and cat "stick-tight" flea. Ordinarily, each of these species prefers a specific host, but will use any warm-blooded creatures as substitutes when the need arises. Fleas may be found on any part of the dog's body, although the "stick-tight" flea more or less localizes in and around the dog's ears.

The flea has a relatively simple life history. The female may deposit her eggs on the dog or in sand, furniture, dog bed, blankets or crevices in the home or doghouse. After a few days, the flea eggs develop into larvae which weave cocoons. These cocoons serve as a protection for the larvae. During the cocoon stage, the larvae turn into pupae which feed on organic matters incorporated into the cocoon. The adult flea emerges from the cocoon in 10 to 14 days, with the whole cycle taking approximately 30 days. One female flea can lay up to 500 eggs in her lifetime.

Before emerging from the cocoon, the flea pupae may stay dormant until favorable conditions exist: when temperatures are above freezing. Very often there are no signs of fleas, then all at once a swarm of adult fleas appear as if from nowhere. The adult flea is able to withstand cold weather, but a severe winter will greatly reduce the flea population.

Adult fleas will stick to the warmest parts of the dog during cold weather. The warmest parts are those with the most hair, such as the chest, neck ruff and root of the tail. Here the fleas congregate until the weather warms up, then they move and spread over the dog's body.

Don't wait until the dog is loaded with fleas and scratching himself raw before doing something about them. By this time, you will have two problems with which to cope: getting rid of the fleas and clearing up the dog's skin. Constant scratching can lead to chronic eczema. Check the dog several times a week, even if you don't see any fleas or he isn't doing any scratching. During the warm weather, keep the dog dusted with a flea powder.

When the dog is heavily infested with fleas, you will have to de-flea him. The standard treatment for fleas consists of using a powder or dip. The dip is more effective, since it has a longer residual time than the powder. A weekly dip or dusting is recommended.

A new method of eradicating fleas (also lice and ticks) and keeping them off the dog has recently been developed. It is an oral medication, in tablet form, and has shown some promising results. Dogs are given the tablet at specified intervals and, as long as they keep getting the tablets, the fleas, lice and ticks stay away.

The concept of oral treatment for the elimination of external parasites is not new. An oral treatment for ringworm and athlete's foot in human beings has been in use for several years. Oral medication for eradicating fleas, lice, and ticks are available only by prescription from a veterinarian. There is a good reason for controlling these chemicals and not allowing them to be sold "over the counter" or as "patent medicines"; an overdose can cause serious trouble, possibly death.

De-fleaing the dog

Dusting: Stand the dog on newspapers and dust him thoroughly with a nontoxic insecticide. One containing lindane, chlordane, rotenone or pyrethrum is safe. Make sure that you get the powder in beyond the outer coat and on the skin. Avoid getting any powder in the dog's eyes. You can protect his eyes with Vaseline or eye ointment. After dusting, comb out the dead fleas onto the newspapers. Roll up the papers and burn them.

Spraying: Insecticides for fleas, lice and ticks also come in sprays that are put into pressurized cans or plastic containers. They usually contain the same ingredients as the powders and dips. The cost is higher, though.

Dipping: While dipping the dog is more of a chore, it has a longer residual effect than either spraying or dusting. Put enough water in the tub to reach the dog's stomach and add a commercial dipping compound. Follow directions on the label as to how much to add. Submerge the dog's body in the solution or pour the solution over the dog, avoiding his face. Again, protect his eyes with Vaseline or eye ointment. After thoroughly wetting the dog, lift him out of the tub and wrap a large towel or old blanket around him and mop up the excess solution.

Don't rub him dry. Allow the solution to dry on him. Keep him in the house until he is dry; then stand him on some newspapers and comb out the dead fleas. The dried solution on his body and hair will afford some protection against reinfestation. If the dog lives outdoors, reinforce the dip with a dusting of insect powder.

Merely knocking the fleas off the dog is only part of the job of flea control. You will have to spray the doghouse or other place where the dog may live. His bed and blanket or bedding should also come under scrutiny and be sprayed or dusted. When spraying the doghouse, make sure that you get the spray into crevices that may shelter flea eggs.

The housedog presents more of a problem. While you can easily de-flea the dog, you have a bigger chore when it comes to the house. Use the vacuum cleaner in cracks and crevices. Bedding, carpets, rugs and stuffed furniture should be sprayed. If you already have an infestation of fleas in the house, you will have to spray at least once a week to break up the 30-day life cycle of the fleas.

Flea collars: In general, the better-quality flea collars do an efficient job of eradicating fleas and—to a lesser extent—ticks. (Since ticks are more stationary than fleas, they do not always come into contact with the collar and insecticide contained therein.) The principle behind the flea collar is a simple one: The collar (usually plastic) contains a pesticide known to be effective against fleas and ticks. When the parasites migrate over the dog's body, they eventually pass under and against the flea collar, thus exposing themselves to the insecticide.

The use of the flea collar is not without some risks. There have been cases in which dogs have had severe allergic reactions from absorbing the insecticide through the skin. Also, it is known that absorbed insecticides from flea collars can interfere with respiration during surgery, especially when anesthesias are used. Watch for any skin reactions, if you put a flea collar on your dog (dermatitis, redness, rash, etc.). Although the flea collar manufacturers state that the collar is effective for as long as sixty to ninety days, our advice is not to leave the collar on for that long a time; remove it just as soon as all fleas are eradicated.

Oral or injectable flea killers: Oral or injectable medication to kill fleas is available through a veterinarian. Briefly, the insecticide is absorbed into the dog's bloodstream and acts as a systemic pesticide; fleas and other external parasites come into contact with the insecticide when they bite the dog or suck blood.

This kind of insect control also poses risks for the dog. In using any systemic pesticide, it is important to maintain the proper balance of the chemical in the dog's bloodstream. An overdose or too high a level can result in death. Even repeated doses over too long a period can deplete the dog's supply of a protective enzyme known as cholinesterase. Oral or injectable pesticides should be used only under the supervision of a veterinarian.

Anyone who has ever had an infestation of fleas in the house or cellar will tell you what misery they went through. You can avoid such an experience by keeping your dog free of fleas. It's work, but it's nothing compared to the work and annoyance that will be yours if a swarm of fleas takes up residence in your house.

LICE

Lice, although they are not as widely distributed as fleas, are just as much of a nuisance. These small, wingless insects are grouped into sucking and biting types. They spend their entire lives, from egg to adult, on mammals and birds. The female louse deposits her eggs on the dog's hair and the eggs hatch in approximately 2 to 3 weeks.

Lice are completely dependent on the host animal for their existence and will not voluntarily leave the dog. They are not as active as fleas and cannot leap from animal to animal. They are transferred by direct contact with the lice or their eggs. When a dog with lice sheds hair containing lice eggs or lice, the hair becomes the means of transmission to other animals. Lice will freely infest different animals, including human beings. Therefore if you have children and a dog (or cat), and one of them has lice, the chances are that the others do. You will have to delouse everybody.

The louse can cause severe anemia in young puppies by

sucking their blood. Puppies usually become infested with lice through contact with their mother, if she is infested. Since puppies are constantly nursing and lying against their mother, the chances of their being infested are great.

Control of lice

The eradication of lice consists of dipping or spraying the dog with a nontoxic insecticide. Oral medication can be used. In dipping or spraying, use the same technique as for fleas.

TICKS

Ticks are eight-legged, hard-shelled parasites that burrow into the skin and feed on blood. They are not true insects. All true insects have six legs. Ticks are very hardy and stubborn parasites, capable of fasting for long periods and withstanding extremes in weather and climate. In some respects, they are more dangerous than either the flea or louse. And they are not easily eradicated from buildings.

A female tick may deposit as many as 5,000 eggs. The eggs are laid on the ground in some sheltered spot. After laying the eggs, the female dies. Three weeks to six months later, depending upon the conditions, the larvae or seed-ticks make their appearance. These seed-ticks have *six* legs. When the temperature and humidity are favorable, the seed-ticks begin their search for an intermediate host. The intermediate hosts are the meadow mouse and other small rodents. When ready to find a host, the seed-tick moves up from the ground, climbing on blades of grass, brush, weeds or other handy vegetation. The seed-tick works its way to the top of vegetation. Here, perched and ready for action, the seed-tick awaits its prey. When a meadow mouse or other rodent comes along and brushes up against the vegetation with the seed-tick, the transfer is made.

When the temperature and humidity conditions are not right, the seed-tick will climb down from the vegetation and become dormant. She will become active only when the conditions are favorable.

After the seed-tick fastens onto its intermediate host,

it digs in tightly and gorges on blood. The seed-tick and adult tick do this by puncturing the skin with the mouth and fastening into the opening made by the bite. Securely anchored, the seed-tick feeds on the intermediate host for 3 to 5 days. After it is gorged, the seed-tick falls to the ground.

Back on the ground again, the seed-tick undergoes a molt and changes into an eight-legged tick known as a nymph. The nymph climbs up on vegetation when the conditions are right and fastens onto a small rodent for 3 to 10 days. Again, gorged to sluggishness, the nymph falls to the ground and eventually molts into an eight-legged adult tick. The adult tick repeats the tactics of the seed-tick and nymph and climbs up on vegetation to await a victim—this time a dog, human being or other animal. You can see that the tick has a more elaborate life cycle than either the flea or louse.

Dogs infested with ticks suffer in a variety of ways. Since ticks gorge on blood, anemia is often the result of a tick infestation. Some ticks inject a toxin that affects the dog's neuromuscular system. Also, infections or abscesses can form at the site of the puncture made by the tick. But, as we mentioned before, it is the tick's ability to carry and transmit disease organisms that make it a very dangerous pest. While any species of tick will fasten onto a dog, it is the American dog tick and the brown dog tick that are the most widely distributed of the group.

Control of ticks

If just a few ticks are dug into your dog, you can remove them by pulling them out with tweezers. Don't try to pull them out with your fingers. This is risky for two reasons: 1) since ticks burrow in very tightly, you may break off the tick's body, and 2) the tick may be a carrier of Rocky Mountain spotted fever or tularemia. Use a pair of tweezers that have wide blunt ends; not the sharp pointed type. Work carefully and be sure to get all of the tick out of the dog's skin. If the head is left in, it may later cause infection. Ticks can also be loosened by wetting them with vinegar, alcohol or acetone (nail-polish remover).

When your dog is heavily infested with ticks, he will have to be dipped. Use the same dipping technique as for fleas and lice. But remember that ticks are very tough and you may have to repeat the dip once or twice before killing all of the ticks. In regions with heavy or persistent infestations of ticks, dogs should be dipped at least every ten days, and more often if the dogs go swimming or are out in the rain.

If you live in an area that is heavily infested with ticks, you will be wise to check the dog every time you take him out. This is especially true if you go into a woods or section with brush and weeds. Be sure to examine between the dog's toes, behind the ears and the root of the tail. These are favorite spots for ticks to fasten. Also, the chest. The dog usually brushes against vegetation with his chest and ticks are sure to get a hold here.

As with fleas and lice, eradicating ticks from the dog's body is only part of the battle. You've got to keep them out of the doghouse and your house. Above all, you've got to keep breaking up the life cycle. Ask your veterinarian to recommend a safe spray, then use it liberally in the doghouse or other infected places, working the spray into corners and crevices. Next, go after the intermediate hosts, the field mice and other rodents. Keep them away from your house and the kennel. Maybe a cat, one that is a good mouser, will be of help. Cut down tall shrubbery, weeds and grass around the property. In short, make life impossible for ticks.

16. Skin Conditions

In addition to irritations caused by fleas, lice and ticks, dogs are often plagued by chronic or acute skin conditions and disease. There are various causes of skin diseases, among them mites, fungi, faulty metabolism, poor diet and allergy. Veterinarians probably treat more cases involving the skin than any other single disease.

Generally, skin conditions are considered to be of parasitic or nonparasitic origin. The parasitic conditions include those caused by insects, mites and minute plants. Fleas and lice are examples of parasitic insects. Ticks and mange mites are parasitic mites. And the fungi causing ringworms and favus are examples of the parasitic plants. The nonparasitic skin conditions include those caused by microorganisms, faulty metabolism, poor diet, mechanical irritation (rubbing and scratching, for instance) and allergy to chemicals, pollen, plants, etc.

The treatment of skin conditions and diseases, especially those suspected of being of allergic origin, is often complex and long drawn out. In the case of some of the minor skin conditions, you will be able to help the dog. In others that are more serious or persistent, you will have to seek veterinary advice.

MANGE

The two major types of mange—Demodectic and Sarcoptic—are caused by mites. Otodectic or ear mange is also caused by mites, although the actual skin condition in this type of mange results more from decomposing secretions and the constant rubbing and scratching by the irritated dog.

Demodectic mange

The mite responsible for Demodectic mange is called *Demodex folliculorum*. It burrows into the skin and causes inflammation and mild irritation. There are two forms of Demodectic mange: 1) the *squamous* form, in which there is a mild inflammation and loss of hair, and 2) the *pustular* form, in which the dog's skin becomes very red with a bloody discharge.

Demodectic mange is characterized by shedding of the hair, a reddening of the affected skin parts, thickened and wrinkled skin, denuded areas around the eyes, elbows, hocks and toes, and bloody or scabby lesions. Unlike Sarcoptic mange, there may be little or no itching. Very often the lesions in Demodectic mange are localized to one area and do not spread to other parts of the body. The squamous form of Demodectic mange is often confused with other skin conditions or diseases. The only positive method of diganosis is to have the veterinarian take some skin scrapings and examine them under the microscope for the *Demodex folliculorum* mites.

Treatment: Demodectic mange is very persistent and should receive veterinary attention. The squamous form responds to treatment much quicker than the pustular form. Also, if the mange is localized, treatment will be more effective. However, you will have to keep in mind that some dogs do not respond to treatment as readily as others. And some cases of Demodectic mange will recur. Treatment usually consists of clipping the dog and washing the skin with a germicidal solution. Next, the affected parts are treated with special mange preparations to kill the mange mites. A good diet is essential during treatment.

You can provide some emergency treatment by clipping the hair around the affected areas, washing them with mild soap and water, and applying a sulphur and cold-cream ointment. Flowers of sulphur is usually available in drugstores.

Sarcoptic mange

Sarcoptic mange is caused by a mite belonging to the genus *Sarcoptes*. We don't expect you to be able to differentiate between these mites, but a knowledge of them and their damage will help you to understand the treatment and course of the condition. Sarcoptic mange often starts on the dog's head, but it may also show up on the lower abdomen, chest, under the front legs, at the root of the tail, and at the base of the ears.

The symptoms of Sarcoptic mange include itching, red dots or blisters, a discharge, scabs and crusts, loss of hair, and a moldy or musty odor. A positive diagnosis can only be made by an examination of a skin scraping under a microscope for the Sarcoptic mange mite.

Treatment: Neglected cases of Sarcoptic mange have proved fatal. So, prompt veterinary attention is vital. The treatment more or less follows that for Demodectic mange. You can give the dog temporary relief by applying a sulphur and cold-cream ointment, but put the dog under the veterinarian's care.

Otodectic or ear mange

The mites causing Otodectic or ear mange live inside the ears. They are often visible to the naked eye as small specks that move. If untreated, ear mange can lead to severe complications.

The symptoms include a tilted head, pawing at the ears, whining or whimpering, poor balance, an ear discharge with a foul odor, and the presence of the mites themselves. Some of these symptoms are also indicative of ear canker and hematoma. (See Chapter 13)

Ear mites require veterinary attention. You can ease the dog's misery by cleaning the ears with mineral or baby oil on cotton swabs.

RINGWORM

Ringworm is a contagious skin disease caused by a fungus. It is transmissible to man and other animals. Two genera of fungi are responsible for ringworm. They have long names: *Trichophyton megalosporon* and *Trichophyton microsporon*. The *T. microsporon* fungus is the type most often encountered in dogs.

The fungi causing ringworm more or less limit their activities to the epidermis or outer layer of skin. They grow onto the hair follicles and in between the hair sheaths, finally killing off the hair and causing it to fall out. Ringworm usually starts on the head, neck, and legs and will spread to other parts of the body.

The symptoms of ringworm are round or oval-shaped lesions on the head, face, legs or body; scabs and crusts;

and loss of hair. The lesions may appear in several forms: 1) as well-defined scaly patches, which form an irregular circle up to two inches in diameter; 2) as small red and raised areas on the hairless parts of the dog's body; 3) as scaly lesions with reddish pustules around the edges or rims.

Treatment: Localized lesions can be treated with tincture of iodine or iodine ointment. Since ringworm is contagious, wear rubber gloves when handling the dog. Stand him on newspapers, clip the hair from around the lesions, and remove the scabs and crusts by washing with a mild soap and warm water. After the lesions are cleaned, apply tincture of iodine or iodine ointment. Wrap up the trimmed hair, scabs or crusts and burn them. Oral medication for ringworm is available and can be procured through your veterinarian.

FAVUS

Favus is another skin disease caused by a fungus. Under the microscope, the fungus causing favus is quite distinct from that causing ringworm; its name is *Anchorion schonleinii*. And like the ringworm fungus, the one causing favus is transmissible to man, birds and other animals.

The favus fungus grows into the hair follicles, over the outer part of the hair and penetrates *between* the layers of the epidermis. In other words, the fungus causing favus goes deeper into the skin. Favus is characterized by cups or indentations found on the face, ears, head and paws. The cups have raised margins that are silver-gray in color. In the center of these cups or indentations may be found stumps of broken hair. A positive diagnosis can only be made by a skin scraping examined under a microscope.

Treatment: Favus responds to treatment with tincture of iodine or iodine ointment. There are also various commercial ringworm and favus preparations that are effective. Treatment should start at the first sign of the condition. Favus is contagious, so wear rubber gloves and follow the same procedure as for treating ringworm. Clip the hair around the affected parts, wash with mild soap and warm water to remove the scabs and crusts, then apply iodine ointment, tincture of iodine or a commercial preparation. If the condition persists, consult your veterinarian.

NONPARASITIC SKIN CONDITIONS

The nonparasitic skin conditions are often very puzzling and in the absence of parasites, the treatment has to be more or less experimental. In many of the nonparasitic skin conditions, the treatment depends on the cause. And it may take some time to locate the cause. We mention this so that you will know that when the veterinarian asks you to bring the dog back for several visits or treatments, he is not trying to stretch out the treatment.

ECZEMA

Eczema has long been a controversial skin condition, both in animals and human beings. It is more a symptom of a disorder than a disease in itself. Various theories have been advanced as to the causes of eczema. For example, dermatologists believe that eczema is caused by faulty diet, hormone imbalance, fleas, lice and ticks, kidney troubles, and vitamin deficiencies. Other factors may be involved. As to vitamin deficiencies, it is well known that a deficiency of vitamins A and E, as well as inadequate amounts of the essential fatty acids, will cause skin eruptions.

The symptoms of eczema can easily be confused with those of other skin conditions or diseases. They include intense itching, pustules, discharge, scabs and dandruff.

Treatment: First, before any treatment can be started, the cause must be discovered. This may require many tests and the subsequent treatment may be extended over a long period. You can give the dog temporary relief by washing off the scabs with mild soap and water, and applying a soothing agent such as calomine solution or cold cream. The diagnosis and subsequent treatment will have to be done by the veterinarian.

ECZEMA NASI (COLLIE NOSE)

This form of eczema affects only the nose, eyes, and the skin surrounding the eyes. It is an abnormal reaction of the dog's skin to bright sunlight. The condition is limited to Collies, Shetland Sheepdogs and mixed breeds containing either of the aforementioned breeds.

The symptoms of eczema nasi are pawing or scratching at the nose; lesions on the nose where the hairless part of the nose blends into the upper hairy section; inflammation of the eyes; bleeding from the lesions; scabs on the bridge of the nose and a loss of hair in the region.

Treatment: Eczema nasi is chronic and should be treated by a veterinarian. You can provide temporary relief by washing off the scabs and crusts, applying calomine solution or cold cream to the affected parts, and treating the inflamed eyes with eye ointment.

DANDRUFF

Dandruff is another skin condition of undetermined origin. Among the suspected causes are too frequent bathings with caustic soap, faulty diet, parasites and other factors.

The most noticeable symptoms of dandruff are dry skin and grayish-white scales or flakes on the skin or hair.

Treatment: The treatment depends upon the cause. Here, again, the dog may have to undergo various tests. And any testing will usually start with the dog's diet. Check it over and make sure he's getting enough fat and the right kind, preferably fat of animal origin. A daily grooming will help get rid of the dandruff that accumulates on the hair or skin. It will not cure it, of course. If, after you've checked and adjusted the diet, the dandruff persists, have the veterinarian examine the dog.

ALOPECIA (BALDNESS)

Alopecia is the loss of hair without any apparent disease or parasites to account for the condition. Among the suspected causes are disease, parasites, friction (such as sleeping or lying on hard surfaces), functional disorders, chemical irritations and dietary deficiencies.

The obvious symptoms of alopecia are either small, localized bald spots or large, irregular bald areas. Alopecia is another skin condition that requires various tests to determine the cause. While there is no discomfort in many cases of alopecia, it is unsightly. And, of course, a poor coat impairs the dog's insulation against heat and cold. Home remedies are useless, unless you know the cause. Consult your veterinarian.

IMPETIGO

Impetigo is an inflammatory skin condition characterized by *isolated* pustules. These pustules are more shallow than those of mange and they break or rupture very easily. Impetigo can be treated with daily applications of an antiseptic powder, such as BFI. The condition usually clears up in a short time.

DERMATITIS

The term "dermatitis" means an inflammation of the skin. Dermatitis is another one of those skin conditions with vague and various causes. Some of the causes may be internal, others may be external. The internal causes include food allergy, faulty diet, metabolic disorders and intestinal parasites. The external causes include insect or animal bites, blows, scratches, chemical irritation (acids, alkalies, plant juices, insect poisons, etc.), and burns, scalds, freezing and excessive sunlight.

A thickened skin, scaling, loss of hair and intense itching are the most prominent symptoms of dermatitis. The itching often becomes so intense, the dog will constantly lick the affected parts and will keep rubbing himself against chairs, tables, walls, etc.

Chronic dermatitis should be treated by a veterinarian. You can relieve the dog's misery by washing off any scabs with mild soap and water, then applying calomine solution or an ointment, such as Panthoderm, to alleviate the itching.

ALLERGIES

The problem of allergy in dogs is a complicated one. Dogs are allergic to all kinds of substances. Among them are pollen, serums, raw horse meat, dairy products, insect stings, plants, plant juices, the dog's own hormone (mainly progesterone) and various other substances.

Allergists have discovered that dogs also may suffer from seasonal allergic rhinitis (hay fever) and this has been confirmed by positive skin tests with offending allergens or substances.

Allergies show up in various ways. Dermatitis, swellings, itching, sores, etc., are all symptoms of allergy. The treatment depends on finding the cause and eliminating it. Most likely the diagnosis and treatment will take some time, so if your dog has a skin condition of undetermined origin, he may have to undergo allergy tests.

17. First Aid for Accidents

First aid is the immediate and temporary help you can give your dog in case of an accident. Do what you can to save the dog's life, then get him to a veterinarian. Don't try to do more than you know.

There are some minor wounds, injuries and accidents in which you may be able to do all that is necessary. But if you are in doubt as to their severity—and we'll repeat a previous warning—let the veterinarian take over.

In rendering first aid, keep cool, work quickly and quietly, reassure the dog and use restraint when necessary. Remember that injured dogs are in pain and have great fear. They will often snap or bite in their pain or fear. When possible, apply an emergency muzzle before handling the dog.

SERIOUS BLEEDING

Cut or torn arteries and veins result in serious bleeding. If the bleeding is not controlled, your dog can bleed to death. Therefore, your promptness in controlling bleeding may save your dog's life.

Symptoms of serious bleeding

Arterial bleeding: You can tell arterial bleeding by the bright red color and the spurting or welling of the blood from the wound.

Venous bleeding: In venous bleeding the blood is dark red and flows steadily from the wound. It may also ooze out.

First Aid

APPLY PRESSURE AT ONCE!

You can apply direct pressure on a sterile pad, clean handkerchief or towel. Place it on the wound and press down firmly. Direct pressure rarely fails to control bleeding, if enough pressure is exerted.

If for some reason you can't check the bleeding by

using direct pressure, then apply pressure at the nearest pressure point.

Should you be unable to control the bleeding at the pressure point, apply a tourniquet. Use a belt, necktie, roller bandage or strip of cloth for the tourniquet. The best tourniquet is made from material that is 2 inches wide. Fasten the tourniquet close to the wound and *between the wound and the dog's heart*. Make the tourniquet tight enough to check bleeding, wrap it around the dog's leg twice and then knot it. Do not remove the tourniquet no matter how long it has been on. Take the dog to a veterinarian and let him remove the tourniquet.

MINOR CUTS AND WOUNDS

Minor cuts, wounds, scratches and the like can be treated by the dog himself. Since his saliva contains a germicide, let him lick those wounds he can reach. The others you can treat. Clip the hair from around the wounds and wash the area with mild soap and water. After washing, apply an antiseptic powder, such as BFI, or a liquid antiseptic, such as metaphen. It isn't necessary to bandage superficial wounds or cuts.

SHOCK

Shock is caused by an interference with the blood supply to the brain and other factors. It usually accompanies severe injuries, burns, snakebite, etc. You should treat for shock as a matter of routine, *but only after you have attended to serious bleeding or stoppage of breath.*

Symptoms

The dog may or may not be conscious. His eyes will be glassy and have a vacant stare. He will shiver or tremble. His breathing is irregular; deep, long breaths alternated with shallow ones. The dog may also vomit.

First Aid

A dog in shock loses his body heat very quickly. This is due to poor circulation. Keep him warm. Cover him with a blanket or heavy coat. If possible, slide some newspapers or another coat or blanket under him. Remember there is an interference with the blood supply to the brain, so try to lower his head. Do this by folding a coat or blanket and putting it under his body, letting his head hang down. If the dog is conscious, keep him quiet. Get him to a veterinarian as soon as possible.

CAR AND TRUCK ACCIDENTS

Dogs struck by cars or trucks may sustain severe injuries ranging from a broken pelvis to internal injuries. Such injuries are not for the amateur to fool around with and possibly cause complications. They require expert treatment. But first aid is almost always necessary, especially when severe bleeding or shock are present.

What to do if your dog is struck by a car or truck

First, remove the dog from the road or street, out of the path of traffic. Remember that injured dogs may bite. If the dog's mouth is not injured, put on an emergency muzzle. Slide the dog onto a blanket, burlap bag or coat and drag or slide him out of danger.

Next, get to work. Control all bleeding. After this, treat for shock. Examine the dog for possible fractures. A break in a leg is usually visible as a large lump or you may see part of a bone protruding through the skin. The dog cannot move the broken part. Do not move the dog or broken part unnecessarily. If there is an obvious break, put a splint on it.

How to put on a splint

Use stiff cardboard, wood, folded newspapers or ¼-inch wire mesh for splints. Gently place the splint against the broken parts, with the upper and lower ends of the splints extending well beyond the break. Fasten the splints above and below the break with roller bandage, adhesive tape or strips of cloth.

If the dog tries to struggle to his feet and can't get his rear end up, he may have a broken pelvis. You can't put a splint on the pelvis. The best you can do is try to keep the dog still. Place him on a board, have someone hold him there, and transport him to a veterinarian.

After you've done all you can for the dog struck by a car or truck, get him to a veterinarian.

TRANSPORTING THE INJURED DOG

Since most veterinarians rarely come out to treat a dog, you will have to get the dog to the veterinarian. Take care in moving the injured dog. Rough or unnecessary handling may result in further injury.

If you have assistance, make a stretcher using two poles and a coat. Broomsticks, mop handles or tree branches can be used for poles. Turn the coat sleeves inside out and slide the two poles, one through each sleeve opening. Button the coat over the poles and the stretcher is ready.

If you happen to be alone, you will have to carry the dog across your shoulders. Lift him up gently and place his body across the back of your shoulders, against your neck, with his head and front legs over one shoulder. His hind feet should hang over the other shoulder. Shepherds often carry sheep and lambs in this fashion.

BREATH STOPPAGE
(Caused by smoke, gas or drowning)

Dogs may be overcome by smoke, gas and excessive water in the lungs. When this occurs, you will have to revive the dog. Speed is essential.

Symptoms of breath stoppage

The symptoms include unconsciousness, breathing stopped, pulse weak or absent (check for pulse at pressure points) and irregular heartbeat.

First Aid for smoke or gas exposure

Quickly remove the dog from the smoke- or gas-contaminated area. Work fast and take precautions against being overcome yourself. There is usually more air three or four feet from the ground or floor.

As soon as you get the dog out into the fresh air, start giving him artificial respiration. Place the dog on his side, with his forelegs stretched out in front, his hind legs stretched out to the rear.

Take your handkerchief and pull out his tongue. This is to prevent the tongue from lolling back and obstructing his breathing passage. Next, put your two hands on the dog's chest, press down, release, wait, press down again, release again, wait again. Do this rhythmically; maintain a press down, release and wait system of thirty times per minute for large dogs, twenty times per minute for smaller dogs. An aid to keeping the rhythm may be as follows: as you press down, say "out goes the bad air"; when you release, say "in comes the good." You may have to work a long time, but stay with it. Treat for shock when the dog revives and then get him to a veterinarian.

First Aid for drowning

First of all, a drowning dog is rare. Most dogs are instinctive swimmers. But there is always a first time.

Here's what to do after the dog has been hauled out of the water:

Take off his collar. If he's not too large, hold him upside down to drain out the water.

Then apply artificial respiration. Have someone call a veterinarian. Keep working on the dog. Treat for shock when he revives.

ELECTRIC SHOCK AND LIGHTNING

Occasionally dogs get electrocuted or are struck by lightning. Electric shocks or lightning strokes can be fatal. However, until a veterinarian certifies the dog is dead, make every attempt to revive him.

Symptoms

Same as for smoke, gas or drowning. There may be burns. Treat for breath stoppage first!

First Aid for electric shock

If the dog is lying across a live wire, find a dry board or stick and pry the dog off the wire. Do this without sliding or pushing the dog over the wire, otherwise you will cause more burns. If the wire is lying on the dog, use the dry board or stick and flip the wire off. If possible, shut off the current.

Next, start artificial respiration. When the dog revives, treat any burns. Get the dog to the veterinarian as soon as possible.

Lightning

Quickly start artificial respiration. When the dog revives, treat any burns. Take him to a veterinarian.

BURNS AND SCALDS

Dogs can be severely burned by exposure to flame, hot ashes, lightning, electric shock or chemicals. They can also be scalded by hot liquids or steam.

First degree burns, in which the skin turns red, are the most common type of burns. Severe burns, in which the skin is charred or blackened, may occur.

Symptoms

First degree burns: skin red or blistered. The hair is singed.

Severe burns: skin charred or blackened.

First Aid

If the burns are small, first degree and localized to small areas, proceed as follows:

Carefully trim away hair from burned areas. Wash the burns with mild soap and water. Apply a thick grease, such as Vaseline, axle grease, butter or commercial burn ointment. Tea has often been recommended in the first aid of burns. Tea contains tannic acid which reduces pain and helps to minimize fluid losses. Fluid losses are the greatest danger in burns. However, tea should not be used in treating large burns or large burned areas, since the tannic acid can be toxic to cells.

If the dog has large burns of any degree, treat as follows:

Should a veterinarian be within an hour's travel, cover the burns with clean cloth and take the dog to the veterinarian.

If you are in an isolated place, you will have to render first aid. Carefully trim away hair from the burned areas, cover burns with thick grease or burn ointment and put a sterile pad or cloth on top. Next, wrap a clean cloth over the first dressing, then bandage the whole dressing with roller bandage or cloth. Treat for shock. Get the dog to a veterinarian as soon as possible.

In treating burns of any degree, do not touch them with your fingers, breathe on them or *apply any antiseptic*. Simply apply a thick grease or ointment to exclude air and prevent fluid losses.

POISONING

Poisoning is always a hazard with dogs, especially if the dogs are roaming loose. Dogs are scavengers and like to root in garbage cans, dumps and other areas that may be treated with rodent or other vermin poisons. There is also the possibility of dogs being maliciously poisoned or picking up poisons around the house. Insecticides, plant sprays and paints should be kept locked up out of the reach of dogs and children.

There are many kinds of poisons and antidotes. Toxicology is beyond the scope of this chapter. But you should know the symptoms of poisoning and the standard treatments.

Symptoms of poisoning

These vary with the type of poison, but the general symptoms are convulsions, burned mouth (alkalies and acids) and unconsciousness.

First Aid

Get to work quickly, you may not have much time. Have someone call a veterinarian and describe the dog's symptoms.

If you know what kind of poison your dog ate, read the label on the bottle or can and follow directions as to antidotes.

If you don't know what kind of poison your dog ate, proceed as follows:

If his mouth is burned, don't make him vomit. If it

isn't, then make him vomit. You can cause him to vomit by giving him a solution of soap and water, equal parts of hydrogen peroxide and water, two teaspoonfuls of table salt in a cup of water, or a regular emetic, such as ipecac, if you have it. Follow directions on label if you use a prepared emetic. Otherwise, put the other solution, whichever one you use, in a bottle and pour into a pouch in the side of the dog's mouth.

After the dog vomits, give him milk or slightly beaten egg whites. Put the milk or egg whites in a small bottle and pour into a mouth pouch.

Follow this by giving the dog a teaspoonful of Epsom salts in a little warm water. Get the dog to the veterinarian as soon as you can.

Lead poisoning

Dogs can get lead poisoning from eating paint.

Symptoms

A dog suffering from lead poisoning will show most of the symptoms of rabies, plus a painful stiffened gait. If you are sure the dog has not been exposed to rabies, treat for poison. Otherwise, handle him as for rabies.

CHOKING

Choking may be caused by a bone or other foreign object lodged in the throat.

Symptoms

The dog with something stuck in his throat will paw at his mouth and try to retch. He may also gag or gasp. There may be a bloody, foamy saliva. In extreme cases, breathing stops.

First Aid

If breathing has stopped, apply artificial respiration.

If you are satisfied that the dog has not been exposed to rabies, try to remove the object from his throat. But, if possible, rush him to the veterinarian.

Go after the object in the throat as follows:

Open the dog's mouth by grasping his lower jaw in your

left hand, pushing down his upper lip so that it covers the teeth, holding them there with your fingers. Next, tilt his head upward, so that his lower jaw hangs open. Reach in with the fingers of your right hand and try to grasp the bone or foreign object. Work quickly and hold his mouth open. If in doubt as to his symptoms, call your veterinarian.

SNAKEBITE

There are four kinds of poisonous snakes in the United States. They are the rattlesnake, copperhead, water moccasin and coral snake.

Just how dangerous are the poisonous snakes to dogs? It all depends on the condition of the snakes and the location of the bites. Also, on the amount of venom injected into the bites. When the writer was a veterinary technician in the Army during World War II, a K-9 dog was bitten by a water moccasin. The accident occurred near a swamp in Georgia, with the dog being bitten on the tip of the nose. Despite emergency first aid (which was difficult because of the location of the bite), the dog died. The snake was very potent and the bite was in a dangerous place.

Symptoms of snakebite

The symptoms of snakebite include swelling, one or two puncture marks, intense pain, weakness, shortness of breath, vomiting, poor vision and paralysis.

First Aid

If the snakebite occurs within a short distance of a veterinarian or medical doctor, get the dog to him right away. Otherwise treat as follows: Keep the dog quiet and still. Too much moving around tends to speed up the heart action and increase the movement of venom toward the heart. If the dog wasn't bitten on the nose, put an emergency muzzle on him.

Remember, the principles of snakebite treatment are constriction, incision and suction.

If the bite is on a leg, tie a belt, handkerchief or strip of cloth around the leg and above the snakebite and swelling. You do this to restrict the flow of venom. *It is not a tourniquet*, but a constriction band. Loosen it if the dog's leg gets cold. Remove for one minute in every fifteen minutes.

If you have a long-haired dog, quickly trim away the hair from around the snakebite. Next, sterilize a knife over flame. Now make ¼ inch cross-cuts or X's through each snakebite puncture. Don't be squeamish about this; your dog's life depends on it. Press the cuts to encourage the flow of blood.

Use suction to draw out the venom. *Do not use your mouth to suck out venom.* If you have a snakebite kit, use the suction apparatus in the kit. If not, make one as follows:

Get a small drinking glass, bottle, vial or canteen. Light up a twisted piece of paper and insert the flaming paper into the vessel. Quickly place the vessel (you can leave the paper inside; it will go out) onto the snakebite incisions, with the open end of the vessel into the bite. Leave the vessel there until it falls off by itself. Repeat this suction routine at least a dozen times.

There is an elementary physics principle behind this technique. Placing a strip of burning paper into a vessel causes the oxygen to be used up. This, in turn, reduces the atmospheric pressure in the vessel, creating a suction. But you've got to slap the vessel down on the incisions before fresh air surges into the vessel. Try this on yourself; it works.

If the swelling near the snakebite begins to spread more than 3 inches above the bite, move the constriction band above the new swelling. Make new incisions here and repeat the suction. Try to get the dog to drink water. Then get him to a veterinarian as quickly as possible.

ENCOUNTER WITH A SKUNK

The skunk is a docile, easygoing animal. He rarely hurries or gets out of your way. He'll let you or your dog approach quite close. And that's why dogs usually get sprayed. If your dog runs afoul of a skunk, you'll have no difficulty in diagnosing it!

Symptoms

First, a powerful and distinct odor. The dog's eyes may be inflamed and he may paw at them.

First Aid

You'll hear of all kinds of treatment to get rid of the skunk smell. Very few of them actually eliminate the strong odor. It just has to wear off.

However, to hasten the process, you can do something.

Wash the dog thoroughly with soap and water. Then wet him down with plenty of tomato juice. Rinse off the tomato juice with a 5% solution of ammonia. Avoid getting the ammonia solution in the dog's eyes. They're already smarting from the skunk spray. Put some eye ointment in the eyes.

PORCUPINE QUILLS

While porcupines are not too common, your dog may happen to meet one. If the dog gets too nosey, he may well end up with his nose and face stuck full of porcupine quills.

First Aid

Porcupine quills are painful to extract. If possible, get the dog to a veterinarian. If necessary, the veterinarian can administer an anesthesia and extract the quills while the dog is asleep.

But if you have to do the job, do it this way:

Have someone restrain the dog; he's going to resent having the quills extracted. If possible, try to get an emergency muzzle on the dog. It may be difficult, and you may not be able to get a good fit, but do the best you can.

Use a pair of pliers or strong tweezers to pull out the quills. Pull slowly and steadily—don't jerk them out. If you have no pliers or tweezers, two large coins—quarters or silver dollars—can be used as substitutes. Place a coin on either side of a quill, press together and slowly draw out the quill. Pulling with your fingers will not do, the quills can be slippery.

After all the quills are extracted, apply antiseptic powder to each quill hole.

BEE, HORNET AND WASP STINGS

Every once in awhile a dog gets stung by a bee, wasp or hornet. The sting can be very painful, particularly if on the end of the nose. Some dogs are allergic to insect stings and will have large swellings at the site of the sting.

Symptoms

A dog stung by a bee, wasp or hornet will suddenly yelp, start forward, then look wildly around for his assailant. He may race away, looking around and behind him. Usually the affected part will swell and itch.

First Aid

If possible, remove the sting with tweezers. Then apply a baking-soda paste. Cold packs (ice or wet cloths) will help to relieve the pain and swelling. Calomine lotion will ease the itching. If the swelling persists a few days, take the dog to the veterinarian. The dog may have an allergic reaction.

DOGFIGHTS

It's the rare dog that doesn't get into a dogfight sooner or later. The canine gladiators usually come out of the fight with various bites. Before you can render first aid, you'll have to break up the fight. Proceed with caution; too many people have been seriously injured trying to break up a dogfight without knowing how.

Remember that in the fury of the fight, both dogs will be snapping and slashing at each other. Neither of them will pay much attention to your shouts or commands. They're concentrating too hard on the battle and in not getting knocked down. You'll have to provide some strong distraction.

Don't ever try to pull your dog out of the fight by

reaching for his collar. That's a good way to lose a hand or some fingers. If you have help, try this technique: Each of you wait for an opening and grab a dog's tail. When you get hold of the tail, pull the dog toward you, quickly swinging him away from the other dog, and heave him as far as you can. If the dogs try to rush back into battle, block *your* dog and give him the command to sit. Have the other person try to chase off the other dog.

If one or both dogs happen to be tailless, you'll have to use another technique. Try banging on a bucket or flinging a chain at the dogs. If near your home, or someone will help you, get out a hose and squirt a stream of water on the fighters.

Dogs usually start a fight very quickly. It can be ended just as quickly, if you can divert the dogs from the battle. Remember, just don't reach for your dog's collar. Use as much distraction as possible, the louder the better. After the fight, you can attend to the dog's wounds. (See pages 219-220).

ATTACK BY A CAT

Cats can do considerable damage to dogs. Usually the dog gets bitten and clawed around the eyes, nose and face, since he more or less leads with these parts.

Before you can give the dog first aid, you'll have to get rid of the cat. When a cat and dog tangle, the cat may use one of several tactics. He may claw the dog in the nose and head for the nearest tree or high fence. Or he may strike at the dog, arch his back and wait for the dog to make the next move. Finally, he may jump up on the dog's back and dig in with his claws.

In the first two instances, you can frighten off the cat by making threatening gestures and loud noises. Given the chance, the cat will be glad to get away. In the latter case, you'll have to get the cat off the dog's back. You may take some of the dog's hair and skin with the cat, but there's no help for it. Grabbing the cat by the tail will not work; he'll simply double up on your arm and sink his claws and teeth into you. The best way to get him off is by using a hose on him. In the absence of a hose, take a stick, slide it under the cat and propel him off.

First Aid

Cat bites are more dangerous than dog bites, since they are small and tend to close up. When they do close up, there is always the possibility of abscesses or tetanus. So, if no artery or vein is involved, let the cat bites bleed freely.

Unless the cat bites and scratches are very jagged and require stitches, let the dog lick those he can reach. You can treat those he can't get at. Just to be on the safe side, apply an antiseptic to each bite and scratch. Do this by rolling absorbent cotton around toothpicks, dipping these small swabs into metaphen and inserting the swab into the cat bite. You'll have to restrain the dog when you do this. It's a good idea to have the veterinarian give the dog a tetanus injection.

HEAT EXHAUSTION

In the chapter on the dog's body and how it functions, you will recall that we mentioned the dog's difficulty in adjusting to excessive heat. Your dog can easily be overcome by heat if you leave him in a hot car with windows closed or in a poorly ventilated building.

Symptoms of heat exhaustion

Heavy and labored breathing, vomiting and prostration are symptoms of heat exhaustion.

First Aid

Remove the dog to a shady and well-ventilated spot. Next, wet him with cold water, particularly his head. When he regains consciousness, give him some diluted black coffee. Don't try to give him any liquids while he is unconscious. Use a small bottle and pour the coffee into a sac or pouch in the side of the dog's mouth. Consult your veterinarian for further treatment.

LAMENESS

Dogs often suffer from sore feet or lameness. Lameness may be caused by sprain, fracture, thorn or other foreign object, rheumatism, injury, etc.

Symptoms

The lame dog will limp, hop on three feet, hold up one foot and whimper. Pain, swelling and bleeding may be present.

First Aid

If necessary, restrain the dog. Gently examine the lame leg or foot. Look for thorns, glass, stones, etc. Check the leg for possible fractures. Remove any foreign objects from the pads or between the toes.

After you've removed any foreign objects, wash the part with mild soap and water. If the cuts are minor, let the dog lick them. If swelling is present, apply icepacks or cloths wet with cold water. Examine carefully for fractures of the toes. These will usually appear as swellings and the dog will be unable to move the broken toes. If there are fractures, or lameness persists, take the dog to the veterinarian.

FIRST AID KIT

A dog first aid kit around the house can be a very handy item in time of accident. It doesn't have to be an elaborate kit. But there are some basic medicines and material you should have. Later, you can add to the kit.

Here are some suggestions for the kit:

Tweezers for removing ticks, thorns, etc.
Roller bandage (1 and 2 inch)
Thermometer (rectal)
Scissors (blunt ends)
Nail clippers
Suction apparatus for snakebite
Hydrogen peroxide

Metaphen
Eye ointment
Burn ointment
Absorbent cotton
Adhesive tape
BFI powder
Insect powder
Sticks for cotton swabs
Mineral or sesame oil

18. Home Nursing of the Sick Dog

Intelligent home nursing and professional veterinary advice will speed your dog's recovery from a serious illness or injury. When the veterinarian discharges the dog from the hospital and commits him to your care, it will be up to you to give medicine, administer to the dog's daily needs and nurse him through his convalescence. The veterinarian expects you to see to it that the dog gets his medicine and he will also expect you to keep him informed of the dog's progress. Fortified with the information in this chapter, you will be able to do a competent job of nursing your dog back to health.

THE SICKROOM

The very sick or injured dog needs peace and quiet, away from household noises and boisterous play of children. If possible, put the dog in a room that is isolated, comfortable, well ventilated (but not drafty) and easily cleaned. You can facilitate the general cleaning problem by removing rugs and carpets and spreading several thicknesses of newspaper on the floor in the area the dog will occupy. Curtains or other materials should be hung over the windows to shield the dog from excessive or bright light. This is important in those diseases or conditions in which the dog has photophobia. (Distemper, for example.) Shredded newspaper, cedar shavings or a washable blanket can be used as bedding for the sick dog. Hang a thermometer near the dog so that you can keep an eye on the room temperature, which should be kept between 70° and 72°F. Place the thermometer so that it hangs a foot or so above the dog's head; the temperature at his level is the most important.

EQUIPMENT AND UTENSILS

You'll need a work area in the sickroom. A small table or bench will prove useful. On it you can keep medicines, food and water pans, grooming equipment and so forth. Keep labels on all medicines and if there are small children in the house, either lock the sickroom door or put the medicines in a box with a lock. Wash and sterilize all pans, dishes and spoons after each use. Use a detergent and germicide and rinse in boiling water. Be sure to wash your hands before and after handling the sick dog.

PROGRESS CHART

Keep a chart or notebook on the dog's progress. It will be especially useful when you report to the veterinarian over the telephone. Make daily entries on the chart of the dog's temperature, dosages of medicine, symptoms and other pertinent information that will be useful to the veterinarian.

Observing the dog's general condition

Make a habit of noticing the dog's general condition. Here are some features to look for:

Breathing: Is the dog's breathing rapid? Slow? Strained? Gasping? Irregular?

Bowel movements: How are the dog's bowel movements? Are they loose? Diarrhea? Bloody? Is he constipated?

Eyes: Are the eyes inflamed? Is there a discharge? Are they weeping? Dull? Bright? Are the eyes affected by light?

Muscular control: Is the dog very weak? Can he turn over? Is he paralyzed? Can he move his legs?

Appetite: How is the dog's appetite? Is it poor? Fair? Good? Fussy? Or does he have no appetite?

Urinary system: Can the dog empty his bladder? How is the urine? Is it colorless? Amber? Dark? Bloody? Does he urinate frequently or sparsely?

Add to these any other symptoms which you notice and that will be of value to the veterinarian in determining the dog's progress.

DAILY TEMPERATURE

The dog's daily temperature is an important diagnostic aid and indicator of progress. Remember that the dog's temperature will fluctuate during the day. It is usually low in the morning and high in the late afternoon and early evening. Therefore, take a temperature reading twice daily; in the morning and later afternoon or early evening. (See Chapter 5)

GIVING THE DOG HIS MEDICINE

Depending on how you go about it, medicating the dog can be an easy chore or a struggle. Dogs are very much like people when it comes to taking medicine. They just don't like it. Some dogs will clamp their mouths shut and struggle fiercely, others will simply regurgitate the medicine if you are inept. The result in both cases is that the dog gets less than the prescribed dosage or none at all. But with a little patience and skill, you can give the dog his medicine with a minimum of wear and tear on your nerves and very little struggle on the part of the dog.

Until you've acquired some skill in administering the medicine, it's best to have someone help you. The assistant can restrain the dog while you give the medicine. When you take the dog to the veterinarian, he usually has you or an assistant hold the dog while he examines or treats the dog. Now bear in mind that the veterinarian is a skilled man when it comes to handling animals. Yet he rarely tries to wrestle with a dog and at the same time give medicine. So there is no reason why you should try to overpower the dog and try to medicate him at the same time. The idea is to get the medicine into the dog, not prove that you are the boss.

When you are working with a very sick or paralyzed dog, the job is not too difficult. The dog will be too weak to put up a struggle. Your main problem here will be to get the dog's mouth open. But this can be done.

Capsules, pills and tablets

The simplest way to give capsules, pills or tablets is to put them into the dog's food or a specially prepared meatball. Since he ordinarily gulps or bolts his food, the medicine will go down easily. Once in awhile, a dog is not taken in by this subterfuge. He detects the medicine in the food and will eat around it. If you have such a dog or one that refuses to eat at all, you will have to put the capsule, pill or tablet directly into his mouth.

Here is the way to give the dog solid medicine:

1. Open his mouth by grasping his upper jaw with your left hand. Push his upper lips down over his teeth and hold them there with your fingers. If he tries to bite, he'll bite his lips.

2. Tilt his head upward. This action will cause his lower jaw to open.

3. Next, place the capsule, pill or tablet well back into his mouth at the base of the tongue with the fingers of your right hand. Hold down his lower jaw as you do so. If you are left-handed, reverse the procedure.

4. When you have placed the medicine, close the dog's mouth and hold it shut with your fingers.

5. Stroke or massage his throat until he swallows. It's important to wait for him to swallow, otherwise he'll spit out the medicine when you release his mouth.

Liquid medicines

Administering liquid medicines is not as difficult as it may seem. A few "tricks of the trade" will help you to give the dog liquids without spilling them. It's best to have someone restrain the dog until you have some experience.

First, pour the medicine into a small bottle or syringe. Make a pouch in the side of the dog's mouth by pulling out the fleshy lower jaw skin or jowels. Now slowly pour the liquid into the pouch, close the pouch and let the dog swallow. If you pour slowly, the dog will usually swallow as the medicine is being poured into the pouch.

CLEANING THE SICK DOG

The very sick or paralyzed dog will be unable to move away from his bed to empty his bowels or bladder. In this situation, he will soil the bed and himself.

Your cleaning task will be easier if you put a washable blanket or cloth under the very sick or paralyzed dog. While cedar shavings and shredded newspaper make good bedding for the ambulatory dog, they complicate the cleaning of the bedridden dog. You can, if you wish, put a diaper on the very sick or paralyzed dog. This may sound ridiculous, but it will save you some work.

After you've cleaned the dog's bed, turn your attention to the dog. Wash off any soiled spots with mild soap and warm water. If the hair is matted, soften it and comb with care. The hair around the hindquarters may be matted and snarled with dried feces. Trim this away, if you can't comb it out. Wash the dog's eyes, nose and ears with warm water. Apply eye ointment when needed. If the dog vomits, wipe his mouth with a mild table-salt and water solution. A gentle brushing all over will help the sick dog spiritually, as well as physically.

The sick dog should be turned over three or four times a day. By turning him over, you will help eliminate strain or discomfort from lying too long in one position. It will also help prevent bedsores.

GIVING THE DOG AN ENEMA

Dogs unable to stand up very often become constipated. If ordinary laxatives fail or if the veterinarian has not advised giving laxatives, you will have to give the dog an enema when he is constipated.

Bedridden dogs usually do not present much of a problem as far as giving an enema is concerned. But the dog that is sick, yet able to move around, may put up a struggle. Don't tussle with him; have someone restrain the dog.

The enema is best administrered in the bathtub, since the mess can be flushed away and the tub washed and sterilized. Use a regular quart-size enema bag with a small nozzle for small dogs and a larger nozzle for big dogs. A small syringe can be used to give an enema to toy or miniature dogs. The enema solution can be ordinary soap and warm water. It should be heated to body temperature (101° to 102°F.).

Steps in giving the dog an enema

1. Fill the enema bag with the soap and warm water solution.
2. Dip the nozzle in Vaseline or mineral oil. Make sure that you don't plug the hole in the nozzle.

3. Open the clamp on the tube to clear out air.

4. Close the clamp and gently insert the nozzle about three inches into the rectum.

5. Hold or hang the enema bag about a foot higher than the dog's body.

6. Open the clamp and allow the solution to flow slowly into the rectum. But keep the pressure low. You can regulate the pressure by lifting or lowering the enema bag. Lift it and the pressure will increase; lower it and the pressure will decrease.

7. When the solution is in the dog's rectum, close the clamp and let the dog hold the solution for a minute or two.

8. Quickly remove the nozzle from the rectum and the dog will expel the enema solution and feces.

FEEDING THE SICK DOG

The dog will need a daily nourishing ration to help him recover from a serious illness. If the veterinarian has placed the dog on a special diet, see that nothing else is fed. A dog recuperating from an injury can usually be given his regular ration.

If the dog has difficulty in keeping his food down, eliminate solid food and substitute broths or beef bouillon. Give them to the dog in small quantities three or four times a day. When you've brought the vomiting under control for 24 hours, gradually introduce solid foods in small quantities. Chopped meat, Pablum or Cream of Wheat will be bland enough to stay down in most cases. Keep increasing the solid food over a three-day period until the dog can eat without vomiting.

Should diarrhea develop, cut out the regular diet and switch to boiled milk, cottage cheese, boiled rice, macaroni or Pablum. A commercially prepared diarrhea medicine, such as Peptobismol, will help in severe cases of diarrhea.

Many seriously ill dogs refuse to eat or just pick at the food. You'll have to force-feed your dog if he refuses to eat. Try tempting him with a variety of food, if he is not on a restricted diet. Beef liver, heart or kidney is appetizing and the more aromatic you make the food, the more likely the dog will be to eat it. Experiment with the food, it's worth the effort. Tomato juice, egg yolks, even brandy, have all been used with success in getting nourishment into the dog that refuses to eat.

The very weak dog may have to be hand-fed. Feed broths by way of a bottle and pouring into a pouch in the side of the mouth. Other soft foods can be fed by putting them back on the tongue (in very small quantities) and stroking the dog's throat to make him swallow. In general, do everything you can to get the dog to eat. The speed of his recovery—perhaps his life—will depend on nourishment.

DRESSINGS AND BANDAGES

Don't fool around with dressings or bandages unless the veterinarian asks you to or they come off. In most cases, the veterinarian will attend to the dressings and bandages. He may ask you to put a protective device on the dog to prevent the dog from tearing off bandages or biting sores. This device is known as an *Elizabethan collar*.

The Elizabethan collar is simple to make. Cut a semi-circle out of heavy cardboard, with the inner or smaller circumference fitted snugly to the dog's neck. Make the outer circumference wide enough so that when the collar is in place, the outer arc extends beyond the dog's nose-tip. This will prevent him from reaching wounds or sores. Punch holes in the straight sides of the collar, insert laces, and lace the collar around the dog's neck, just below the jawline. When the collar is in place, it will resemble a rat guard on a ship's dock line.

To sum up: nursing your dog through a serious illness or injury requires time and devotion. But just think how devoted the dog is to you. He's willing to lay down his life to save yours. You ought to be willing to help save his.

Part Six

REPRODUCTION

19. Mating and Prenatal Care

Mating, while a perfectly natural action, is not always as simple as you would think. Inexperienced dogs, most often the male, have difficulty in consummating the sexual act. True, most males readily mount a female and go through the motions of the sexual act, but they fail to penetrate the female. On the other hand, nervous bitches may make it difficult for the male to copulate. They may refuse to stand for the male or they snap at him, thus not only making things difficult, but discouraging him. These are some of the complications of mating.

In Chapter 11, we gave a brief summary of the reproductive process, including the main parts of the male and female reproductive systems. Before we discuss the actual mating process, some information on the sexual behavior of the male and female is in order.

THE MALE

The male is more or less sexually active all year round. His interest in sex starts early in puppyhood. Pups as young as three months old show sexual interest. They will mount your leg or the backs of their litter mates. These sexual actions on the part of the male pup don't necessarily mean that he's oversexed or showing abnormal behavior. These may come later on, when he's mature and cannot get rid of his sexual energy. Early mounting and interest in sex are instinctive reactions. Nature is preparing the pup for his future role of procreator.

As the pup matures he will show more and more sexual interest. The desire to mate increases with age. The awkward pup will show more interest in other dogs, both male and female. He'll carefully examine their genitals and mount them, going through the motions of the sexual act. Most of the time this mounting and simulating the sexual act is nothing more than a "dry run." The young male is usually too inexperienced to actually copulate. Believe it or not, he will probably need some help to achieve a complete mating.

Unless the male is kept under control, his increasing interest in sex can get him into trouble. Sex and food are two topics guaranteed to start a dogfight. Nowadays, most dogs are well fed and don't often get into a fight over food. Not so with sex. Just let a female in heat go by and she will quickly have a large following of males, ranging from pups to grizzled veterans. The competition for her favors becomes fierce and fights break out. Usually the best fighter does all of the mating, or at least gets the first chance.

This sexual competition among males is another one of Nature's plans to perpetuate a strong species. The weak and ineffectual males are weeded out in the fights. Only the strong get a chance to mate in the wild dog packs; the weak ones have to be content with the role of onlooker.

But the survival of the fittest is not an issue among domestic dogs. You are not interested in having your male eliminated. Nor do you want him to be injured. And he can get injured if he tangles with huskier and more sagacious dogs while competing for a female. All of this is a good reason why you should keep your dog at home.

The average mature male getting a balanced diet and adequate exercise is capable of mating up to the time he is 10 to 12 years old. He should not be mated under 1 year of age nor over 10 years. The American Kennel Club will not accept puppies for registration when the sire is under 7 months of age or over 12 years. The over-1-year and under-10-year regime is best to follow.

Cryptorchidism

Cryptorchidism among dogs is not uncommon. It is a condition in which both testicles have not descended from the body into the scrotum. Cryptorchids are sterile. They cannot breed since the undescended testicles are either atrophied or the spermatozoa are killed or rendered immobile by the body heat.

Monorchidism

Occasionally, you will see a dog that has only one descended testicle. Monorchids are not sterile. They can mate and produce offspring just as well as the dog with two testicles. But the condition is a fault. Geneticists beleive that monorchidism is hereditary; consequently, if you have a male with one testicle, your chances of mating him to a purebred bitch are nil. There is too good a chance that a portion of any litter sired by a monorchid will inherit the fault.

THE FEMALE

The female or bitch, as we stated in Chapter 11, comes into heat twice a year. Like the young male pup, the female will show sexual interest at an early age. She will indulge in juvenile sex play, perhaps even mounting her litter mates or examining the genitals of both males and females. Later, as she matures, she will grow out of this juvenile sexual behavior and settle down to a rhythmic pattern of coming into heat twice a year. She will restrict her sexual interest to the heat periods.

You will recall that the bitch's heat period is divided into phases. During the first phase, you will notice that her vulva or external genitals are swollen. The bitch will pay attention to this swelling by constantly licking the parts. She may also be slightly nervous or uneasy. Her appetite will vary from day to day; in fact, as her heat cycle increases, she may skip a meal or two. Males will be interested in the bitch during the first phase, but she will not encourage them. Most likely she'll do the opposite; discourage them by snapping or growling at them.

There is no need to be concerned that the bitch might be hurt by males when she acts like this. No matter how fiercely she resists the advances of eager males, they will not retaliate. No male will ever attack or bite a female— in or out of heat—unless he is berserk or rabid. This is the law of the pack and no male in his right mind ever violates it.

At the end of the first week after the vulva have become swollen, the second phase starts. This is characterized by a discharge. The discharge is bright red at first, later changing to a pinkish fluid (or colorless fluid) five to nine days after the discharge starts. With rare exceptions, the bitch will attend to the matter of cleaning herself and her bed. But there is always the possibility that she will stain rugs, carpets and furniture. It's best to keep her in a place that is easily cleaned during her heat period, especially during the discharge phase. There are special sanibelts for bitches, available in pet stores, but these irk the dog and are more bother than they are worth.

Toward the end of the second phase, the bitch becomes very coy and playful. She will be very solicitous to all males. But she is still not ready to stand and be mated. There is some risk though; some overzealous and impatient male may corner and mount her. And since conception may take place, keep her confined if you don't want her mated or are planning to mate her with a particular dog.

The discharge ceases at the beginning of the third phase. The bitch is now reading for mating, usually between the 9th and 14th day from the onset of the heat period. Conception has its best chance between the 11th and 14th day, with the 12th and 13th days considered as the optimum. During the third phase, the bitch will encourage all males and will stand to be mated, thrusting her tail aside. Here, again, you will have to keep a close watch on her if you don't want her to mate or wish to avoid a mismating. The urge to mate will be very strong at this time and the bitch will make every effort to get out.

A bitch can be very troublesome when she's ready to mate. Taking her for walks on a leash can be hazardous. You'll have to be constantly on the lookout for males. They will not be far away; "word" get around very quickly that there's a bitch in heat in the neighborhood! Despite your efforts, a male can be on top of the bitch before you know it. And 63 days later, you'll be the owner of some puppies.

Young bitches should not be mated before their second heat period; larger breeds should be allowed to reach the third heat period. Saint Bernards and Irish Wolfhounds are examples of large breeds that should be permitted to attain maximum growth before being mated. These and other very large breeds are slow to mature. The American Kennel Club will not accept puppies for registration from a bitch that is under 8 months or over 12 years of age. But even though a bitch may be capable of breeding up to her 12th year, it's best to stop breeding her when she's 7 or 8 years old.

Spaying

If you decide you do not want to mate your bitch, you can have her spayed. Spaying is an operation in which the bitch's ovaries are removed. This eliminates the heat periods and the possibility of conception. In the hands of a competent veterinarian, the operation is a simple one.

Spaying is a form of birth control among dogs. When you consider the large number of stray and unwanted dogs in this country, you'll agree that some form of control is necessary. There have been some arguments advanced against spaying; some of them on moral principles, some on physical grounds. They range from the argument that spaying interferes with Nature to the argument that spaying makes a dog fat and lazy.

Concerning the argument that spaying interferes with Nature, we'll leave that to the philosophers and moralists. As for spaying making a dog fat and lazy, there just isn't enough evidence to support this argument. Overfeeding and lack of exercise will make both spayed and unspayed bitches fat and lazy.

Spaying has some decided advantages. If the operation is performed correctly, there will be no more heat periods, no more males hanging around the yard and no litters of unwanted puppies. In most communities, a license for a spayed bitch costs less than for an unspayed bitch. Also, in the case of those breeds or individuals that tend to be nervous or snappy, spaying a bitch when she is six months old often has the effect of curbing these tendencies. Finally, it is believed that spayed bitches have fewer breast tumors than unspayed bitches.

There are some disadvantages to spaying. The main

one is that you can't breed your bitch if you should change your mind. This is something to think about before you rush your bitch to the veterinarian and ask him to spay her. Since a dog's life is comparatively short —10 to 12 years—you might possibly want to have a puppy from your bitch to raise after she goes. Also, a spayed bitch cannot be shown.

Another disadvantage to spaying is that some bitches develop a urinary incontinence. It doesn't happen to every bitch. As some spayed bitches grow older, they lose control of their bladder and urinate frequently. Many of these cases, however, have been helped by hormones.

PLANNING THE MATING

You will be wise to plan the mating of your dog well in advance. Remember the age factor: mate a male after he is one year old and the bitch on her second or third heat.

If you own a bitch, it will be up to you to start negotiations for mating. This means you will have to survey the field, make arrangements to bring your bitch to the male when she comes into heat, and take her home again. For intelligent planning, you will have to keep a record of the bitch's heat periods. Guesswork will only lead to frustration.

Breed your purebred bitch to a purebred male or stud. A suitable male in the neighborhood will simplify matters. But make sure the male is in good health and not a monorchid. Also, try to pick a male that is somewhat like your bitch in size and type.

Matings are usually done at the home of the stud. There are some good reasons for this requirement. Most males perform much better when on their own home grounds. And if the male is being used for other matings, travel will sometimes affect his potency or ardor.

Perhaps you may want to breed your bitch to one of the professional studs of the breed. If you do, your arrangements will be more formal. The professional studs are usually advertised in the dog magazines, such as Dog World, Popular Dogs and Dog News. Some of these studs are for restricted use. When they are, the advertisements will specify that the stud is available to "approved bitches only." Now, this is not a snob motive. Many of these professional studs have produced outstanding progeny. Their owners naturally want to continue this policy. They have to; their livelihood depends on quality puppies.

The usual procedure when you answer one of these ads offering the services of a professional stud is to send a copy of your bitch's pedigree. You may also have to include a photograph of the bitch, since the breeder may want to see what she looks like. If your bitch measures up to the breeder's standards, she will probably be accepted for mating.

It's your responsibility to get the bitch to the professional stud and home again. No matter if the stud lives in your state or clear across the country, you will have to ship your bitch. You can ship the bitch by rail or plane. But query the breeder and the commercial carrier before shipping the dog. Both usually have special requirements, especially as to health and rabies certificates. A note of caution: shipping your bitch a long distance can be both costly and hard on the dog. So make sure that she is in the right stage of heat and will be ready to mate upon arrival. Sending her too soon will result in a boarding bill from the breeder. Likewise, don't send her when she's on the way out of heat.

Professional breeders have certain requirements and practices insofar as mating and fees are concerned. Fees range up to $500 or more, depending on the stud and his record. Or, instead of a fee, the breeder may ask for the best pup in the litter resulting from the mating. The "pick of the litter" pup is usually claimed when he is 6 to 8 weeks old.

Regardless of whether you mate your bitch to a neighbor's male or send her off to a professional stud, you should have a written agreement. Very few professional breeders will accept your bitch without one. And the terms of the mating will be set down in black-and-white, including the method of payment. The agreement will also state that your bitch is entitled to a return service, if the first mating fails to result in conception. But that's all the return trips or rain checks she will get. If she doesn't conceive after the second mating (upon her next heat period), there's something wrong with the bitch, or else you are making an error as to her heat period. You can assume that the stud is potent; professional studs are proven sires and are examined for potency.

You will still have to pay the stud fee even though the bitch fails to conceive after two matings. After all, the breeder can't guarantee conception; just two matings. He takes a gamble if he asks for a pup from the litter and no litter is forthcoming. Technically, if only one pup is born, the breeder who has specified that he wants a pup can claim the lone pup.

Make sure that you understand all of the terms of the mating agreement. Ask questions. You'll find the dog breeders are congenial people and willing to help you out.

If you own a male dog and want to mate him, you'll have to shop around for a bitch. Pass the word along to friends and neighbors or put an ad in the classified section of your local newspaper. When you get a response, work out the arrangements and put them in writing.

THE MATING

If you use the services of a professional stud, then you will not have anything to do with the mating. The breeder will see to it that your bitch is mated and you can rely on him. All you have to do is deliver and pick up the bitch and pay the fee when due. But if you are using a local male, then you may have to help with the mating, especially if the male is inexperienced. The chances are the owner of the local male doesn't know much about mating the dog. You both will have to learn the facts of a dog's life.

Don't feed the bitch on the day she is going to be mated. Ask the owner of the male to withhold food from his dog. A full stomach is not conducive to sexual activity. This is true of other animals besides the dog. Bring the bitch to the place selected for the mating; a cellar, shed or garage will do, just so long as the dogs can have reasonable privacy (despite the fact dogs will copulate in public on the street!).

Before introducing the bitch to the male, take the precaution to put an emergency muzzle on her. This is to prevent her turning on the male and snapping at him. She can easily ruin his ardor by such tactics. It's quite possible that you miscalculated as to her readiness to stand for mating. When the muzzle is on the bitch, let the male come over and get acquainted. He'll soon show signs of interest and will sniff her genitals, wag his tail and get aroused. Watch the bitch. If she shows signs of nervousness or irritability, talk to her and reassure her. If she is ready to mate, she'll whisk her tail aside and stand still. If she doesn't, then you made a mistake.

When the bitch shows her willingness to stand, let the male mount her. Let him do it his way at first. That is, providing he is not trying to mount the wrong end. And this frequently happens with an inexperienced male. If he's confused as to direction, have his owner lead him around to the right end. Allow him to make another attempt. But if he gets too excited and doesn't seem to be getting anywhere, have his owner take him outside.

There may be a physical disparity that is holding up the mating. For instance, the bitch may be too short or too tall. If this is true, you'll have to do something about it. And as hilarious as it may sound, you'll have to prop up the bitch if she is too short or bolster up the male if *he* is too short. In the case of the bitch, you can hold her rear end up to the male. As for the short male, fold a blanket or coat and place it under his hind legs.

When the male seems to be doing all the right things, but still fails to penetrate the bitch, he will have to be guided. The best method is to take hold of the bitch with both hands under the abdomen, move her rear end to the right or left or up and down to facilitate entry by the male. In cattle breeding, the handlers often take hold of the bull's penis and guide it into the cow's vagina. But size is a factor in cattle breeding and a similar technique is not always feasible with dogs. You will have to be patient and keep helping the male. But don't make a marathon out of it. If the male fails to penetrate the bitch after an hour or two, give him a break. When you do separate the dogs, don't give them any water. And after three or four hours of failure, call it off and bring the bitch back the next day.

Upon penetrating the bitch, the male will be "locked

in." What happens is that the bulbous end of the male's penis becomes greatly enlarged. At the opening of the bitch's vagina there is a sphincter muscle. As the male's penis pushes past this sphincter and enlarges inside, the sphincter muscles traps the penis. The male will ejaculate. But he cannot withdraw his penis until the swelling has subsided. This takes some time. Consequently, the male and female are locked together. Doubtless, you've seen two dogs locked together—maybe rear to rear—on the street. This is Nature's way of making sure that fertilization takes place.

There is nothing you can do but wait until the dog's unlock themselves. Under no circumstances should you try to hasten the process. You can seriously injure one or both dogs. While being locked together may seem an abnormal position for the dogs, it doesn't hurt them. All they have to do is think of something else to speed up the unlocking process.

The bitch may tire of the male's weight on her back and she will try to lie down. Don't allow this. Most males will swing their right or left leg over the bitch's back and thus have two feet on the same side of the bitch and on the ground. If the male doesn't do this, have his owner do it. Keep the emergency muzzle on the bitch until the dogs are unlocked. Don't let her jerk away or move unnecessarily.

Occasionally, two locked dogs get twisted around so that they are rear-to-rear. This position looks very ludicrous. But it can be painful and injurious to the dogs, especially if one dog starts dragging the other. If mated dogs do get into the end-to-end position, see that they do not struggle and injure each other.

Although the male mated with your bitch the first day you brought them together, you will be wise to bring her back the next day. This is just to "make sure." If you mated her at the correct stage of heat (9th to 14th day), she will still be receptive to the male. After the final mating, keep her confined. She will still encourage males and it is possible for her to mate again and have a litter sired by more than one male. After the 20th or 21st day from onset of heat, the bitch will no longer be willing to mate.

PRENATAL CARE

Naturally, your aim is to have the bitch produce healthy and vigorous pups. The prenatal care that you give her will determine whether she does or not. For the next 63 days, you should see to it that the bitch has every opportunity to bring forth a healthy litter.

Before we go into the prenatal care of the bitch, we should mention false pregnancy or pseudocyesis. This is a condition in which a bitch shows many symptoms of being pregnant, yet she is not pregnant. She may have milk in the breasts, gain weight, have a desire to make a nest and other symptoms of the pregnant bitch, but it's a false alarm. False pregnancy is common in high-strung or nervous bitches. A bitch need not be mated to have a false pregnancy. The symptoms usually appear 50 to 70 days after the bitch has gone out of heat and may persist for as long as several months. The treatment consists of giving the dog sedatives or tranquilizers and catering to her mistaken maternal desires. Give her an old shoe or toy to mother during her false pregnancy. Hormone injections sometimes help alleviate the condition; the only sure way to prevent a recurrence is to have the bitch spayed.

Now, assuming that you have had the bitch checked for pregnancy, we can return to her prenatal care. The bitch should be in the best health possible, and that means free of skin diseases, internal and external parasites. Remember that ascarids and hookworms can be passed to the pups while they are still in the uterus. If the bitch wasn't wormed before mating, you can worm her up to the beginning of the third week of pregnancy. If you don't do it by then, postpone it until after she whelps.

The pregnant bitch's diet is very important. Feed her a high-quality dog meal supplemented with fresh meat. Vitamins and minerals are necessary for the bitch and pups. If you give her a vitamin supplement, select one that is high in calcium. Extra calcium will help prevent a condition known as eclampsia after the bitch whelps.

(See Chapter 20) See that the bitch has access to plenty of fresh water.

The pregnant bitch can have moderate exercise. Take her out only on the leash and avoid strenuous romps, games or roughhousing. While you don't have to keep the bitch confined to the house during her pregnancy, you do have to use good judgment and see that she isn't injured. Injuries can result in miscarriages, abortions and stillborn pups.

As her pregnancy progresses, the bitch will gain weight and her appetite will increase. Toward the end of the 5th week, her breasts will become larger and firmer. Some bitches have enlarged breasts with swelling and caking over the nipples. Milk may also leak out. You can relieve the swelling and caking by squeezing out some milk in the morning and evening, and applying baby oil to the nipples.

The bitch may be constipated. This is common during the last week of pregnancy. Use baby suppositories to relieve her. Don't use laxatives or mineral oil!

Near the end of pregnancy, about the 7th or 8th week, you can feed the bitch three times a day. But don't over-feed her. Watch her weight. You can judge her weight by observing the flesh on her ribs, back and shoulders. This is where she will "bulge."

At the end of the 8th week, you can make some preliminary preparations for the whelping. Clean the bitch's breasts with mild soap and warm water, then soften them with baby oil. If you have a long-haired dog, trim the hair around the rectum and vulva. Also, clip hair around the breasts and teats.

The average period of gestation in the dog is 63 days. But it may vary a few days either way. During the last week of pregnancy, the bitch will undergo a change in behavior. She'll lie around more, her appetite may be poor and she'll show signs of uneasiness. These are all indications that the pups are not going to be carried much longer.

It's a good idea to fix up a whelping box for the bitch during the last week of pregnancy. The whelping box should be square and large enough for the bitch to turn around. It should have sides at least 8 inches high, be draft-free and easily cleaned. If your bitch is going to whelp in her doghouse—and this isn't advisable in the winter—make sure that she has plenty of clean litter. Put an 8-inch board across the doorway of the house to keep the pups from falling out. You can put tarpaper down on the doghouse floor and then cover it with a thick layer of shredded newspapers or cedar shavings.

You can also start setting up your equipment. Clean towels, blunt-end scissors, extra newspapers, absorbent cotton, Vaseline, hot-water bottle, thermometer, baby bottle and nipple, eyedropper, these are things you may need during whelping.

After you're all prepared and the bitch is using the whelping box to sleep in, you and she can settle down to waiting for the big event.

20. Whelping and Care of the Newborn Pups

Thousands of dogs give birth to litters of puppies every year with little or no difficulty. Occasionally, there are difficult deliveries, stillborn pups and Caesarian sections. With a little knowledge of the whelping process and possible difficulties, you will be in a better position to handle an emergency.

Puppies are usually born between the 61st and 65th day after conception, with the average time being 63 days. If your bitch goes beyond the 65th day without any signs of labor, consult your veterinarian.

LABOR AND WHELPING

Be on the alert for signs of labor during the last week of pregnancy. While 63 days is the average, the bitch can whelp sooner or later. A day or so before she is due, the bitch's vulva will become enlarged. She will be uneasy and will spend a lot of time making a nest in the whelping box (if she's taken a fancy to it). Keep an eye on her but let her alone. She'll probably drink more water than usual and urinate more frequently during the last few days of her pregnancy. If she is constipated, *do not give her any laxatives*. Add more bulk to her diet, such as leafy vegetables.

About 24 hours before whelping, the bitch's temperature will drop a degree or two. If you want to use this as a sign of approaching parturition, start taking her temperature twice a day during the last week. The bitch's appetite will fall off and she will probably refuse food anywhere from 24 to 12 hours before whelping. Don't try to make her eat; she knows what she's about and what's good for her. You can expect her to be very uneasy, fidgety; possibly shivering and trembling. A discharge from the vulva will herald the event.

When all is normal, you can expect the first pup within 2 hours after the above-mentioned symptoms. Now, as to the important question: what should you do while the bitch is whelping? Our advice is for you to do nothing—unless the bitch is in difficulty or fails to perform certain functions, which we'll mention. Too much attention and fussing will lead to confusion, possibly injury to the pups. Some nervous bitches have been known to kill or hide their pups because of too much human intervention. But while too much attention is not advised, you should not ignore or forget the bitch. Stay with her during the whelping and be ready to lend a hand if she needs it. Your presence will help reassure the bitch who may be whelping for the first time.

The bitch's restlessness will build up as the moment nears and her anxiety increases. Then the first labor contractions start. These will be involuntary and very noticeable. During the contractions, the bitch will pant, move around in the whelping box or even leave the box to go get a drink of water. As the contractions become more frequent, the bitch will pant harder between contractions. Let her alone; this is normal.

The first pup should be born within 2 hours after the contractions speed up. If the first pup doesn't emerge within 2 hours, give the bitch another hour of labor, and then if no pup appears, call the veterinarian.

In a normal delivery, a pup emerges headfirst. When a pup comes out feetfirst, it is a breech delivery. (Breech deliveries are not at all uncommon.) Each pup is born encased in a transparent sac or membrane. This sac or membrane will be the first thing you see as the pup is expelled. It will be bulgy and transparent and you will see the pup inside. The sac will be attached by a cord to the placenta, which should come out after the pup. The placenta or afterbirth is the means by which the fetus is nourished within the uterus.

If the sac breaks on the way out, quickly bring the pup to the bitch's attention, if she hasn't already gone to work on it. Ordinarily, the bitch will break the sac with her teeth and gnaw off the navel cord to within one inch of the pup's navel. If the bitch doesn't break the sac or chew off the navel cord, you will have to take care of these. Pick up the sac with the pup inside (use a clean cloth) and break the sac near the pup's head. Do it by gently stretching the membrane or hooking a finger into it and carefully pulling it apart.

Next, put the pup down where the bitch can lick and clean it. It is imperative that the pup be cleaned. When the sac is broken, the pup should gasp for air. Breathing may be impeded because of mucus in the pup's nose, throat or lungs. This mucus must be removed. If the bitch will not clean the pup or it doesn't gasp for air, you will have to take over.

Quickly wipe any excess mucus from the pup's mouth. Open the pup's mouth, take a medicine dropper and suck out any mucus. Rub the pup vigorously with a clean, dry cloth, both with and against the lie of the hair. The rubbing will help to stimulate circulation.

If, after these administrations, the pup still doesn't gasp for air, you'll have to use more drastic measures. Wrap the pup in a clean cloth, hold it cupped in your two hands, with the head toward your fingers, and swing the pup downward in an arc in front of you. Stop the swing suddenly, but hold on to the pup. The centrifugal force plus the sudden stop usually clears out the mucus.

Another emergency measure to get the pup breathing is to use a rubber tube and syringe to withdraw the mucus. Insert the tube well into the pup's mouth and squeeze the syringe to aspirate the mucus. Keep working on the pup and don't let it get chilled. A hot water bottle wrapped in a cloth will provide heat.

Artificial respiration is not always practical. But you can insert the rubber tube in the pup's mouth (take off the syringe) and try forcing your own breath down. When you try this, proceed as follows: breathe air into the tube, stop, then press gently on the pup's ribs in the region of the lungs. Be careful, you can easily break the pup's rib cage. Keep working to make the pup breathe; don't give up too quickly.

The placenta

New dog owners watching their bitch whelp for the first time are often alarmed or disgusted when the bitch eats the placenta or afterbirth. Eating the placenta is neither harmful nor abnormal. Various theories have been advanced as to why the bitch (or any animal) eats the placenta. Among them are that the bitch eats the placenta to clean up any evidence of whelping (this is important in the wild state where predatory animals may scent the birth and attack the bitch and pups); and that the bitch eats the placenta to provide temporary nourishment, since she cannot leave the pups to forage for food. Regardless of the motive, your bitch may eat the placenta.

You should keep track of the placenta and the number of placentas should correspond with the number of pups born. Sometimes a placenta is retained. This happens when the cord between the placenta and fetal sac breaks, leaving the placenta inside the bitch. If the bitch doesn't expel the placenta, you can gently pull it out. Take a clean cloth and carefully withdraw the placenta (the broken cord may be hanging out of the vulva and you can take hold of this). A retained placenta will interfere with the birth of the next pup and if left inside will decompose.

As labor continues

Subsequent pups may come rapidly or there may be 2 hours between each pup. Remain with the bitch. If she labors for more than 3 hours between pups, she may be in trouble. If she doesn't deliver the next pup after 3 hours (or if there are more than 3 hours between each pup) call the veterinarian. He'll want some information; to wit, when the first pup was born, how was it born (normal or breech delivery), how long the bitch labored with the first pup, how long the bitch has been laboring with the difficult pup, etc.

SOME OBSTETRIC DIFFICULTIES

There are various reasons why a bitch may have a difficult time in whelping. Some are due to physical conditions of the bitch herself, such as a weak pelvis, disease, etc. Others may be due to the conformation of the pups, such as a large head, large body—or two pups may arrive in the birth channel at the same time. Breech deliveries often cause difficulty, too.

Breech delivery

As we stated before, the breech pup comes feetfirst. Usually the head of a breech pup is large and the bitch has trouble in expelling the pup. You may have to help her. As she strains to deliver the pup, grasp the pup's feet and part of the body, if possible, with a clean cloth. Gently pull the pup and *only when the bitch strains*. Be careful, you can easily injure the pup. If you are not getting anywhere, don't delay; call the veternarian.

Caesarian section

A Caesarian section is usually performed by cutting through the abdominal wall into the uterus and removing the pups through the opening. The technique was so-named because Julius Caesar was supposed to have been delivered in this manner.

Caesarian sections are usually necessary when the pups are too large to be delivered in the normal way. It's possible to tell before birth whether the pups are too large and a Caesarian section can be planned. Many times the operation is done after a bitch in labor gets into difficulty. After straining for hours, the uterine muscle simply loses its power. If your bitch labors for more than 6 hours without any results, get her to the veterinarian as soon as possible.

THE NEWBORN PUPS

When all of the pups are born, make sure that each one has a chance to nurse. Remember that newborn pups need the colostrum-milk to get immunity against disease. Place each pup on a teat, if they haven't already found one. The bitch may become so absorbed in licking a pup or herself, that she may forget to nudge the pups toward the teats.

The navel cords

Under normal conditions, the bitch will chew off the navel cords. If she doesn't, you can snip or break them. But do not cut them any closer than one inch from the navel. The navel cord stumps usually dry up and fall off in about 2 or 3 days. Once in a while, a cord breaks off too close to the pup's navel and a small rupture ensues. The rupture may heal as the pup grows or it may have to be surgically repaired. As a precaution against navel infection, you can apply an antiseptic to each of the navel cord stumps. Tincture of iodine will be satisfactory.

Checking for an unborn pup

Just when you think that all the pups have been born, the bitch may go into labor again. She may be trying to expel another pup or a retained placenta. Let her alone and see what happens. If she works for more than an hour or two without any results, call the veterinarian. Sometimes you can feel an unborn pup on the underside of the bitch's pelvis. More often you merely feel the swollen uterus.

When it's all over

When you are satisfied that no more pups are due, let the bitch rest. She's just been through a strenuous experience. She may want to go outdoors to relieve herself or she may not want to leave the pups. But let her make the move. If she does go outside, don't leave her out too long. Later on, she'll get back on her regular house-training schedule.

Next, clean up the whelping box, clear away the equipment and let the new mother take care of her pups. You might try her with some food; warm milk or warm milk and Pablum will be nourishing. Don't be surprised if she refuses to eat. It will not be long before she is looking for her meal, especially when the pups start nursing in earnest.

The next few days

The bitch will have a discharge for the next week or ten days. If all went well during whelping, the discharge will be red or dark in color. But a greenish discharge means trouble. A placenta or portion of a placenta probably has been retained. (You may have miscounted them in your excitement!) Serious infection can result from a retained placenta. This infection can cause the bitch's milk to dry up and the bitch and pups may die. Don't waste any time when you spot this greenish discharge; get her to the veterinarian or call him for instructions.

For the first few days, you will have to keep a close watch on the new pups. Make sure that each one is getting enough to eat. The rear teats usually hold the most milk, and the larger pups will shove the weaker ones aside to reach these well-filled teats. If the litter is a large one —over 8 pups—it will be necessary to feed the pups in shifts. Divide the litter into two groups and feed one group at a time, three or four times a day.

Some bitches can't or will not nurse the pups. When this occurs, you have two alternatives: 1) find a foster mother; or 2) hand-rear the pups. Your veterinarian may be able to help you find a foster mother or perhaps the local humane society will help you out.

In using a foster mother, proceed cautiously. First, make sure she is in good health. Second, see that she has enough milk to feed the litter. And third, remove the natural mother when using the foster mother.

Many foster mothers will not allow strange pups to nurse. You'll have to use some subterfuge. Squeeze out some milk from the foster mother (do this in another room) and rub it on each pup. This usually deludes a foster mother into thinking the pups are hers when she sniffs them and smells her own odor. Shepherds use this trick when they put an orphaned or rejected lamb on a foster mother. They go a bit further, though. Usually a ewe used as a foster mother has lost her own lamb. So, the shepherd will skin her dead lamb, tie the hide over an orphaned or rejected lamb, take some of the foster mother's milk and smear it over the hide covering the lamb. It all sounds complicated, but it works.

ECLAMPSIA

A serious condition known as eclampsia or milk fever may follow whelping. It affects nursing bitches. The depletion of blood calcium is suspected as a major cause. The condition is characterized by excessive panting, nervousness, restlessness, loss of appetite, a stilted walk, temperature about 103° and as high as 108°, collapse and convulsions. Don't waste time—call the veterinarian:

There is nothing you can do. The veterinarian will have to inject calcium into the bitch and it should be done as soon as possible.

HAND-REARING THE PUPS

In the absence of a foster mother, you will have to hand-rear the pups. While this will take time and patience, it can be done successfully.

Feeding by hand

The pups can be raised on a formula fed with a bottle. In feeding newborn pups, it is necessary to approximate the bitch's milk insofar as possible. Fortunately, a commercial formula, Esbilac, manufactured by the Borden Company, is available. It is a complete formula and just needs the addition of water. Esbilac can be purchased in most drugstores.

You'll need the following equipment for feeding the pups: baby bottles, nipples, mixing bowl, measuring cup (graduated in ounces), a baby scale and some spoons. The nipples should have the holes made larger so that the formula will ooze out.

The feeding schedule

Contrary to what you may have read or heard, the pups do not have to be fed every 2 or 3 hours. Three times a day will be adequate. And as the pups grow, you can reduce the number of formula feedings. Here is a guide to feeding the formula:

Birth to 3 weeks of age: 3 feedings per day.

3 to 5 weeks: 2 feedings per day. (With other food)

After 5 weeks: you can cut out the formula or continue to feed it.

Start each pup on ¼ ounce of the Esbilac formula per feeding the first day. Increase the amount gradually, so that by the 4th or 5th day, each pup is getting ½ ounce of the formula per feeding each day. Weigh the pups daily to keep a check on their progress. Also, keep an eye on the feces. If any of the pups has diarreha, reduce the solid part of the formula; that is, add more water to the mix. You can reduce the solid part of the formula mix by as much as one-half. When the diarrhea is cleared up, gradually increase the solids.

Sanitation

Proper sanitation is important for the health of the pups. Wash your hands before mixing the formula or handling the pups. After feeding the pups, wash all bottles, nipples, pans, etc., in hot water and detergent; then rinse them in hot water. Esbilac is perishable and must be kept under refrigeration. Heat the formula to 100°F. before feeding to the pups.

Introducing solid foods

The pups—regardless of whether they are hand-fed, nursed on a foster mother or fed by their natural mother —can be given solid food when they are 2 to 3 weeks old. Start weaning them on Pablum and milk, with some finely chopped or ground beef mixed in. Introduce all new foods gradually. After 5 weeks, you can eliminate Pablum and the formula and gradually substitute a high-quality puppy meal supplemented with chopped meat and cottage cheese.

GENERAL CARE OF THE PUPS

The bitch will usually take care of the newborn pup's immediate needs, such as stimulating him to evacuate and then cleaning up afterwards. If she doesn't do it— or in the absence of a mother—you will have to perform these functions. Dip some absorbent cotton into warm water and massage the pup's abdomen. This will stimulate the pup to have a movement. Wipe the pup clean after the bowel movement.

Grooming the very young pups should be kept to a minimum. Wash any soiled eyes with warm water or boric-acid solution. Trim any sharp nails. You can rub baby oil on the pups' bodies once or twice a week. But, in general, don't fuss with the pups; it's more important for them to eat and sleep.

Pups reared without access to colostrum-milk will be protected about one week against distemper. This immunity is passed to them while they were in the uterus.

Pups receiving colostrum-milk will be immune for a longer period, of course. Therefore, its important that the hand-reared pups receive a live-virus distemper injection at 2 weeks of age.

A final note of caution: the bitch will be very protective about her pups. Very small children and strangers should not be allowed to come too close to the bitch and pups. The instinct to protect her pups is very powerful and she may misinterpret a move and attack a child or stranger. And she'll do this even though she and the children have been great friends. So, use good judgment; keep the children and strangers away—at least until the bitch shows that she doesn't mind having spectators.

Part Seven
OLD AGE

21. Care of the Aging Dog

Aging in dogs, as in human beings, is composed of gradual and constant biological changes. The aging process begins when the dog is born and continues until his death. While the dog is always aging, the process becomes more noticeable after the dog reaches 6 or 7 years of age. Now, this doesn't necessarily mean that a 6- or 7-year-old dog is decrepit or senile; far from it, many dogs this age are very alert and active. But age is upon them. The 6- or 7-year-old dog may be compared to a 40-year-old person: both have telltale signs of age.

Most dogs manage to remain in good health up to the time they are 6 or 7 years old, even beyond that. They still have good eyesight, hearing, hair, teeth and muscular coordination. But when they go past 6 or 7 years, the aging process makes heavy inroads.

With reasonable care, your dog can live to be 12 years old. Many dogs live to be 14 to 17 years of age. Some live to be 25! But these very old dogs or canine centenarians are usually the exceptions—and they are usually small or toy dogs. There is a definite relationship between the size of the dog and longevity. In general, the smaller breeds mature earlier and live longer than do the large breeds. And another actuarial fact on canine longevity is that males outlive females. This is the reverse of human beings. For the sake of comparison, a 17-year-old dog is equivalent to a 100-year-old person.

A few years ago, the Gaines Dog Research Center, New York, conducted a survey on the longevity of dogs. The Center was mostly interested in "canine centenarians"— dogs 17 years old or over. Five hundred dog owners with dogs 17 or over were queried as to what they attributed the dog's longevity. The consensus of opinion was that good care, a sound diet, plenty of affection and a congenial environment were the most important factors contributing to longevity. Of course, genetic and freedom-from-disease factors contribute to longevity, but even these must be supplemented with good care.

The Gaines survey dealt only with dogs 17 years of age and over, but many of the conclusions drawn from it can be applied to dogs 6 years and up.

PHYSIOLOGICAL CHANGES IN THE AGING DOG

When the dog gets beyond 6 or 7 years of age, he begins to show definite physiological changes. He may be in good flesh, with a stout appearance, or he may be emaciated, depending on how he's endured the years. His hair will be dryer and sparse, especially on the abdomen; resulting from a reduction in the skin gland activity. The hair around the old dog's muzzle turns white or gray. Skin tumors make their appearance and the skin thickens with age. Calluses are common in old dogs and form on the hocks, elbows and other bony parts. The old bitch's breasts sag or hang down and the nipples become wrinkled and enlarged. Deafness and blindness come to the old dog. Cataracts are most always present in dogs over 10 years of age. Finally, the old dog's teeth are worn down, broken or riddled with cavities.

There is a generalized loss of muscle tone in the aging dog, with accompanying muscular atrophy. The respiratory, cardiovascular, digestive and urogenital systems all undergo changes and deterioration. The old dog has less resistance to disease or stress than younger animals. And he doesn't adapt too well to changes in his routine or environment.

CHANGES IN BEHAVIOR

Like the aging human being, the old dog becomes "set in his ways." He gets crotchety, grumpy, even irritable at times. In some instances, he may even be snappy. Any change in his routine will upset him. He's simply used to doing things a certain way for a long time. In brief, he's getting old. Humor him as much as you can.

The old dog can be very jealous and possessive. After all, he's been the center of your pet world for years. He'll resent children and other animals, particularly when you show them affection. Keep up the old dog's morale by letting him know that he is still important. And caution children and visitors about the old dog's feelings, disposition or infirmities.

Many dog owners get a young pup while they still have an old dog. As to the advisability of this, we don't have any opinion one way or the other. The decision is up to you. But we do think you should handle such a situation with care and tact. There's no doubt about it, the old dog is going to be very jealous of the new pup. Keep them separated—especially at mealtimes—until you see that there will not be any fights. Above all, keep reassuring the old dog and let him know that he's still the *number one dog*. The pup will have plenty of time to get his share of praise and affection when the old dog is gone.

GENERAL CARE OF THE OLD DOG

The old dog is slowing down, so do everything in moderation.

Exercise

Old dogs tire very easily. Adjust the walks and exercise periods to the old dog's pace. Don't overdo them—strenuous play or long hikes may overtax the old dog's heart. If he doesn't want to walk or exercise, don't force him. And if he insists on sleeping, let him; he's earned his place in the sun.

Feeding

The caloric requirements of the old dog are considerably less than those of the younger dog. This reduction is due to the lessening of activity and a lowering of the metabolic rate. Avoid overfeeding. Obesity in the old dog is just as dangerous it it is in aging human beings. You will definitely shorten your dog's life if you allow him to put on excess weight. If your dog tends toward overweight, cut down on his daily intake of food, but not the quality. The old dog still needs a complete and balanced diet, albeit in reduced quantities.

You can go right on feeding the old dog a high-quality prepared dog meal and meat ration. The old dog still needs moderate amounts of protein and carbohydrates. But his fat intake should be kept to a low level, about 4 or 5 percent of the total daily ration. He'll need vitamins and minerals, too. If the veterinarian puts the old dog on a special diet, stick to this diet. The old dog's life may depend on it. The best feeding policy is to divide the total daily ration into two parts and feed one in the morning and one at night. This will keep him more contented.

Grooming

The old dog will probably need more attention as far as grooming is concerned. Brush him daily, oil his skin and keep him free from fleas, lice and ticks. Remember, he can't stand much stress and an infestation of parasites will put him under stress. Avoid bathing him, except when absolutely necessary and then only on very warm days. If he has a doggy odor, use one of the spray cleaners and deodorizers on him. Watch his nails and trim them when they get too long. If his eyes weep, wash them with boric-acid solution and soothe them with an eye ointment.

Teeth

Tooth decay can cause misery for the old dog. Have the veterinarian remove any decayed teeth. Avoid giving the old dog big bones or hard toys that may break his teeth. Accumulations of tartar should be removed from the teeth. This is best done by the veterinarian.

AILMENTS OF OLD AGE

Rheumatism

Rheumatism usually shows up when the dog reaches 10 or 11 years of age. Stiff joints, difficult movement and irritability are the most common symptoms. Your veterinarian can prescribe medication to help relieve rheumatism. You can help the old dog by giving him a warm and dry place to live and sleep. Keep him out of drafts and dampness.

Otitis

Old dogs frequently suffer from chronic otitis or inflammation of the external, internal and middle ear. The condition can be very painful and will make the dog very irirtable. He may refuse to eat. Otitis is more often seen in those dogs with long or pendulous ears, such as the Dachshund, Cocker Spaniel and Setter. Upon close examination, the ear will be inflamed and there may be a discharge. Don't try to treat this condition, take the old dog to the veterinarian. Surgery is very often necessary.

Deafness

Otitis may lead to deafness. But deafness is caused by other factors, such as disease and injury. If—after you've had any ear infections or injuries taken care of—the old dog has difficulty in hearing, you can attribute the loss of hearing to advancing old age. There isn't much that can be done for senile deafness. In rare cases, deaf dogs have been provided with hearing aids. But these are costly and not really necessary.

Once you know the old dog is deaf, you'll have to make some adjustments in the daily routine. Since he can't hear, the old dog will be easily surprised when napping or lying down. Move quietly and try not to startle him. Caution children and strangers about the dog being deaf. He may snap or bite when startled. Also, take care that he doesn't get out onto the street where his impaired hearing will expose him to danger.

Blindness

Blindness is common in the very old dog. Cataracts are the main cause of blindness. They usually follow a chronic course. Cataracts may be seen in the form of cloudy spots resembling the solid white of an egg, and are visible through the pupil or hole in the center of the eyeball. Cataracts can be removed by surgery and a major portion of sight restored.

It may take you some time to catch on to the fact that your old dog is blind. A blind dog can move about amazingly well, particularly in familiar surroundings. He can move without bumping into chairs or tables because he relies on his scent. Most dogs retain a good sense of scent until the end. Outdoors, however, the blind dog gets into trouble. Never let him out of the yard alone. Keep him on the leash when you walk him.

Nephritis

Some degree of chronic nephritis or inflammation of the kidney is present in most old dogs. Nephritis may range from the nonuremic type, in which the old dog drinks a lot of water and frequently urinates, to the more dangerous uremic type. Both types of nephritis require veterinary attention. The dog with chronic nephritis will probably have to be on a special diet for the rest of his life.

Other ailments

Prostatitis, pyometra and ascites—ailments of the old dog—are discussed in Chapter 13. While these conditions are usually found in old dogs, they may be present as symptoms of disease in younger dogs.

BOARDING THE OLD DOG

Our advice is to board the old dog as few times as possible. Old dogs become depressed and refuse to eat when placed in strange surroundings. Veterinarians and boarding kennel operators are not too happy to take an old dog for boarding. Their reluctance is understandable: an old dog that refuses to eat and pines away to the extent of emaciation isn't good for reputations. Too many owners have accused veterinarians and boarding kennel operators of starving and mistreating their old dogs.

The writer has had considerable experience with this situation. As manager of the Bide-A-Wee Home for Animals in New York, he supervised a special boarding and "pension" section. Not too many old dogs were boarded, but the "pension" kennels had as many as fifty old-timers on a daily basis. It took all of our ingenuity and dog know-how to get these old "pensioners" to eat. None of them was ill; they were just getting old—many of them 10 years or more. We had to resort to special foods, fancy cooking, intravenous feeding—even having the old dogs fed by women. Many dogs have been fed by women all their lives and will refuse to eat when fed by men.

It may be asked at this point why these old dogs weren't

put to sleep instead of being boarded out or pensioned off. Well, there were some good reasons. First, Bide-A-Wee has the policy of never destroying dogs unless incurably ill. Second, many of the owners of these old dogs were forced by housing laws or family circumstances to give up their old dogs. They just couldn't bring themselves around to having the old dogs put to sleep. So, in lieu of euthanasia, these people were happy to pay a yearly fee to keep their old dogs at Bide-A-Wee where they got excellent care and medical attention.

And this brings us up to the question of euthanasia, or putting the old dog to sleep. Should you have the dog put to sleep when he gets too old? The question is one with which the writer grappled almost every day of his six years as manager of Bide-A-Wee. There are too many facets to the question for a pat answer. The decision is yours alone —no veterinarian will tell you that the dog must be put to sleep.

Why not look at it this way: if the old dog is in fair health for his age and it is possible for you to keep him, there is no need for euthanasia. But if he is infirm and seriously ill, possibly in pain and misery, then perhaps the kind thing to do would be to have him put to sleep.

We are aware of the controversial nature of euthanasia. But we can only point to Nature's way of taking care of the situation. In the wild dog packs (and with other animals), the old are never allowed to go on. When an old dog becomes infirm and goes down, he is killed by the rest of the pack. And while this may sound like a specious argument, certainly the old dog doesn't expect more than to be put away when he becomes decrepit and infirm. But —as we said before—*you* must make the choice.

If you do decide to have the old dog put to sleep, have the veterinarian administer euthanasia. We can assure you from long experience that the dog will slip peacefully into a long sleep and never wake up.

BIBLIOGRAPHY

American Kennel Club, *The Complete Dog Book*. New York: Garden City Press, 1961.

Baker, J. A., "See Key to Bitch Immunity and Pup Vaccinations in Blood Test," *Gaines Dog Research Progress*, Fall, 1958.

Baker, J. A., et al., *Development and Expectations of the New Vaccines*. New York: Gaines Dog Research Center, 1957.

Deutsch, H. J., and McCoy, J. J., *The Dog Owner's Handbook*. New York: Thomas Y. Crowell Company, 1954.

Edgar, S. E., Jr., "Dogs in the Sight of the Law," *Gaines Dog Research Progress*, Fall, 1960.

Evans, H. E., "A Dog Comes into Being," *Gaines Dog Research Progress*, Fall, 1956.

Hayes, F. A., "Canine Ascarids and Related Problems," *Gaines Dog Research Progress*, Winter, 1959-60.

Kirk, R. W., "Puppies: Prenatal Care and Pediatrics," *Gaines Dog Research Progress*, Fall, 1959.

Lorenz, K. Z., *King Solomon's Ring*. New York: Thomas Y. Crowell Company, 1952.

Lorenz, K. Z., *Man Meets Dog*. Boston and New York: Houghton Mifflin, 1955.

McCoy, J. J., "Should You Keep a Dog in the City?" *Bide-A-Wee Quarterly*, 1961, 10, 22-27.

Miller, H., *The Common Sense Book of Puppy and Dog Care*. New York: Bantam Books, Inc., 1956.

Montague, A., "Origin of the Domestication of the Dog," *Science*, 1942, 96, 111-12.

Morgan, C. T., "Introduction to Psychology," Chapter 23, *Animal Behavior*. New York: McGraw-Hill Book Company, Inc., 1956.

Pavlov, I. P., *Conditioned Reflexes* (tr. by G. V. Anrep). London: Oxford University Press, 1927.

Riser, Wayne H., D.V.M., and Miller, Harry, *Canine Hip Dysplasia and How to Control It*. Philadelphia: Orthopedic Foundation for Animals, 1967.

Scott, J. P., "Abnormal Behavior in Dogs and Other Animals," *Gaines Dog Research Progress*, Winter, 1957-58.

Scott, J. P., *Animal Behavior*. New York: Doubleday, 1963.

Tinbergen, N., *The Study of Instinct*. London: Oxford University Press, 1951.

Wolters, R., *Gun Dog*. New York: E. P. Dutton and Company, Inc., 1961.

INDEX